Praise for *A Traitor in the FBI*

"Wayne Barnes took concepts I developed for criminal profiling and used them on his Cold War intelligence targets. In this case they were crucial for a successful outcome."

—John Douglas, the "Mindhunter," former FBI Behavioral Sciences Unit Supervisor, and author of over a dozen books on criminal profiling

"A gripping true tale of high-level espionage, Wayne Barnes shows his mastery of investigation in the cat and mouse struggle to root out one of the most destructive spies in US history. This story is nothing short of sensational!"

—Robert K. Wittman, former FBI senior investigator and *New York Times* bestselling author of *Priceless* and *The Devil's Diary*

"I am glad Wayne finally received permission to have this one, *A Traitor in the FBI*, published—a bigger-than-life story—about what Wayne does best—catch spies!"

—Michael A. Ledeen, Former Special Advisor to US Secretary of State Alexander Haig (1981–82)

"FBI Agent Wayne Barnes lived every pulse-raising moment of the spy/counterspy drama that is the heart and soul of one of the greatest espionage thrillers that will ever deprive you of sleep. Combine a real-life hero with an innate flair for bringing a story to life in print, and you can forget about an early bedtime."

—John Dobbyn, author of the
Knight and Devlin thriller series

"I was one of the three FBI agents who flew to San Diego in 1998 to ask Wayne to do what everyone thought was impossible—but he did it anyway."

—Gene McClelland, FBI
Supervisory Special Agent, retired

"Imagine the lead domestic intelligence agency in the United States, responsible for protecting the nation's highest-level secrets, believing there was a mole in their organization. This is how Wayne Barnes fit the pieces of the puzzle together to end one of the most difficult and consequential intelligence cases in the history of our country."

—Marc Weber Tobias, Physical Security Expert

"*A Traitor in the FBI* is compelling reading, full of never-disclosed FBI insights of the spy-catching world that only a twenty-nine-year professional FBI special agent would know. With seemingly no leads left to cover, Wayne always found some and solved his cases.

—Thomas V. Cash, former Special Agent-
in-Charge, Drug Enforcement Administration

A TRAITOR IN THE FBI

THE HUNT FOR A RUSSIAN MOLE

WAYNE A. BARNES

A REPUBLIC BOOK
ISBN: 978-1-64572-124-6
ISBN (eBook): 978-1-64572-125-3

A Traitor in the FBI:
The Hunt for a Russian Mole

Cover Design by Cody Corcoran
Cover Illustration by Biba Kayewich

This is a work of nonfiction. All people, locations, events, and situations are portrayed to the best of the author's memory and knowledge as actually occurred in the story. Over two dozen true names are mentioned in the book, all of whom gave their consent to have their names published. A few have passed away, and the names of some were replaced with aliases, to protect their identities and privacy.

Republic Book Publishers
New York, NY
www.republicbookpublishers.com

Published in the United States of America
1 2 3 4 5 6 7 8 9 10

This book is dedicated to the loyal and hardworking men and women of the FBI—who daily, fight crime and keep our country safe—for their many years of service and patriotism.

DISCLAIMER FOR THE READERS, FROM THE FBI PREPUBLICATION REVIEW UNIT

In accordance with my obligations as a former FBI employee pursuant to my FBI employment agreement, this book has undergone a prepublication review for the purpose of identifying prohibited disclosures, but has not been reviewed for editorial content or accuracy. The FBI does not endorse or validate any information that I have described in this book. The opinions expressed in this book are mine and not those of the FBI or any other government agency.

CONTENTS

FOREWORD BY JOHN DOUGLAS

Wayne Barnes and I entered on duty in the FBI a year apart, for me in 1970 and Wayne in 1971. While my path involved the criminal world and years in profiling, his trajectory was in foreign counterintelligence. However, it wasn't until more than twenty years later, in 1992, that we finally met.

I had been traveling on FBI business in the far East and stopped in San Diego on my way back to Washington, DC. As coincidence would have it, after his long career in the nation's capital, Wayne had transferred to San Diego just a couple of years before.

I was asked to give a presentation in the field office and was glad to meet so many FBI colleagues. One aspect of my talk was to mention the concept of "Bureau family." That is, there is a closeness among those who carry FBI credentials, and dozens of others in important support positions. I asked, rhetorically, whether the Bureau really was a "family." Somewhat facetiously I added, "The director of the FBI never sent me a birthday card!"

This got a lot of laughs, but when the raucous died down, a baritone voice called out, "When *is* your birthday?"

This was followed by silence from the big group, and I looked around to see who asked the question. I saw an agent standing along the back wall, who had a straight face. He seemed to be serious, so I said my birth date out loud.

It never occurred to me that anything would come of this. After all, I was just passing through and would retire in three years, so I thought nothing further about it.

Months later, on the next June 18th, I received a very nice card at my office—from that agent in San Diego, who had asked when my birthday was. It was from Wayne Barnes. I had to smile, recalling my presentation and that moment. I should note, no one else sent me a birthday card, not faulting anyone, but receiving this one was certainly an anomaly.

This began what has become a thirty-year friendship. Wayne has never missed a year for sending me a birthday greeting, even though I retired over twenty-five years ago.

My path in the Bureau, in pioneering profiling, began with interviewing notorious serial murderers who were spending the rest of their lives in prison. The Behavioral Science Unit went on to profile violent sex offenders and even arsonists.

Wayne's path was in foreign counterintelligence which, in the Bureau, is very much a separate category from criminal investigations. But he took some of the same concepts from our criminal profiling in dealing with his many cases, especially Cold War intelligence officers from the KGB and Eastern Bloc countries, who were targeted for recruitment.

In counterintelligence, the term "profiling" might not apply the way we did it, but he came up with two categories that really did need to be looked at more carefully: 1) What is the personality of a Soviet Intelligence Officer who the FBI can recruit? And 2) What is the personality of someone working for a defense contractor, who begins to commit espionage, and sells our nation's secrets?

After conducting a lot of research, Wayne concluded that in both of these circumstances, the susceptible individuals had a crisis in their lives. For a Soviet official, a child born in the US, needing immediate surgery, which only an American doctor could successfully perform. For the American, a financial need, often based on a costly medical procedure for a loved one, which they could not pay for, or even secure a loan for the surgery. "Helping" these individuals was one way to begin a recruitment process for one, and to end the national security threat for the other.

Whether in criminal matters or counterintelligence, there are concepts in profiling that are similar, because they all boil down to a simple formula I developed early on, and profilers have used for years: Why + How = Who. That is, why was the act committed, and how was it done, which will lead to narrowing down the suspects to a certain set of individuals in the category of those who could be responsible for the evil act, be it a serial murderer, or someone involved in long-term espionage.

The corollary to this is, "behavior reflects personality." To understand the artist, you must look at their artwork. If we want to fully comprehend the mind and motivation of the criminal, we must look at the specifics of the crime. This concept was also applicable in espionage investigations.

In Wayne's story, *A Traitor in the FBI*, he took his years of experience in working undercover cases and, after several encounters with his subject, created a very specific profile. This was an important tool in determining how to pitch his intelligence target, without which, the case would not have been successful. It was a nice blend of the knowledge from our two careers.

John Douglas, author of *Mindhunter*, Behavioral Analysis Unit Chief, FBI Special Agent (1970-1995), retired

PROLOGUE

Sergei Motorin was marched down a long tunnel in the bowels of Lubyanka Prison in central Moscow. The four soldiers around him were not crowding him, but he couldn't get away either. They seemed to walk forever.

Sergei was a major in the KGB and had been assigned to the Soviet Embassy in Washington, DC, in the early 1980s. He met, became friends with, and secretly began to work with one of my colleagues in the FBI, Mike Morton, "Salt" to his friends.

Some might call what Sergei did "treason," but if you were repulsed by the system you worked for—believed you were *part of the problem*—of what made the Soviet Union such a terrible place, you saw it differently. Providing sensitive KGB information to the FBI was his piece of the puzzle to subvert that system, and he was glad to do it.

A uniformed officer slowly came up behind Sergei, falling in step with the other guards. He raised a 9mm Makarov handgun to the back of Sergei's head. As old as the Cold War, this weapon had been produced to remove enemies of the state.

Sergei thought he would survive this short trip back in Moscow. After he would return to the States, and months later, just before he was to go back to the Soviet Union for good, he planned to defect with his family. Driving to the Washington National Airport, at the last turn, he would veer off the main highway and down a back street to meet his FBI friend.

I had worked the Motorin case with Salt for months, planning each next move, analyzing audio tapes from many meetings, figuring new topics of discussion, and determining how best to reach into the Russian's soul. We wanted him to see clearly which side he was on, not from his birth in Moscow, but from the experience that was America, which he had now seen with his own eyes. *They* had been lying to him about life in the West, he realized, and he resented it.

He was one of the Golden Youth in Russia, everything handed to him, benefiting from the very best their system had to offer. But it was corrupt, and he began to detest it. So, he met with Salt and gave away his country's secrets. Unbeknownst to Sergei, he had been found out. He would no longer have the sun shine down on him in America. There would be nothing but darkness around him for the rest of his life—which would be only for a few moments longer.

The officer pulled the trigger.

The crack of the gunshot reverberated like thunder. The bullet penetrated Major Motorin's skull and he crashed forward, dead before he slammed into the stone floor.

When we learned about this months later—Salt, Jim Stassinos, our KGB squad supervisor, and me—it was a crushing blow. How had Sergei's connection to us been blown? Was there a misstep in our tradecraft or something we had overlooked? What we did not know, didn't even suspect, with perhaps an astounding level of naiveté, even with our combined fifty years of counterintelligence experience, was that our precious source had been undone by someone who worked—actually *lurked*—within the FBI: a turncoat of our own.

I swore I would find out what had happened, who had done this. It would be fifteen years before a grand plan was created to try to make things, well, not *right*, but as close as I could get—to learn who the spy was in the FBI.

PART ONE

CHAPTER 1
THE OVERTURE

Every day may start like thousands that came before, but once in a great while, a life-changing moment sets the wheels in motion for something dynamic. For me, it was on a sleepy Sunday morning in San Diego, in the spring of 1998, when my phone rang.

"Wayne, it's Gene."

"H-e-e-e-e-y, Red Pop! How's it going?"

Gene McClelland and I had worked in the Washington Field Office of the FBI catching Russian spies in the 1980s. His handle, Red Pop, reflected the color of his hair and good nature.

"We're coming out on Tuesday," he said. "Let's meet early afternoon."

"Sure, what have you got?"

"I'm coming with Dave and Mike. Can you recommend a hotel?"

The heavies, I thought. Dave Greb and Mike Rochford had been around a long time and were senior people in the FBI's Intelligence Division.

"Yeah, the Bahia down on Mission Bay."

"We want to see you, and only you," Gene stressed. "It is important that no one else knows we're coming, not even your supervisor, and especially no one on the counterintelligence squad. Take leave or come between leads. Find a way to fit us in."

I was incredulous. Management had always seen me as a maverick, an outside-the-box thinker—well, outside of *their* box.

"Can you tell me more?"

"Not now, and not on the phone."

"You're coming all the way out here just to talk to me?"

"Be patient," he told me.

"Okay, but not even a clue—maybe a codename?"

When a case is assigned a codename, there are considerable funds and manpower dedicated to the operation. What Gene didn't say, because I really did not need to know, was the codename—*Graysuit*. My part of this much larger operation would be called *Bowsprit*.

"Just don't discuss this with anyone," he said, gravely. "That's all. See you at the Bahia on Tuesday at two."

Beginning in 1974, I worked on a counterintelligence squad in Washington against Romanians, Czechs, Poles, Bulgarians, Hungarians, and Yugoslavs. After seven years and a great deal of success, I was moved to work Soviets for a decade. That was Gene's specialty, and we quickly became friends. When he called me in 1998, I had already been in the San Diego Division for eight years.

After the Berlin Wall came down in 1989, the Bureau cut back spending on counterintelligence—the "peace dividend" it was called. I was currently assigned to healthcare-fraud cases. Actually, *relegated* was how I felt about it. Don't get me wrong, the work was good, but once you've caught spies for a living in the nation's capital, little else measures up. It would be easy to meet with my old colleagues. I could catch a scamming medical lab or cheating doctor another day.

The Bahia, on Mission Bay, is a pleasant expanse of low buildings in a garden setting with colorful sailboats on one side and a slew of tennis courts on the other.

Gene was in the lobby. His trademark red hair now blended into gray at the fringes, but he still exuded his good nature.

We shook hands warmly and exchanged smiles. No one nearby could possibly know our long history together and strong bond.

He said, "Come on, they're waiting."

We took a trail around an enclosure with California sea lions, walked between fragrant bushes, and reached a set of stairs up to their room.

Dave and Mike sat at a table near a balcony window overlooking the bay. These guys were all business but couldn't help admiring the Jet Skis and bikini-clad water-skiers. It was certainly different from their office views back in Washington.

Dave and I had been on the Eastern Bloc squad in WFO, the Washington Field Office, when it was in the Old Post Office with its iconic bell tower. He was assigned to work Polish Intelligence, while I dealt mostly with Romanians. I knew him early in his career when he first became an agent. He would come into the squadroom with his slender build, white shirt, and tie—"Bobby Bureau," we joked—always the straightest arrow in a room full of straight arrows. Now he had sallow cheeks from years of smoking, and his hair had gone all gray. The intensity of counterintelligence work in the nation's capital could age an agent.

Mike had an all-Soviet career without the satisfaction of the successes of the Bloc agents. He had a feature that would have made him the picture-perfect villain, had he been written into a spy novel.

Several years before, a surgical procedure on his cheek went awry and a nerve was severed. The left side of his face collapsed, lifeless. This gave an odd twist to the right side of his mouth, a pose you could hardly make if you tried. The curious thing was, after a while, this new persona *became* Mike Rochford.

They got up and we all shook hands.

Mike was in charge and got right to it.

"We have a penetration of US Intelligence. We think he is a senior official at the CIA, but he might be in the FBI. We hope not the latter, but we don't know. Over the last few years, we received information from independent sources that there is still a big one out there."

He explained that they had conducted a detailed analysis of the information CIA turncoat Aldrich Ames had given to the Soviets over the decade before his arrest in 1994. He had phenomenal access as the internal auditor at Langley. But the mole they were now looking for, the unknown subject—"unsub" in FBI parlance—had passed the Russians information Ames never saw. US Intelligence sources within the KGB, who Ames could not have been aware of, had not just been compromised—they had been executed.

Mike paused to let me take it all in.

Ames had been the last big spy caught working for the Soviets, and it shocked the Intelligence Community. One response to his treachery was setting in motion five-year background updates for anyone with a government clearance. It was a program of mind-boggling size but long overdue.

Were you spending money but couldn't explain where it came from? What kind of contacts and friends had you acquired since you first received your clearance? Was there a pattern to your foreign travel unlike what you had before? And how come, as a grade-five clerk, you just pulled into your driveway in a brand-new red Lamborghini?

There were dozens of similar questions which had to be asked of everyone with a US government clearance, thanks to Aldrich Ames. But in spite of all this, there was still a mole working in the Intelligence Community, and at a senior level.

Mike went on.

"We have a squad set up at WFO. To get to our space, you have to pass down a hallway through two doors with cipher locks. All the agents assigned to me are polygraphed every week to make sure they haven't discussed our work with anyone. If they have, they are banished from the squad and still have to keep our secrets. It's the most sensitive squad in the FBI. No one who is not cleared for this case gets into our area or knows what we are doing. You see, our unsub could be working right down the corridor."

Mike paused to look back and forth at his colleagues. He wasn't trying to impress me because he knew, as a longtime Cold Warrior, I had seen a great deal. But I also knew nothing like what he described had happened before.

"How can I help?"

"We tried to narrow our search using the parameters of the information the unsub gave away."

This was a shocker. Almost every Eastern European intelligence defector would tell us they had the FBI penetrated, which we assumed was BS. It was something they were told during training to prevent them from being recruited by the West. But one KGB officer had come out with photocopies of actual FBI documents which the unsub had provided to them, which set off the alarm bells and changed everything.

Mike went on. "Based on who had access to those documents, we made a list of potential suspects in US Intelligence that stretched across the Intelligence Community. Believe me, that wasn't easy. It included what the unsub read as it crossed his own desk, but also, what a colleague sitting nearby, who stepped away to get coffee or use the bathroom, left open on his desk that the unsub might have seen.

"Another factor is what cities he was assigned to, because we had some of that information. And I know what you are thinking—the unsub never gave his name to his handlers, so even the Russians don't know who he is."

With that, Mike brought out a folder from his briefcase, a black one, the kind used to turn in high-school projects. He opened it to show a dozen black-and-white mug-shot-type photos of men, all middle age to a little older. He asked if I knew any of them.

From 1983 to 1986, I was assigned to a very special squad, CI-11, with the codename "Courtship." It was composed of three FBI special agents and three CIA case officers, all working under an FBI supervisor at a regular business location in Springfield, Virginia, but with no apparent connection to the federal government.

There had never been a time when the FBI and CIA worked well together. Then one day, around 1979, Admiral Stansfield Turner, the CIA director, met with William Webster, the FBI director, who was also a former federal judge. They decided to put the discord between the agencies behind them and combine forces. They authorized the creation of a squad with the sole objective of recruiting Soviet intelligence officers.

You couldn't volunteer to be assigned there but were handpicked from a pool of the most experienced agents in the office. They took "Court" from the judge, and "Ship" from the admiral, and created "Courtship." Of course, in the field, we liked to think the name suggested we would charm our targets.

I briefly scanned the photos and pointed to the only man I knew.

"That's John Knox. He was a CIA guy at Courtship in the mid-eighties. Is he a suspect?"

Again, Mike looked back and forth at his colleagues and then at me.

"Tell us about him."

"John was a pain in the ass. You couldn't know him for more than ten minutes before he told you he scored an 800 on his English SAT more than twenty years before. He has an ego even larger than your typical CIA officer, but nothing I could see to justify it.

"One day he came into the office all excited and told us we had to come down to look at his new car. He had gotten the Mercedes-Benz he always wanted and was beside himself.

"As I went down in the elevator, I was wondering how a CIA guy could afford a new Mercedes. Then I saw it and understood. It was the newest, but absolutely the smallest compact Mercedes model they made, a 190E. It looked almost like a Toyota Corolla, light blue and nothing special to me, but it was the apple of his eye."

"How about his work?" Mike asked.

"Eh, nothing momentous, just a big talker. He was full of himself. My recollection is no case he ever worked went anywhere."

Again, there was reflection among the three Washington agents. That could be the pattern of a Soviet spy. Get on the most sensitive squad and be aware of what is going on with everyone else's cases, but do nothing productive yourself.

Mike said, "Anybody else?"

"Nope, that's it. Are any of these guys in the Bureau? I can't imagine there could be too many senior people I've never seen."

"Well, most of them are in the CIA, but don't worry about that," Mike said. He took a deep breath.

"We did a study of all the Soviets who were assigned to the US, Washington, in particular, but also New York, over certain periods of time. After a helluva lot of man-hours, we came up with a list of Soviet officials—just over a dozen—who could potentially identify our unsub. Some were in the security or counterintelligence section of the Soviet Embassy and might have dealt with him. Other names surfaced through different kinds of assessments. That was the first part of our plan.

"The second was tracking the movements of these men and getting advance notice when they were scheduled to travel outside of Russia. If one of them was taking a trip to Tokyo or London, we could get someone there before he arrived who would try to meet him."

I know my brow must have knitted because Mike paused and said, "The goal is to recruit one of these Russians who might be able to identify our unsub."

I was astounded. Having worked in counterintelligence for over twenty-five years, it was clear that one of the most difficult things to do—in all of human endeavor—was recruit a Soviet official during his four-year assignment in the United States. These were, after all, *Russians*! By and large, they were certain they were citizens of the best superpower and would never consider helping the US, which, at embassy meetings, they always referred to as the *glavnyy vrag*—the Main Enemy!

Mike went on. "We recently learned that one of these Russians is traveling to Los Angeles to attend a conference. We want you to go there and find him, meet him, befriend him, recruit him, and get him to identify which guy in these photos is the spy."

I stared at Mike for a long moment, then at Gene and Dave, and back to Mike.

"How long will I have to do this?"

"Eight days."

CHAPTER 2

SPECIALIZED TRAINING

It had been more than a decade since my last undercover assignment, so I was mandated by the powers that be to attend a specialized training school in Los Angeles. But did I really need to be there?

Back in Washington, I had been an instructor at the undercover school, was the undercover coordinator in the Washington Field Office, and had set up backstopping for undercover counterintelligence agents at several dozen companies, including many defense contractors. I'd also had a record number of hours of face-to-face, undercover (UC) meetings with counterintelligence subjects. Along with several colleagues, we had great success recruiting Eastern European intelligence targets and causing defections through the 1970s and early '80s. But no matter, that was then, and this was now. So, I was bound for Los Angeles for a full day of "training," a block that, administratively, had to be checked.

I believe there are two basic components for a successful foreign counterintelligence operation: working undercover and recruiting.

The undercover aspect gets you up close and personal with your target so you can make a psychological assessment—What makes him tick?—which leads to a recruitment effort. If successful, this final step gives US Intelligence the most valuable source: someone who lives deep within enemy territory, but whose heart lies in the West.

In 1989, my daughter, Natalia, was born with spina bifida, a major birth defect. I received a transfer to San Diego, where orthopedic surgeons worked their magic on her feet, legs, and spine over several years. This was why I was now far from Washington, where I had worked for so long.

When this case began in 1998, I had five children: three boys and two girls, seven through eighteen years old. Preparation time for my part of this case would mean long-hour days and many away from home, which can be stressful on a family. That comes with the job.

The drive on I-5 North to Los Angeles to attend specialized training was an easy two hours. It gave me time to relax and ponder before things started to move quickly.

In 1972, my training agent in Los Angeles was George Aiken, an old-timer who gave me sage advice. When I was driving our Bureau car, referred to as a "Bū-car," and a red traffic light seemed too long, I was always anxious to get going and cross the intersection.

In his easy Alabama way, George said, "Mr. Hoover is paying you to sit here and wait for the light to change. And then he is paying you to go on the green and cover our lead."

Essentially: Follow the bureaucratic rules, but still get the job done.

At WFO, there was a dividing line between the criminal and counterintelligence "sides of the house." Between the FBI and

CIA, this would be described as a firewall, but within the FBI, the difference was simply based on a need-to-know.

Agents working criminal cases right down the hallway had no more knowledge of what the foreign counterintelligence agents were doing than the tourists who walked past the Old Post Office on Pennsylvania Avenue, the home of WFO. When it came to specialized training, in the FBI, it was the same. The criminal side had theirs, and we had ours.

One day my old friend Harry Gossett, a criminal supervisor, invited me to speak at his undercover class. He was my link to the criminal world, and I was his into counterintelligence. This was the first time an effort was made to share crossover knowledge.

One thing FBI agents hate is reinventing the wheel. If the counterintelligence agents had an easy way to secure undercover identification, and criminal agents could secure other sorts of alias ID, why duplicate the effort?

At the criminal undercover training in the late 1970s, the instructor described their targets—mobsters, pimps, conmen, and other nefarious characters. Most were not well-educated and had gotten as far as they had in life on their street sense. They were not, he emphasized, "rocket scientists," which brought laughter from the class.

Then it was my turn to explain what counterintelligence agents faced in our operations. Our targets were Soviet intelligence officers who had been to college and often graduate school. They spent many months in intelligence courses and learned from instructors who told them about the KGB's seventy years of experience at stealing secrets from the West, often involving highly technical subjects. So, many of our targets *were* rocket scientists!

This, too, got a laugh, but the point was made. How you dealt with a mobster, as opposed to a Soviet intelligence officer, was very different, but there were also similarities. They were still people, with personal issues, conflicts on the job, families, and foibles.

When I arrived at the hotel in Los Angeles and entered the conference room, it was nearly filled with agents, but no one else from San Diego. That was odd because all new agents want to get their feet wet in undercover work.

San Diego was the sixth largest city in the country, and there should have been at least a couple of other agents from the field office. It was not until much later that I learned this was due to the very sensitive nature of the case *I* would be working. Someone very high up in the Bureau had kept all of the other San Diego agents out of the class, so no one in the field office knew what I was doing. It may not seem like much, but this was an unheard-of security precaution.

At fifty years old, I was like a father figure to my classmates, who wondered: Who does he know? They thought it was just a free day off for me, some sort of reward from my supervisor. They had no idea of my background, nor was it something I would discuss with them. Even though I was currently assigned to healthcare fraud, I was the only agent in the room who would soon be working undercover to recruit a Russian target.

Speakers came in to talk about their cases. One agent from Mobile, Alabama, went undercover in a construction-fraud case. A company was supposed to install culverts for drainage along miles of highway and had dug some of the trenches. But it was not laying the large cement pipes and had pocketed hundreds of thousands of dollars. They were also bribing county officials.

How they thought they could get away with this, especially when, sooner or later, it would rain and roads would flood, was beyond me. That was an example of criminal targets—*not* rocket scientists.

There were other speakers, and the day wore on.

A session was given on documentation for undercover activities.

Back in 1986, after my three-year assignment at Courtship, I volunteered for the midnight-to-eight shift at WFO. In most field offices, this is the graveyard shift, but not in Washington.

FBI Headquarters does not communicate with the public, only field offices. So, if a call came in from Helsinki, Finland, that a US plane had been hijacked and was bound for the States, it would be patched over to the field office and connected to me. With a staff of four clerks, and the chatter of the teletype machine never seeming to stop, every evening was abuzz for the first few hours.

Just before dawn, when the call volume was low, I wrote a "How To" manual for undercover counterintelligence operations. I answered all the questions that peppered my mind. How do you pick the name you will use in your case? How do you pick a house or apartment? Do you buy or lease one, may you use your own, or borrow one from a friend, just for an evening, to convince your Russian target you are a *real* person? How do you use alias credit cards, and what are proper expenditures? There are dozens of questions, easy to answer if you have done this for years, but not if you're new at it. I have said many times, "Don't try this by yourself the first time."

To get into the FBI you need a good deal of education and a clean background. After that, it is almost 100 percent on-the-job training. There is absolutely nowhere else to learn what FBI agents do. Reading all available books on the subject and watching scores of TV shows will not put you face-to-face with a bad guy who would just as soon shoot you as look at you if he knew who you really were. It might be someone with diplomatic immunity, who could not be prosecuted, and would fly home, scot-free!

I completed the manual over six months of night-duty work—a hundred pages—and submitted it to headquarters to be used by the Training Unit in the Intelligence Division. I also printed out a copy for each squad's small intelligence library. The feedback was so good I thought of having it copyrighted in 1986, but that was not something you did in the FBI.

At a break in the class, I spoke with the agent in charge of the day's training, who had flown out from Washington. On his table, from the suitcase of items he had brought with him, I saw something that looked very familiar. It was a "How To" manual for undercover activities. I spun it around and saw the author: Thomas A. Reilly, Unit Chief, Intelligence Division.

Tom had been my supervisor on Courtship for a year in the mid-1980s. Then he transferred out to take over the Training Unit at headquarters. My old friend, Gene McClelland, had told me years before that he had seen my manual there, but was reluctant to discuss it, which I found curious. Now I understood. Tom Reilly had put his name on my six months of work and published it within the Bureau.

Agents will tell you the letters F-B-I actually stand for "Fidelity, Bravery, and Integrity," the words on the ribbon at the bottom of the FBI seal. So much for the fidelity and integrity part for my old supervisor.

But the FBI is a big place, and I had a job to do. I was more interested in making this undercover case work than seeking credit for what I had done to help those who came after me. If the UC manual could be better promoted with someone else's name on it, so be it. I figured, as long as no one was making money from it, did it really matter? Above everything else, I was happy the pages of knowledge I had passed on were still being used, now a dozen years later. And, *I* was the one they asked to work this undercover case, not my old larcenous boss.

I pointed at the manual. The man in charge lifted it in two hands and held it near his chest, like it meant something to him. He said it was his primer on "this stuff," and it was easy for me to get a good feeling from that moment. He would never understand what had happened, and might not have believed me if I told him.

I asked what was planned for the rest of the day. He had the same perception of me as the rest of the agents did—and was also many years my junior. But he would not ask about my case. That was need-to-know, even here.

He said we had a psychological test, not pass-fail, but just to see how we would do. They would compare our answers with a set of guidelines they had been using for almost twenty years. It was to gauge our ability to work undercover, how we got along with people, did they like us, and did we have genuine relationships? Were we leaders or followers, and more.

When the test was handed out, it was similar to one I had taken many years before. The thirty-nine agents who had made up the old Soviet Bloc squad, led by legendary supervisor Don Gruentzel, included several who were very successful recruiting embassy officials. Our camaraderie was extraordinary and, together, we compromised most of those Warsaw Pact intelligence services. It was that small set of agents who had been given this test, but we had no idea what they did with the results.

During this day's test, I found my answers were different than how I had responded nearly two decades before. Now, I had a family with five children. Did I always see myself as a leader? When I came home, tired from work, and called out that it was "pizza night!" they all followed me out the door. But if any of my children suggested where to eat, or what movie to see, I would always give them reinforcement so they developed as individuals. That included from the oldest down to the youngest.

I finished the test, still tossing over its similarity with the one from years ago. I waited until all the other agents left before I approached the man in charge.

"Where did this test come from?" I asked, adding, "It's not the normal Minnesota Multiphasic Personality Inventory." The MMPI was developed by psychologists to gauge various personality traits, and had been modified and recrafted over the years, based on the objectives of those administering the test.

The agent was reluctant to talk about it, but finally said it had been created at the FBI Academy in the Behavioral Sciences Unit from testing they did "way back during the Cold War."

I asked what the testing involved. He said there had been a particular set of agents who had taken the test, after which they remodeled a new, specialized test from their responses. That was what we took today.

"And who were those agents?" I asked.

He honestly did not know, only that their accumulated knowledge and experience had become the standard for gauging all FBI undercover operatives from then on.

What I knew, but he did not, was that those agents were me, and my old squadmates, who had been so incredibly successful at recruiting intelligence targets.

I thanked him, adding that I hoped the hell I passed.

He smiled and said he was sure I did fine.

I glanced once more at my erstwhile "How To" undercover manual and shook his hand.

I left the training day hoping I was able to pass a psychological test that was based, at least in part, on me! It was worth a smile, but was just the first bureaucratic hurdle to jump over before I would get to the real nitty-gritty.

CHAPTER 3

BACKSTOPPING

Jack Valenti

For those who are addicted to adrenaline, the most stressful thing is...*doing nothing*!

I continued investigating healthcare fraud in San Diego in my normal way—hard-charging as ever. My supervisor was completely unaware of my undercover operation.

If there was even the slightest possibility that he might have spoken with one of his buddies at FBI Headquarters and mentioned a "big UC operation," and he found out that the undercover agent was me, our unsub might learn about it. Then our case could be over before it began.

For the first time in my twenty-five-year career in counterintelligence, practically no one needed to know what I was doing. The paperwork for my time away from the office would list some sort of administrative leave with no explanation.

Meanwhile, Gene McClelland was busy in Washington covering bases for the next step.

The event our Russian planned to attend was sponsored by the American Film Market, a marketplace for the film industry lasting eight days. Unlike a regular film *festival*, here, production and distribution deals were the main focus. It would be in Santa Monica, where Los Angeles slides down into the Pacific Ocean.

Gene learned that Jack Valenti, the longtime head of the Motion Picture Association of America, had an office in the nation's capital. Surely, he would have access to information about the film market. We wanted to learn anything we could about our subject's connection with the festival.

Who was he coming with? How many were in his group? Where were they staying? Who paid his conference fee? What sessions was he planning to attend? There were a dozen other questions that would need answers once the basics were learned.

Surprisingly, Gene had little trouble getting an appointment to see Valenti.

He had been a World War II bomber pilot, been awarded several medals, and had even been in the motorcade in Dallas when President John F. Kennedy was shot. This is the kind of past that usually leads one to be supportive of the FBI.

Following the assassination, Valenti worked as a special assistant for newly-sworn-in President Lyndon Johnson. He might have been affected by some of the leftover bad feelings between Bobby Kennedy, then-US Attorney General, and J. Edgar Hoover, the FBI's longtime director. But this was the 1990s, and there was also the "Hollywood factor," which inclined movie people to shy away from helping the FBI.

It was up for grabs which way Valenti would go, but it was incumbent upon Gene to give it his best effort.

Gene met Valenti in his office, A-space, to be sure, on I Street in Northwest Washington, DC. Gene wore what we call

"Hoover Blues," a navy-blue suit, white shirt, and dark blue tie. We named this "uniform" out of respect for how Mr. Hoover wanted his agents to dress—professional, neat, and clean.

Valenti wore an immaculate suit that likely cost more than Gene's entire wardrobe. He came around his desk to meet Gene with a warm handshake.

Valenti always reminded me of James Cagney: not merely his face, but the strong, jutting jaw and short stature, which he overcame with the force of his personality. He was clearly a man to be reckoned with, and it would be good to have him on our side.

Gene asked Valenti to keep what he would tell him in the strictest confidence. In light of Valenti's past, that seemed like an easy request.

Then Gene laid out the minimal information necessary for what we needed.

We were interested in a Russian who was attending the AFM event in Santa Monica in a few weeks. Any information he might be able to provide about him, and the circumstances of his attending, would be very much appreciated.

On the face of it, this sounded easy. If it was couched in terms of a mere *interest* in the man, Valenti might or might not help. There would seem to be little downside. But if Gene told him how significant this matter was to the FBI and, ultimately, that it was the highest priority for our national security, that might have gotten the Hollywood man's attention. But did he really need all of that information, and who else would he tell?

In the end, Gene said it was an important investigation. Why else would he be meeting with *Jack Valenti*? He also downplayed the actual impact of the case and how many hundreds of man-hours and hundreds of thousands of dollars had already been dedicated to it.

There seemed little doubt that Valenti could help, and he said as much to Gene. He would make some inquiries and call Gene when he learned something.

Valenti told Gene, "Trust me!"

Gene left feeling very pleased and reported his results to the small circle of agents working on the case.

Then he waited, and waited, and waited.

Nothing.

Then Gene called Valenti.

He was not available.

Valenti did not return phone calls, and the AFM was soon to start.

Gene never heard back from Valenti. It was as though he had fallen off the face of the earth.

We later estimated the Hollywood factor was probably the deciding issue. If it became known that Valenti had accepted an overture from the FBI, and then assisted *the feds*, it could have embarrassed him and his entire organization.

But he never admitted to that, or anything else.

Only later, when I became more involved in the Hollywood aspect of this case, did someone clue me in on an important point.

In Hollywood, when someone says, "Trust me!" he actually means, "*Fuck you!*"

Jack & Polly Platt

You never know from what unlikely sources great benefits might come.

For years, Gene had been friends with Jack Platt, professionally and socially. Jack had made his career in the CIA and had the street handle "Cowboy." I had minimal contact with him but liked him a lot. I hadn't seen him in a decade, but Jack was one of the good guys.

During a secure phone call, when Gene was updating me on his meeting with Jack Valenti, he said he wanted to bring Jack Platt "into the loop," but only so far.

We could certainly tell Jack that a former Soviet was the target of our case, but the ultimate goal need not be revealed. Another reason could be crafted for why we would want to get close to a Russian that would be acceptable to a longtime member of the Intelligence Community, even so long after the Berlin Wall had come down. Jack was so good, we believed he would go along with whatever we needed. It was simple—we trusted him and he trusted us.

Gene told me that, long ago, he had learned Jack's sister was a Hollywood insider. She was a member of the Academy of the Motion Picture Arts and Sciences and had even been nominated for an Academy Award for Art and Set Decoration for *Terms of Endearment* in 1984. She wrote the screenplay for *Pretty Baby* and discovered Brooke Shields for the title role. Years before, she had been married to famed film director Peter Bogdanovich.

Gene solicited my thoughts about asking Jack for his sister's help.

Unlike the overture to Valenti, a man with no particular reason to help the FBI, other than the obvious one—*Patriotism*!—in Jack's sister there would be a family connection. It was a bond that might enable a Hollywood insider to cross the line. Still, it was a wait-and-see game. I would be happy to work with whatever Gene could provide.

My plan was to go to the film market with a not-yet-created backstopping and my best street-sense on full alert. Anything more would just make my job easier.

A couple of days later, Gene called. It was a "go" with Jack's sister, Polly Platt. The only catch was she had to meet the undercover agent before making her final decision.

That was fine and quite normal. Why would anyone risk their reputation and livelihood with their eyes closed? Her request merely confirmed she was a prudent person.

When I was assigned to the Courtship squad in the 1980s, our supervisor, Jim Stassinos, was promised an undercover position in a large company with its headquarters in Boston. The last piece of the puzzle to seal the deal was for the CEO to meet the undercover operative.

Stass was a full-blooded Greek and, as he told it, not the kind portrayed by the iconic statue of the Discus Thrower. He was one of the shorter, squatter, endomorphic Greeks. He had barely made it over J. Edgar Hoover's height requirement of 5′8″ for getting into the FBI.

He was proud of his heritage, but without the athletic body shape of most FBI agents, he had a bit of angst on his flight to Boston.

He finally arrived at the top floor of the corporate headquarters and introduced himself to the CEO's secretary. She asked him to wait while she went through a beautifully crafted doorway adjacent to her desk.

In a moment, she motioned Stass to come in.

In his Hoover Blues, he stepped across the threshold into an enormously long room with hardwood floors, exquisite furniture, a large Persian rug, ornate chandelier, sculpture, artwork on the walls, and a full library lined by floor-to-ceiling shelves.

At the far end of the room, the CEO stood behind his massive desk, talking on the phone. He was silhouetted by a panoramic view of Boston. He signaled Stass to move closer.

When he was about halfway to the man, the CEO spoke into the mouthpiece, "Hold on," and pressed it against his lapel.

He looked Stass up and down and asked, "Are you the guy who will be representing himself as an employee of my company?"

"Yes, I am," Stass said.

The CEO did a second sizing-up and trumpeted his lips.

"Yeah, okay."

He went back to his phone conversation and the meeting was over.

Stass wondered if it had been worth the roundtrip ticket for this twenty-second encounter, but he knew it was. It finalized the long-sought cover slot. There are few milestones in undercover work that are more essential to get the ball rolling.

Now I would drive from San Diego to Los Angeles to meet an actual Academy member, much more than the meeting Stass had, which I hoped would enhance our chance of success.

Meeting Polly Platt

Polly Platt's office was at the Carsey-Werner Studios in the San Fernando Valley. She left word at the gate to let me in. The lot looked exactly like they are portrayed in the movies—strangely costumed people walking around and golf carts everywhere, moving people and props.

I cannot deny that I felt exhilarated. In my mind, the wheels were turning as to how the meeting would end. Could a cover position be crafted to get to the next step?

I entered through the only door in an enormous wall of a warehouse. Pathways and corridors led through a maze of partitions, each holding different scenes for television shows I was familiar with. The lights were dim.

Right across from the stage set for *That '70s Show* was the door I was looking for.

I knocked, and a young lady answered.

I had not yet chosen a name I would use in this undercover role, but it is best to use your own first name. As a longtime FBI agent, with the great likelihood that my name was on a list in Dzerzhinsky Square in Moscow, at the former KGB Headquarters, I would need a different last name.

I didn't want to upset Polly, but the fewer things the uninitiated need to remember, the better. My actual last name was one of them, so in her office I was just "Wayne."

Fortunately, this did not seem too terribly abnormal: one of the benefits of dealing with Hollywood. Their standards and methods are so outside-the-box, compared with the rest of America, well, anything goes.

Polly's brother, Jack, was a good-sized man with a significant chunk of flesh under his belt, and nearing the end of his CIA career. But the petite woman who rose from behind her desk was the opposite. She was a few years older than me and had a neat blond pageboy. Her office was filled with various awards and honors from her industry, although not displayed in a garish way. It was more like, "I have to put them someplace, so it may as well be here."

To say that Polly Platt was gracious would be an understatement, and she took me at face value. It was not at all that she wanted to be involved in the excitement of helping the FBI catch a criminal or a spy. She had made a promise to her brother, and that controlled all.

She was quite clear that this had to be a confidential matter. She felt comfortable with her reputation in her community and wanted nothing to change it.

Part of the reason was the infamous Black List in Hollywood, instituted in 1947, when those linked with communism could not find employment. The pendulum had now swung back the other way.

For years she had kept hidden that her brother was in the CIA, actually part of *his* job description, but the rest was due to Hollywood politics. When she found herself in the middle, she leaned toward her brother, for which I was grateful.

My mother's maiden name was Johnson. It was an alias I had last used twenty-six years before and, coincidentally, in Los Angeles. I had been a card-carrying member of the Black Panther Party—even as a blond-haired, blue-eyed white guy.

Because it would be easy for me, and also for Polly, we went with "Johnson."

It was worth discussing because, as I told Polly, I did not want her to think I was lying to her, although a certain amount of deception was required for what we were doing. Should any of her colleagues want to find out more about me, the ruse would also protect her.

In my ordinary life, if two people I have met want to verify that I am the same person, all either one has to ask is, "Did he show you a picture of his family in the first ten minutes?"

I like to pull out a wallet-size, annual Christmas photo for a number of reasons. If the interviewee is a woman and has children, or siblings, it reflects similarities in the two of us.

Because of the obvious closeness between Polly and her personal assistant, I thought I could induce that family-related conversation with the photo.

I like to hear the *oohs* and *aahs* that the cute, wholesome family photo evokes. But then I also like to learn about the family of the one holding the photo.

By the time it is back in my wallet, we are several degrees closer, and that could not have been accomplished without it.

Polly's assistant turned out to be her stepdaughter, Kelly Wade. Polly invited her into the office to look at the photo. That demonstrated their closeness, even if not blood-related, and their shared common set of values.

Kelly also knew I was a friend of "Uncle Jack."

It wasn't that I was using the tricks of my trade on someone who was not my target. You use them on everybody—and all the time. It's just what you do.

If I were potentially going to rely on Polly for so very much, I had to be certain about what made her tick. However, by the end of our two hours together, her genuineness was quite apparent. It was almost as though she had wanted to do something courageous like this for years, but it would never happen solely within her very large circle of Hollywood friends.

Hearing my plan, Polly realized I needed to learn some basics about the movie industry.

She went into nomenclature about movie distribution at home and abroad using terms like "having legs." That's how a movie plays in other countries.

She gave me copies of several screenplays, almost all 117 pages long. Whether from a Jane Austin gothic novel, or a Star Wars action movie, this demonstrated there is only so much dialogue in any movie.

By the end of our meeting, it was like we were reacquainted, long-lost friends.

It should be noted I did not mention Jack Valenti. Had she learned of that overture, and his not coming through for us, it might have given her second thoughts. Now, she had become an essential part of our operation.

There was something else about Polly that I liked. She was sincere—but never uttered the words, "Trust me!"

I left her with a good feeling, but now I had even more on my plate than before. I had to dream up a cover that would be acceptable to her—something to use at the film market—and also of sufficient interest so a Russian would want to be my friend. How the hell would I come up with that?

History with George Ramonas

It was time to piece together the backstopping for my cover position.

When you are confronted with a unique set of facts and need to insert yourself right into the middle of something quite big and complex, there is no cover position preordained for such an operation. You cannot just reach into an undercover closet, pull one out, and put it on.

No, each case that comes down the pike requires something brand new, created just for that operation. It must fit as perfectly as you can get it to meet your needs. Time spent fabricating such a cover takes all the brain cells and mental alacrity you have, plus a quarter of a century of experience to fine-tune whatever you eventually come up with.

Some think having the ultimate cover position is half the battle. Even so, it is *only* half the battle, for then you must wear it and charge into the actual battle—with confidence that you will succeed.

The Bureau expected me to walk into the AFM festival, locate the Russian, become friends, and recruit him—at least enough for him to identify a photograph.

I had no contacts in the movie industry, other than Polly. I felt privileged for her help, but it was too much to ask her to support my backstopping as well.

In 1974, George Ramonas came to Washington to be part of President Gerald Ford's election campaign. He was an attorney in Cleveland and had clients who were Romanian émigrés. He didn't know it, but that put him squarely in my crosshairs to be interviewed. I had been to language school, spoke Romanian, and worked those cases.

He went to the embassy on Massachusetts Avenue with the goal of reuniting his clients' families. But the intelligence officers in the consular section were looking for something quite different. To meet with an American attorney, wine-and-dine him, and possibly have a source in the White House, would be a choice contact.

If he was interesting to the Romanians, he was interesting to me.

When we finally met, we were both young lawyers from big cities who had recently passed the bar. We had a myriad of shared experiences, as though we had known each other for years. Importantly, George was willing to assist our investigations. In return, I could explain the Romanian Consulate's bizarre rules for dealing with émigrés, his clients, and how he could solve their problems.

By the time Jerry Ford lost to Jimmy Carter in 1976, George had acquired a taste for the Washington political scene. He earned a spot on the staff of Senator Pete Domenici of New Mexico. This made George a juicy morsel for Romanian Intelligence to meet with and have a "continuing dialogue," meaning regular lunches together. I would have my own dialogue with George soon thereafter, teaming up against Romanian Intelligence.

That is how George was: helpful and patriotic, nearly to a fault. Our close relationship led me to turn to him after almost a decade since I moved away from Washington.

Many years before, my partner, Warren Rowlands, and I were meeting with George in his Capitol Hill office. After three interruptions from people wanting a piece of his time, I commented on how much in demand he was, and that we appreciated the time he gave us.

He looked back and forth at us, and then at each one of us directly in the eye. He told us we did not understand—not at all. I was taken aback.

He said every person on Capitol Hill, and every lobbyist, wanted something from him. And there was always an ulterior motive which would benefit them personally.

He leaned back and told us we were the only ones whose requests were solely for the benefit of the United States and the people of America.

He had instructed his secretary that, if we called, to rearrange his schedule so we could meet with him and deal with whatever crisis was barreling toward us.

He looked over at his doorframe, and down at the floor, even pointed at it. He said, "You are the only ones who cross that threshold who I can say that about. You are welcome anytime."

With that as our history, it was an easy decision to go to George for help, once again.

Meeting George Ramonas

I called George from San Diego. Ours had become a Christmas-card-exchange relationship in the years since I left Washington.

Once back in touch, it was as though no time had passed since we last spoke. I told him I would be in DC in a couple of days and hoped he'd be free for lunch. He said he would make reservations "at the usual place."

That would be the Old Ebbitt Grill, across from the Department of the Treasury, just down the street from the White House. My favorite anytime meal was eggs Benedict. Even if it wasn't on the menu, George would call ahead to make sure they could whip up some fresh hollandaise sauce for one of their best customers.

In two days, I walked into George's office, high in a building on I Street. I told the receptionist I was "Wayne for George" and was sent through to his secretary. Astonishingly, this was the same woman he had brought with him from the senator's office years before, and she remembered me. More importantly, she knew that, once again, something was afoot.

George came through his doorway and we proceeded to lunch.

At the Old Ebbitt Grill they made our eggs Benedict to perfection. We caught up on the intervening years, but when it was time for business, we lowered our voices.

I made reference to one of our operations from fifteen years before, where he had been able to assist our case in a dynamic way. Nothing like it had ever been done, but it wouldn't have been for lack of imagination. Any fully functioning agent would have known that the kind of plan we concocted was way outside the bounds of what might be authorized.

But Courtship was a squad for highly qualified agents with the goal of recruiting Soviet intelligence officers—the hardest target. So, an undercover role that was outside the box seemed completely appropriate to me.

The sensitive nature of that operation precludes me from going too far into the details, but suffice it to say, an important aspect of the plan was that Soviets were not familiar with the actual workings of the democratic election process in the West. They were prone to projecting their system onto ours. How long had it been since someone from a party *other* than the Communist Party was "elected" in the Soviet Union?

Right: never, all the way back to 1917.

In the US, the Soviets had seen the Democrats win both houses of Congress since almost back to World War II—and why should it change?

In 1980, when Ronald Reagan was elected, he swept in a Republican Senate majority. The Russians were in a state of shock.

They thought it was a trick. The trick, of course, had been that Jimmy Carter brought the country to what Reagan called a general condition of "malaise." The former California governor was elected to come to the rescue. None of this was in the Soviets' realm of understanding.

Worst of all, when they realized the Democrats no longer controlled the Senate, they began knocking on Republican doors. *Surprise, surprise*—nobody was home!

In an ingenious way, we were able to leverage that situation to our advantage. But would FBI Headquarters go along with it?

At Courtship, the naysayers were everywhere.

I made my best effort to describe what the project was intended to do—head off the herd so we could wrangle Soviets to their new sources—a slew of undercover FBI agents.

Many days went by. When we finally heard back from FBI Headquarters, there were so many caveats and proscriptions, it looked like we would have to call it quits. But I soon realized their caveats did not really affect our goal.

My responding teletype may have been the shortest on record: FBIHQ requirements and caveats noted. Approval is appreciated.

I am sure there was cringing at FBI Headquarters, but I have always said, "It takes so much effort to fight the bureaucracy, when you finally succeed, catching the bad guys seems easy."

Meeting and reminiscing with George gave us the inspiration to conceive of a plan I could implement. I would be a financer of independent films, ostensibly backed by Texas millionaires who had no knowledge of the film industry but wanted to dabble in it.

My "investors" would rely on my supposed expertise to pick the projects where their money would be spent.

Win or lose, my backers found excitement in it. They knew the stock market was gambling, as was where to drill when searching for oil. It didn't matter that looking for a hit film was just as risky, and they could certainly afford it.

I was the keeper of the purse strings of a non-existent fortune and could pick and choose who I would talk to and what I would tell them. In the right circumstances, I would be the most popular person in the room.

CHAPTER 4

A CHILDHOOD THAT LED TO THE FBI

Even in a government agency, where everyone has to pass the same tests and meet certain criteria, there is still an extraordinarily diverse set of individuals. What was it about me that caused three FBI agents to fly all the way across the country to ask me to take on a mission that any unbiased observer would have seen as next to impossible?

My father would probably have said "upbringing." He was raised in orphanages and swore to himself that if he ever had children, he would raise them right. While he was wise and calm, my mother was the one who, for any project, charged right ahead, striving to "get it done, now!" I like to think I'm a nice blend of the two.

We had little money, and the narrowest of rowhouses in a working-class neighborhood, but there was never a question about where the next meal would come from. I give my parents credit for instilling in me *the desire to be somebody.* But what do you do with an upbringing that enables you to open doors for yourself, often even when they seem closed and locked, but reach out and throw them wide open?

When I first arrived in San Diego in 1990 and was assigned to the counterterrorism and counterintelligence squad, my personnel file also arrived. It is like a thick, in-house resume.

My new supervisor went through it. When he finished, he picked up his phone and called my last supervisor in the Washington Field Office, Jim Stassinos. He said he had only one question. "Did Barnes really do all this shit—all of it?"

Stass told the man, "When Wayne is working a case and has covered all the leads, he will walk up the stream turning over rocks, looking for more. He will splash around and find what no one else would see, or simply create leads that didn't exist, anything to make the case work. I'd take ten Waynes if I could find them."

***

Life for me began in the inner city of Philadelphia. I had one brother, Ken, two years older. He was a once-in-a-generation intellect. A couple of examples are worth noting.

As a senior at Penn State, he took the Graduate Record Exam, necessary when applying for graduate school. He walked out of the test and told me it was easy. The rest of the test-takers were still in the hall sweating bullets.

Two weeks later he received a letter from the Educational Testing Service in Princeton. He was the first person who ever answered all of the questions and got them all right. He broke the national curve. Where the highest score was an 800, he was awarded an unprecedented 810.

When he took the test for Mensa, not only did he qualify, he scored in the 99.6 percentile, the top 2 percent of the top 2 percent, a "Double-M." I was smart, but he was a genius, with an IQ measured at *165*.

This is not to brag about him, but every year of my life, until high school, every teacher would ask, "Are you Ken's little brother? Are you as smart as he is?" It drove me nuts!

There was a test you could take to qualify for Central High, the school for "smart boys" in Philadelphia, administered in the eighth grade. On the day of the test, I made a decision which only later would I realize was a life-changing moment. But I saw it as my path to get out from under second-child syndrome and become my own person.

That night, my father asked, "How did the test go?"

I gathered my courage and told him, "I didn't take it."

That was perhaps the angriest I had ever seen him. He could not afford to send me to a private school. From having gone to Pennypacker Elementary in our local community of West Oak Lane, then Leeds Junior High in Mount Airy, I would now attend Germantown High. Three miles away, it was in one of the roughest neighborhoods in the city.

My father feared for me, and my mother cried.

At fifteen years old I was five feet tall and weighed a hundred pounds, the smallest kid in a school of four thousand, where 85 percent of the students were Black. I was a little blue-eyed white kid whose hair was platinum. It flowed down over my forehead like the shiny satin edging of a baby's blanket. None of my friends could pass me by without petting it. This, too, drove me nuts! But at least no teacher ever asked if I was Ken's little brother.

Germantown turned out to be one of the best things that ever happened to me. Not following my brother became less important than what I faced there, and how I faced it.

In Germantown High, if you weren't Black, you were Jewish, and if you weren't Jewish, you were me! With all the talk of "minorities" in later years, I had checked that block in high school. If you studied hard, one day you could leave Germantown behind. It was not a good place to *be*, but it was a very good place to be *from*, a character builder—if you survived.

The first week was pretty scary. Between classes I went to the boys' bathroom. It was filled with smoke from big guys standing around, lighting up. As I waited for a urinal, one of the tallest boys in the school approached me. Everybody knew Freeman Washington, great-grandson of a slave and a mean customer. He towered over me and looked down into my face.

He pointed a finger at me and his deep voice said, "Gimme a smoke."

I had no idea what he meant.

"Smoke? I don't smoke. I don't have any cigarettes."

Freeman stayed calm. It was *his* bathroom.

He pointed his finger at my shirt pocket. "Gimme a smoke," he said again.

That was the moment I realized I had to communicate with him. He could have slapped me silly, but he waited. I didn't want to disappoint him, but I didn't want to die, either.

"I don't have a cigarette," I told him. "If I did, it would be yours."

He slowly put the end of his long finger into my shirt pocket, not saying a word. Then it clicked. Every day I had a red box of Sun-Maid raisins in that pocket, about the same size as a pack of Lucky Strikes. I took it out and held it up to him.

"They're only raisins," I said. "Want some?"

He took the box and stared at it, then looked inside. He thought I was hiding cigarettes, but there were only raisins. He put some in his mouth.

"Raisins," he said slowly, and nodding. He repeated it louder, smiling with his big white teeth. He looked around and all his boys laughed.

"Keep the box," I said, sweat running down my sideburns. "I'll bring more tomorrow."

"Okay, Raisins," he said. "Come on back tomorrow."

The beauty is that he had gotten something of value, even if it wasn't what he was looking for, and I managed to escape with something more than just my life. I had made a friend who everyone feared, and I was *his* new friend, "Raisins."

This was a lesson that would help my FBI career. No, it didn't involve the world of spies, but it *was* about recruiting someone: Who benefits, and how?

Freeman would get his raisins, and I was glad to give them to him. It began a friendship that lasted two years. I actually took a liking to him, and he to me. But what did I get out of it? I went home each day unhampered in the hallways and bathrooms and fared better for having known him. The benefit to me far exceeded whatever Freeman Washington got from the deal.

I went on to be on four athletic teams: swim, gym, soccer, and track. I dove from the one-meter springboard and pole vaulted. In my senior year I was offered a gymnastics scholarship to Iowa State University. But for an inner-city boy who had never been across the Mississippi River, and hardly beyond the Susquehanna, it would have been like going to college on Mars. For extracurriculars, I was also involved in Scouting and earned the rank of Eagle.

Along the way, I grew—a lot. When I graduated, I had grown thirteen inches in three years and gained sixty pounds. My mother had been wise enough to buy pants with extra material in the cuffs and lowered the hems every few weeks. During my eleventh-grade growth spurt, I grew six and a half inches, with six gray hemline marks down my pant legs that all my friends joked about.

I got involved in school government and, in my senior year, was elected president of the student body. This was a poser for many, but I got along with everyone. The proof was in the ballot box.

My escape from the inner city was to attend Penn State in the center of Pennsylvania. Studying my keester off, I was accepted at the Villanova University School of Law but could ill afford it.

On a sunny Saturday morning in the spring of 1968, I donned a jacket and tie and put my thumb out on the road, hitchhiking 215 miles to Philly and the house of Joe Bevilacqua, the Villanova dean of men. At a picnic table on his back lawn, he sized me up as big enough and fit enough for the task. I was given a counsellorship and assigned to Austin Hall, the freshman football-scholarship dorm—a.k.a. Animal House! But it paid for room and board for three years and enabled me to earn a Juris Doctor degree. From there, it was a short leap to an FBI application for the Special Agent position and a career I could not have dreamed of.

My first office was Los Angeles in 1972, assigned to the Extremist Squad.

A couple years before, there had been a shootout between the LA Police Department and the Black Panther Party. Several months later, the militant organization was in disarray. Two leaders emerged from the rubble, each supported by a block of followers:

Huey Newton and Eldridge Cleaver. Cleaver was a wanted fugitive and had left the US for Algeria. A group of Cleaver-faction Panthers started a new group, the "Nation of Nigretia." They described themselves as a country without land, descendants of slaves brought from Africa and now spread throughout the US. It took little time for a sixth investigative sense among the agents on our squad to realize something was afoot.

Back then, the Bureau had few Black agents, and all were well known in the Black communities. At a squad meeting, we tossed around ideas about how to learn what the Nigretians were up to.

I spoke with my supervisor and the lead agent and told them of my past in Germantown. They were shocked, but I was given the go-ahead. They made clear what the dangers were if my real identity became known.

"They would just as soon shoot you as look at you," I was told.

With fifteen weeks of FBI training, the only actual "training" I needed for this assignment was to have attended Germantown High.

I drove out to San Fernando Valley State College and bought a gray T-shirt with the school's name on it, then put it through a few cycles in a washing machine to fade it a bit. I sat in on several classes, like an auditing student.

A few days later, I walked into Black Panther headquarters, armed with only my gray college T-shirt and whatever chutzpah I could muster. I explained that I was a graduate student in sociology and was writing a master's thesis on an American ethnic group. I had chosen them.

The man behind the reception desk stood up, smiled, and put out his hand.

"Welcome to the Black Panthers!"

For the next six months I was a card-carrying Black Panther. Not bad for a blue-eyed, blond-haired, white guy.

At one meeting of the Nation of Nigretia, held in the home of the High Priestess of Nigretia, in South LA, there were fifteen in attendance, many of whom I had met before. The dining room had been cleared and chairs set up in rows. Of course, I took notes, diligently, ostensibly for my master's thesis, but really to prepare for an FBI memo the following morning. I had become the Nation of Nigretia's ad hoc secretary.

At a break, the High Priestess came in with her college-age son, Rodney. While it seemed as though I had been accepted, this would be the test I had foreseen, although not in this form. He was an undergraduate student at San Fernando Valley State.

Oh, shit!

With his mother and three others nearby, Rodney asked about my classes and instructors. I easily told him about the advanced "sosh" classes I had and said things so he knew I was familiar with the campus.

Then I turned the tables and asked Rodney about his classes. He mentioned a few professors, one whose advanced class I had actually sat in on.

I told Rodney the man was an old, fat, bald, Jewish, white guy who didn't know what he was talking about. I clarified that with some esoteric sociology issue recalled from his class and then stopped.

There were five blank faces staring at me.

"What's the matter?" I asked, truly puzzled by their reaction to what I had said.

Rodney was the first to respond.

"We never heard a white person defame another white person."

Humorously, I thought, they didn't get out very much!

I just smiled and shrugged my shoulders.

Easy conversation continued, and it seemed I had passed their test.

I did realize that many of these Black Panthers were of the mentality that they *would* just as soon shoot you—*me*—as look at me, if they knew who I really was. But this is why you backstop your cover and prepare and prepare, never letting your guard down.

At the next meeting, Rodney greeted me like we were old friends. Afterwards, he pulled me aside and said, "You know what this is really all about?"

I had no idea what he meant and gave him a blank stare.

He said Eldridge Cleaver was a fugitive in Algeria and was trying to create a way to get back into the United States without being arrested by the FBI. The Nation of Nigretia had just been recognized by four African nations, including Senegal, which had even granted four acres of land so there could actually be some territory to call "Nigretia."

With these recognitions, Nigretia was petitioning to gain admission to the United Nations. Once received, they planned to bring Eldridge Cleaver back to the United States as the Nigretian ambassador to the UN.

"He would have diplomatic immunity," Rodney explained, "and could not be arrested by the FBI!"

"Wow!" I told him. "That's great!"

I added that would mean "we" would have an easily recognizable name to lead Nigretia, and the membership would soar.

Rodney jumped up and down and slapped me on the back with a big smile, seeing I really did understand. It was a good moment—but it was also time for me to get the heck out of there.

The next morning, I wrote a communication summarizing what had happened in the last few months and provided the specifics of what I had learned the previous evening. The details from Rodney were set out with their plan to bring fugitive Eldridge Cleaver back into the United States, with the objective of circumventing US laws.

The communication was signed out by my supervisor and transmitted to Washington.

Apparently, it was well received at FBI Headquarters and disseminated to the State Department, from which it was sent on to the United States Mission to the United Nations.

I was told it would have landed on the desk of the US ambassador who, at the time, was George H. W. Bush.

In faraway New York City, within just a few days, Ambassador Bush read the communication. It was he who walked it down the hallway in the UN building and met, individually, with the four ambassadors from the African nations that had officially recognized the Nation of Nigretia. I was also told he stood there with each ambassador as they read the communication. Within a few days, each of those nations withdrew their recognition, and the Nation of Nigretia quietly slipped away from the international sphere.

At the time when I was nearly buried under working the Black Panthers, I had also become involved in a second, very contrasting, undercover role. I was the inside man in a white-extremist group that was planning to kill President Nixon at the Western White House in San Clemente. Eventually, both groups were stymied, and neither that plot, nor the one with the Nation of Nigretia, ever became known to the public—probably a very good thing.

The FBI director gave me a letter of commendation, but the story doesn't end there.

A decade later, in 1982, a senior Soviet KGB officer, who had previously been assigned to their embassy in Algeria, defected to the US. By then, I had gained a niche in debriefing defectors and interviewed this one.

I raised Eldridge Cleaver's name. The defector recalled a Soviet embassy reception in Algiers in the early '70s which Cleaver attended. He had made an overture to speak privately with someone in the KGB. Our defector accommodated him. Cleaver explained he had a plan to return to the United States without fear of arrest. He asked the Soviets to supply him with weapons "to foment revolution."

The intelligence officer sent a telex to the KGB's Moscow Centre reporting the request. A few days later, Moscow replied that they first wanted to see Cleaver successfully enter the US—safely. Only then would they provide him with the requested arms. It was not at all certain they would have come through as agreed, but the point soon became moot for, thanks to the Black Panther undercover operation, the Nation of Nigretia had quietly faded away.

I was the only person in the FBI who knew both halves of this story, and it was written up in an official letterhead memorandum. The Black Panther undercover role had been my first, followed by a dozen more. The current one, with a Russian target, would be my last. I would do everything I could to make it the icing on the cake of my FBI career.

CHAPTER 5

SANTA MONICA

The American Film Market is a big deal, where many come to sell their movies. In 1998 it was staged at the Loews Santa Monica Beach Hotel with over four hundred rooms and suites. It is five stories high at the Ocean Avenue entrance but rises to eight on Appian Way to the west. The building does not get any taller, but the property has a steep slope down to the beach and provides a spectacular view of the Pacific Ocean.

Santa Monica is a dozen miles down the boulevard from Hollywood, the recognized world headquarters of the movie industry. For anyone not actually from there, the festival felt like it was held at the center of the motion-picture universe.

The event was an eight-day affair and the clock was ticking. I missed the first couple of days because of something that should have been easy to get, but wasn't—my business card.

This had to be professionally printed, with my alias name, the proper logo, and, especially, my phone number—which rang on the recently installed instrument in my bedroom in Solana Beach. I could not look like an amateur when I finally met the target and had the opportunity to give him one. That meant *not* writing my information on the back of a paper napkin. A proper-looking business card was essential—the perfect "proof" of my fictional identity.

I sat in my house in Solana Beach, waiting for the special delivery of five hundred business cards and could feel the dynamics of the festival passing me by. How many opportunities was I missing a hundred miles to the north where things were going on without me?

When the cards finally arrived, I called Gene McClelland to tell him I was almost out the door. He told me to stop in at the Los Angeles FBI field office before going to Santa Monica. Fine, I thought, but let's get moving!

The drive north was a good time to settle into being someone else. Had I not done this in more than a dozen cases, I would have been much more stressed. When one assumes a different *persona*, even if only short-term, precautions must be taken.

You have to answer to your cover name, but you must *not* answer to your own. If you think this is easy, try it sometime. A couple seconds of hesitation can spell disaster when you hear what is supposed to be your name.

"Mr. Jones, how good to see you again!" *Oh, right, today I am "Mr. Jones."*

"And it's so good to see you, as well."

How long does it take your brain to adjust to that?

How far through your signature—when paying for a meal with your credit card, and your subject is right beside you, watching—would you realize you were signing the wrong name?

That is beyond the carefully laid plans of dozens of other aspects of your backstopping, beginning with your driver license, and it included years of taking just the right family photos. You must keep in mind where your cover story diverges from your real job—FBI agent!

Your legend includes vignettes of every shape and dimension about all of the experiences you should know off the top of your head: here, the role of a big-time movie financer. It takes a while to get your brain enmeshed into being someone else.

I thought back to my first undercover role, also in Los Angeles, in 1972, when I was in the Black Panthers. Today's case was different, but in some ways, the same.

While there was no particular danger in the present operation, more hung in the balance than even I knew. Our most valuable sources in Soviet intelligence had been executed, and the compromise of US security was completely unacceptable. The problem had needed fixing for a long time, but it had taken years to realize there even was a problem. Then there were myriad steps to try to do something about it. I was enthusiastic to be part of it—and with this degree of orchestration.

Are you lying? Yes, of course, but for "God and country." A Supreme Court case ruled that an undercover FBI agent is allowed to lie to bad guys in the process of catching them for the bad things they are doing. So, don't worry that promises made will never be fulfilled, and don't lose sleep over them. There are more important things to worry about.

It had been a quarter of a century since I had been in the LA field office at 11000 Wilshire Boulevard. Back then, the top three floors were the home of the FBI. By 2007, it would be nine floors and they were looking for more space, even to have the building demolished and replaced by the FBI's own twin towers. But that hadn't happened yet.

Much of the large lobby is taken up by a US Post Office. We all have many regrets in our lives, usually for something we did which, perhaps, we shouldn't have. I recalled one missed opportunity I did not realize which existed at the time.

One day in 1972, as a young agent, I was in line in the post office. The man in front of me was about an inch shy of my height, but twice as broad in the shoulders.

This was before Disneyland-inspired, single-queuing lines were used in banks and post offices. Parallel lines fed each window. People nearby were gawking at the guy ahead of me. I peeked around his left shoulder at the stack of business envelopes he was holding. The return address was "Mr. Olympia, Mr. Universe," and other "Misters" I could not decipher.

He was, of course, Arnold Schwarzenegger, five years before his breakout movie, *Pumping Iron*. On that day he was seen not as the millions of moviegoers would see him in the future, but as more of a freak show. Gold's Gym was just down the road, but few went there and did what Arnold did.

As we waited, I should have followed my own rule, "Interview everyone you ever meet." It wouldn't have changed my career in the FBI, but it would have been an interesting moment with the future megastar and California governor.

Today, when I reached the floors of the FBI, I was met by Supervisory Special Agent Clark Harrison, and his agent on the case, Philip Jing. They briefed me on the events in Santa Monica. The only photo we had of our target was from his fifteen-year-old file in Washington, so they secured a new one from an overture made to the people who ran the film festival.

I cringed, hoping the person interviewed could be trusted, and what that really meant to Hollywood insiders. I also hoped the FBI had asked about *all* of the visiting Russians, and not just our target, so he wouldn't stand out. But what was done was done, and I was not there to interrogate or criticize. There was way too much on my mind.

I met my contact with the LA Special Surveillance Group, the SSG, also called "the Gs." He reported that the subject had been under observation for a day and a half. I was raring to go.

Then I learned something that surprised me—but shouldn't have. This was the FBI, and you never know what bureaucratic proclivities will overrule just plain old good sense.

During my first meeting with Mike, Dave, and Gene in San Diego, they told me of the much larger effort to contact any former Soviet Embassy official who might be able to identify our unsub. This had been going on for several years. Sadly, they had all been "cold pitches." In the world of counterintelligence, that is tantamount to an insult—offering an individual you have never met before a suitcase full of money to betray his country. While we were only looking for one very specific piece of information—pointing at the photograph of an American traitor—using a cold pitch has a very small chance of success.

One of the beloved Assistant Special Agents-in-Charge in the Washington Field Office during the 1980s was Nick Walsh. When he had supervised CI-3, the Soviet Military, GRU squad, he developed a program called "Pitch-A-Bum-A-Month!" It worked like this:

Put several Washington-based GRU officers under surveillance during the third week of the month. Wait until one of them was in a restaurant and eventually got up to use the men's room. A moment later, an FBI agent would follow him in and, as the Russian was peeing, come up beside him at the next urinal. The agent would identify himself to the Russian as an FBI agent and ask if he was willing to sell Soviet secrets. Further statements would be made until the Russian became red-faced, zipped up, and marched out of the bathroom, then out of the restaurant.

Russians were reluctant to report such a pitch because the person in charge of their embassy security would not look at it the way others might. He would ask himself, "Why did the FBI pick *this* officer?" and, "What weakness did they see in *him*?"

The problem for the Russian using the urinal was, if he and his family were sent back to Moscow, his wife would scream at him for doing something stupid. She would no longer be able to shop in American stores! It was a no-win situation for the officer, but with such an overt pitch, Russians felt compelled to report it.

This went on for eight months, and each Russian skedaddled out of the restaurant to tell his tale of woe to the security chief. Then, in month number nine, we didn't pitch anyone. The month after that, we went back to pitching a-bum-a-month, always with the same results.

The problem for the Soviet security chief who received monthly incident reports was there would be no report of an American pitching one of his officers in the ninth month. His question—and it would eat at him—was, "Which one of my GRU officers did *not* report a pitch, and *is he now working for the FBI?*" To say the least, he would have felt deep consternation.

It was a great program, but what would have happened if a GRU officer accepted the offer? Probably, we would have quickly pitched someone else who would report a pitch that month. But the program would still have worked with the sheer goal of unnerving the Soviet security chief. Cold War fun!

Now in Los Angeles in 1998, what I had not known was that this same cold-pitch scenario was planned to take place with the man who I saw as *my* Russian target. I was told there would be a two-prong approach: overt and covert.

The overt effort would consist of two veteran FBI agents: former colleagues from counterintelligence squads in Washington in the 1980s. I wondered how they had been chosen for this assignment. I had to participate in this conversation while stifling my own thoughts because I was quite outraged.

Thaddeus ("Ted") Suchan headed up the squad handling Soviet satellite countries in the Washington Field Office, a generation of supervisors after I had transferred off the squad. He was later transferred to a Soviet desk at FBI Headquarters and happened to be the one who read the paperwork from the field about the Russian who was now attending the film festival.

The other agent was David Cardillo. Like Ted, a very decent guy, but neither had experience on the front lines, face-to-face, recruiting Eastern Bloc intelligence officers. Neither one had had their psyches pasted into the remake of the Minnesota Multiphasic Personality Inventory test as the standard for who might be successful at recruiting targets. So why would these two be chosen to make the overture?

Simple! The bureaucracy declared that if Cardillo had been the case agent fifteen years ago, he should be the case agent today. And he *was* an experienced agent; never mind that he didn't have one-on-one skills in meeting and finessing a conversation with a Russian. Worse still, Suchan's having read Cardillo's paperwork, which was minimal, seemed to qualify him to come to Los Angeles, fifteen years later, to pitch the Russian!

The sad thing was that my part would be the covert prong. The undercover operation was relegated to a support role for the pitch to be made by Suchan and Cardillo.

It was now my job to learn the Russian's schedule for the pitch boys. When would he leave the conference for his hotel where they might make their overture? But I could do little to help them. For instance, if the Russian only wanted to shower and change to get ready for another meeting, that might be the worst time to knock on his door.

Picture the Russian opening his hotel room door, hair wet, naked but for a bath towel around his waist, and confronted by two men in suits with a suitcase full of money….

I decided not to have any angst and thought of the poem I would recite for my children's elementary school classes:

Patience is a virtue,
Virtue is a grace,
And Grace is a little girl
Who doesn't wash her face.

Light humor, but the concept helped swallow the bitter pill a bit more easily.

This was one job which required, perhaps, more patience than any other. I reflected on Mr. Hoover, who used to pay me to wait for red lights to turn green, and tried to layer that over what I had just learned. I would do my part as well as I could. But at the Bureau's request and expense, I had put in a lot of time for my cover: travel to Washington, meeting Polly in Los Angeles, attending the day of "training," setting up the UC telephone in my bedroom, and much more. It was just too much work only to play the role of a support position for a ploy that was—in my experience—almost doomed to fail.

Besides three FBI agents—Suchan, Cardillo, and me—there was a plethora of other FBI personnel in Santa Monica for this occasion, members of the SSG. Teams were from Washington, LA, and other cities, a couple of dozen strong. They had dedicated their lives to seeing others who would not see them—and were very good. But not everyone was in the loop about the ultimate goal. They would watch the Russian target and not wonder why, so many years after the Berlin Wall had come down. And they never would know.

Their job was to report to Suchan and Cardillo, but their information would not have the same value as someone's who was personally in touch with the target and might know where he was going next. For my part, I wanted to create a scenario where I could bump into him and meet him.

I still knew several of the older Gs. The most senior one from Washington had the handle "Hooker." He was a Civil War buff whose street name came from the hard-partying General Joseph Hooker. His troops were followed by "comfort women" as they moved from one encampment to the next, and these women would become known as "hookers."

Hooker and I had a warm reunion, and he called me by my street handle, "Captain Cosmic." He recalled my scams and that I would do all I could to make an operation work, even if I wasn't the one bringing it to the desired conclusion. Every piece of the puzzle helped make the whole picture. He had been around long enough to realize, as I did, that it was unlikely Suchan and Cardillo would meet with success.

I felt a bit second-fiddle as I drove west on Wilshire Boulevard out to Santa Monica and checked into the Holiday Inn. I freshened up and was soon marching down the street, feeling better. At last, I would finally begin what had taken so many weeks of planning.

Finding Ivan

The visage of the Loews Santa Monica Beach Hotel was quite something. It had enormous panels of glass up to a gable shape, topping off a spacious, high-ceilinged atrium lobby. The penthouse suites had their own gable ends, and windows were everywhere, the better to see the glistening ocean and magnificent Pacific sunsets. Exquisite cuisine was served around fireplaces and multi-tiered dining and lounge areas, and every variation of stylish place to recline was the norm. Lush vegetation, vines hanging from balcony walkways, and tall palm trees gave the feeling of a botanical garden.

A few days before, Gene McClelland had flown out from Washington to have an in-person liaison with the LA office, which was still not in the loop on the ultimate reason for the investigation.

Gene and I had walked around the hotel, getting the lay of the land before the festival began.

How important would a case have to be for someone from Washington to fly all the way across the country just to meet with the agents there and stroll the area of the planned encounter? Weren't there secure phones for such conversations, and couldn't I have done the strolling alone? Wasn't I trusted to do that?

The simple answer is, among those in the tightly held loop of the most sensitive and important case in the FBI, no one wanted any screw-ups. Even the planning stage was planned!

I had never heard of such elaborate coordination. And this was not some sort of bonus for Gene or a case of simply having a friend at FBIHQ who could authorize his travel. That is not how the highest echelon in the Intelligence Division worked.

If Gene came to LA, there was a justifiable reason. He was to coordinate this effort—personally. One might argue that we were all sophisticated and educated people with decades of experience. No matter. Every precaution had to be taken so it would go smoothly.

There was something else that was astonishing to me, even if kept behind the scenes. All of this effort, the enormous amount of time by so many top operators, and the mounting expenses, needed to have paperwork supporting it, but in a way so it would not come to the attention of the ultimate unsub. If he was in the FBI—and not the CIA, as most believed—and would be on the alert for any *sub rosa* operation mounted against him, he would be looking for a paper trail. All of these massive expenses had to be papered as though they were for some other fictional operation. This level of covertness inside the FBI was unprecedented.

Now, as I walked into the Loews Hotel, it had been completely transformed for the festival. Every room had been converted into an office. All of the beds and accoutrement for overnight accommodations were replaced with sofas, tables, and whatever was necessary to play trailers—previews or coming attractions—of movies made by the exhibitors.

In the cathedral-like atrium lobby, all the plants remained, but everything else had changed. It was now divided into cubicles, partitioned for different filmmakers to show their wares, their "one-sheets" (movie posters), and there were separate tables for those less well-financed. Would-be stars loitered, hoping to be discovered by someone who actually mattered.

The place was frantic, now on the second day of the festival. With only six more to accomplish the mission, I became embroiled in the turmoil.

An SSGer came inside to point out our target. But when I got up close, he was not our Russian, and he wasn't Russian at all!

This was dismaying. The Gs had been following the wrong person for a day and a half! So, we were back to square one. But how would *I* find him?

I took another look at the updated photo and put it back in my pocket. I glanced around the immediate area. There were hundreds of people moving in all directions: a beehive of activity. There was almost no organization to what was going on, and the din of near and distant conversations made any one of them unintelligible.

I found an information table and checked for anything related to Russians. There was one room—more significant than a cubicle—with a Moscow film company. I found it down a hallway. There were posters in Cyrillic and English, wild scenes from their latest action movie, and three men manning their posts.

I schmoozed with one and learned that five individuals were in their group. Could I hope that one of the two missing men was the Russian I sought? I had no time for options.

I told him I had met a man earlier named Ivan and asked if he was part of their group. No, none of them was an Ivan. Great lead, I thought, but no positive outcome.

Trying to look like a man with places to go and things to do, I marched down each hallway, searching from room to room. This took some time, but—nothing. I went around the atrium and into every cubicle with the same results.

I could have no contact, official or otherwise, with the administration of the American Film Market about Ivan. I, personally, could do nothing to show specific attention to our subject. I thought of how nice it would have been for Jack Valenti to come through for us.

Wasted time.

I began to wander around, seemingly plying my trade. I had come to the market as a financer of independent films and should have some experience at it by the time I met Ivan.

I went to a centrally located cubicle with two men and two women showing promotional items of their movie project. The men were the business part, while the women were absolutely gorgeous, decked out to present their own wares in the very best way possible. Both "babes" were pictured on the cubicle's back partition in the one-sheets. The space-effected scene was intended to bring thoughts of *Star Wars*, although with less skill and technology.

With the men, I discussed financing for their film, already completed, or "in the can," as we movie moguls say. But they were looking for the backing of a major motion picture studio to distribute it. That wasn't me, but it was good to hear more movie lingo.

Out in the large open area, I eavesdropped on several conversations. This was completely acceptable and even desired. There was no lack of aggressiveness in this crowd, and a downright passion to become involved in the movie-making process. Most were would-be producers and directors, but also many actors who had vaguely familiar faces, their names just beyond the tip of your tongue.

Over in a corner, with a white-sheet backing and bright lights, were two chairs and a couple of cameras ready to roll. A Hollywood man in a sharp navy-blue blazer, wearing enough makeup for me to realize he was about to be on camera, stood looking nervous. He was waiting for someone to sit in the second chair and be interviewed.

A humming came from the crowd a distance away, which grew louder as it approached, and then applause broke out. Through the mass of people appeared a petite Lea Thompson, famous as Lorraine McFly in the *Back to the Future* movies. The attendees went wild.

In such moments, I like to stand back from the masses and watch the reaction to what's going on. My father once told me that if more people had done that over the millennia, world history would have been radically different.

When Ms. Thompson got up that morning and brushed her teeth, when she dressed and drank her coffee, she was just Lea. But walking through an adoring crowd of movie fans, she became *"Lea Thompson."* This is not a bad thing, but one simply has to have the perspective of the periphery.

While all the others looked toward the interview, I scanned in the opposite direction. I saw a face I recognized. He looked a little older than his photo from the 1980s—and now matched the one I had been handed just a few hours before. In the midst of all the hubbub stood Ivan Fyodorovich Kurylenko.

CHAPTER 6

THE BASICS OF THE TOUCH

The touch is a very special moment in an undercover operation. After months of planning, when you finally meet your target, he must feel comfortable and completely unaware he is a target.

He must think he initiated the contact, and later, kept it going. There must be no hint of a grand scheme swirling around him, not the surveillance teams flooding the area, or the many vehicles down the street. He cannot be aware of the binoculars trained on him from a distance, or secreted Handie-Talkies relaying his every move. Learning such finesse is years in the making—and necessary when the results will actually make a difference. Here, they would.

An important part of this clandestine procedure is for the subject to be aware of you by the time you first make contact. You put yourself in front of him so he cannot help but notice you. It doesn't have to be a close encounter, just a basic familiarity with you. That is, the first time he shakes your hand cannot be the first time he has seen you, because it might carry the subliminal message that a plan is in motion working against him. He must be aware of your existence, from an hour before, or the day before, but in some way, of your presence at the film festival. He should have no reason to believe you ever laid eyes on him. He must feel that *he* has the upper hand in the relationship that is about to begin, and *you* are the naïve one.

Ivan was in his late forties, fairly fit and trim, and neatly groomed. He wore a long-sleeved white shirt, normal in most business settings but very different from what everyone else was wearing here. That was the first bit of personality assessment, but there was more.

He was in the crowded atrium, with most of the two thousand attendees surrounding him. Sunlight streamed in a sublime way, and everyone was in a good mood, including Ivan.

Did he even know who Lea Thompson was? I didn't think so, but his reaction said he had an interest in whatever was going on around him. He wanted to be an active participant and would have an open mind. It wasn't a perfect profile, but it was the beginnings of one, and this was in the first fifteen seconds.

Keeping Ivan in my peripheral vision, I moved through the crowd to find Hooker. I couldn't carry a Handie-Talkie, so we had to make personal contact for me to point out Ivan. This was years before everyone had a cellphone, which would have made all of this much easier.

Once nearby, I flicked my eyes and raised my chin to Hooker, who made his way through the crowd to me. We pressed our shoulders together but didn't look at each other. I told him what Ivan was wearing and where he was. I moved back through the mass of people with Hooker trailing to get an eyeball for himself.

From there, the dynamics for his team changed from a search-and-find to strictly surveillance. They would monitor his location for Agents Suchan and Cardillo's overt effort, needing up-to-the-minute information.

Most importantly, I could never be observed watching my target. If he happened to notice me—well, it could get creepy and end the operation before it began.

I made my way to a phone to call Polly and trigger the plan to insert her into our scenario.

No Kim Philby Redux!

There is a concept which comes well before you get to the time in a case where someone will make "the touch." It has to do with something I had not even considered when so many parts were moving around me. That is, *who* will make the touch? And, exactly, *why* had I been the one chosen for this undercover role?

At one point, when Mike Rochford, Dave Greb, and Gene McClelland verified that Ivan was coming to the US, a major issue which confronted them was: Who would be chosen for this one-on-one UC contact with the Russian?

The three agents had sat around a table, thinking and pondering for many minutes, seemingly getting nowhere.

All of a sudden, Gene sat up. A lightbulb had gone on in his mind.

"I know who," he said.

Dave and Mike looked at him, expecting him to spit out a name, but he wanted them to come to the same conclusion he had. He gave them hints, crumbs to follow to get to the prize.

"Who has been involved in recruiting intelligence officers from more than one country?"

No one, the other two seemed to think.

"Who has been working counterintelligence for twenty-five years and most of it in Washington, but he's not here now?"

Still nothing.

"Who was really successful working the bloc countries, then Soviets?"

Mike had nothing, but Dave reviewed who had been on his old Soviet Bloc squad that handled Czechs, Poles, Hungarian, Yugoslavs, Bulgarians—and Romanians.

Then Dave had it.

"Oh, no," he said, "I know." But he, too, would not say the name out loud, although both he and Gene knew there was only one person in the Bureau who fit that description.

Mike was still in the dark, and finally Dave said, "Barnes."

All were silent for a moment, and I know what they were thinking. This would involve bringing someone new into their most sensitive and tightly knit squad, but it was more than that.

There was a story that had circulated in the Intelligence Community about Kim Philby, who had been the senior British Intelligence officer in MI6, posted to the British Embassy in Washington in 1950. At one point, the Brits in London realized Philby was a Soviet agent. They sent a telex to their embassy in Washington with the instruction, "Arrest Philby!"

It turned out that Philby was the one who decoded that message, and the next time he was seen, he was walking down the street in Moscow.

The lesson was: Don't send the spy you are trying to catch to recruit a Russian who would name that agent as the spy you are looking for.

(Later information came out that this was not exactly the sequence of events regarding Philby, who did eventually make a covert departure from London, right under the nose of British Intelligence, and was then seen on the street in Moscow.)

So besides having to find an FBI agent capable of attempting the mission at hand, they also had to make sure the agent was *not the spy*!

Fortunately, information in the file indicated the unsub we were trying to identify had been active in 1992, while I had transferred to San Diego two years before, in 1990. That is, I had not been in Washington, DC, during crucial moments when the unsub was committing espionage in the nation's capital—so I was not the bad guy.

For my part—not to say I had been naïve—I never imagined I might be under suspicion. The agents running the massive case, however, had to think about all the possibilities. I had worked closely with Dave and even more so with Gene over the years. While they did consider the issue, I don't believe they ever thought I had such an unpatriotic deception within me. For the record, I didn't.

Getting in Front of Ivan

Polly knew it was showtime. I would pick her up at two and drive to the film market. In the meantime, I had to set my own stage.

During my earlier walks around the atrium, I had spoken with various people about their projects, covering my search for Ivan. When I mentioned that I financed independent films, a small crowd had gathered around me. Then they formed a line in front of me. I felt like a Disneyland attraction.

The two closest to me were in their early twenties, shaggy hair and slender, like they had passed up a few meals, so dedicated they were to their project.

"Our story takes place on a fictional planet," one of them said. "Monsters attack an intergalactic ship from Earth the moment it lands. It's good versus evil."

His partner went into all sorts of gyrations to describe the scene to me, but they had lost my attention at "monsters." This was clearly entertaining to those who were right behind them, with the end result that I accepted their business card, but not their screenplay.

The more aggressive of the two asked for my card, but I told him he couldn't have it. He seemed hurt and asked why not.

I said, "If I give you my card you will call me. If I want to speak with you, I will call you!"

His final plea was that his project required "only $4 million," and he already had $2 million. He was looking for the other two. After a short redux of our discussion about business cards, they walked away.

The next fellow in line said he wanted to talk about his movie idea but needed to tell me about the two guys who just left.

"They said they have a $4 million project, and need only two more, but that's bullshit! Theirs is a $2 million project, and they don't have *any* money. They want you to finance the whole deal!"

Nice, I thought. The last words out of the mouths of the men pitching for money had been a lie, and the first words from the next guy were to turn them in to curry favor with me so I would finance *his* project. This was the world I had entered.

Using this scenario to my advantage, I found Hooker and we had a powwow in an out-of-the-way place with half a dozen Gs. I wanted to get in front of Ivan with something similar to what had happened earlier.

I was fifty years old at the time, one of the older people at the film market. Most of those running around looking for contacts—to find investment money or be discovered—were half my age, as were many of the Gs. I guessed that Ivan, closer to my age, would be less likely to see them once and remember their faces.

For our little drama, I wanted to make sure to use FBI people who had no distinguishing features, like curly red hair, or bright clothes. However, this was their life's work, and part of the job description was *not* to stand out so their targets wouldn't remember them. Looking at the Gs before me, even I hadn't been able to pick most of them out of the crowd as part of our team. I should not have underestimated them.

We got a signal from the G with the eyeball on Ivan that he was approaching the atrium. I set up shop about fifteen feet inside the open area and began to hold court. I addressed my group of six Gs in a commanding tone—which some friends call my "FBI voice."

"Okay, you're first. Tell me what you have," I said to Hooker.

"I have a science-fiction motif, but with a romantic twist. It takes place a hundred years from now and involves time travel between two lovers."

"Fine. How much funding are you looking for?

"Right now, about two and a half million, but I would accept a mere million for a ten-percent share of the profits."

"Too little percentage for the amount you want," I told him. "Next!"

A female G said she had a romantic comedy, "along the lines of the television show *Friends*, but in Los Angeles and not New York."

This had been one of the most popular shows in America since 1994, particularly for her age-set. It might work as a concept, at least for a made-up movie project. Good for her.

As this was taking place, a small crowd gathered who were not part of our FBI scam. They genuinely wanted to make quick-pitches for funding their hoped-for movies.

Important for our illusion was for Ivan to walk past so he could not help but see me. Also, he couldn't help hearing the back-and-forth where I was the focus of attention. And then, there he was, right on the periphery of our little play.

He stopped for a few moments to observe and listen to our small gathering. Then he moved on. That was all I needed—all I had wanted. And—no eye contact! I forced myself to do absolutely nothing that would indicate I recognized his existence.

Even after Ivan was out of sight, we continued for a few more minutes. Then I gave my apologies to the real *and* made-up wannabe movie-makers and stepped away.

Enter Polly Platt

Polly lived in Venice Beach, less than three miles down Ocean Avenue from Santa Monica. This was convenient and enabled me to avoid the often-brutal LA freeway traffic.

I updated her and described the scam we had put on for Ivan as he walked past. She had not known about the more comprehensive effort with so many on surveillance, inside and out of the film festival, and especially not the overt-prong agents. When she became aware of many of the goings-on, she handled it professionally and took it in stride. But even Polly would not be told the ultimate reason for the undercover case—seeking to identify one of the most damaging spies in US history. Still, hearing about the morning's events ratcheted up, in her mind, the magnitude of the operation. It also made her realize she was one cog in a much larger wheel.

If a person does not think the weight of the world rests on her shoulders, she will play her small part much more readily, no matter how significant it might really be. Polly knew she was there as a showpiece to draw attention and assist my bona fides. That she had an open mind about all of this made her a dream to work with.

We chose a different set of Gs for the next stage, but the precaution was unnecessary.

The American Film Market had a cost for admission to the entire festival of $725, which I purchased for myself. A daily pass was $125, which I bought for Polly. But if you only wanted to enter the entrance area of the atrium, there was no cost. There, you were more of an onlooker and didn't have a name badge hanging around your neck.

My vignette with the Gs earlier in the day had been in the atrium, so only Hooker and a couple of others needed day passes. Polly and I would be walking through the free area and into the main event section, requiring the badges.

Even with such a seemingly small decision, spending $725 versus $125, and how many of the latter, necessary to pull off the next stage, there was a feeling of government angst.

Every FBI agent is circumspect about spending US taxpayers' money. It is often said that agents are cheap, but it is really a mental constraint, knowing that an administrator will later second-guess their paperwork about how much they spent and for what reason. No matter the value of the operation, which could be incalculable for US security, we would later hear, "Did you really need to buy *five* daily passes instead of *four*?"

Polly was a diminutive lady, always dressed stylishly, and had navigated the Hollywood circuit for over four decades. With several major and minor award nominations, and a few big wins, she would be in her element at the festival, more than I realized. She didn't need my show-fans to make her presence known.

Polly and I went through the glass entry doors, her hand through my arm, and entered the sunlit atrium. Two of my SSG plants turned around, seemingly surprised to see Polly. One of them, Crab, called out, "Hey, it's Polly Platt!"

My role-players began to trail behind as we walked. But then so did others who were not in on the scam, and were not paid by Uncle Sam. They said just about the same words and joined in, like a reenactment of the Pied Piper of Hamlin—with Polly in the lead.

Of course, all of this was coordinated with the Gs who had the eyeball on Ivan. They had him at a spot farther back where we would stroll by. There were now over a dozen people following Polly. My Gs could have dropped out of her retinue, and there would still have been plenty of others following her to make my point. That is, Polly *was* somebody! She made that statement quite well without any help from us.

From a position right beside Ivan, a female G, Pepper, sang out, "Look, it's Polly Platt!" Two others came forward to see better, and everyone in the area focused their attention on us.

Only Ivan had been our target audience, and he couldn't help but observe what was going on. Way beyond my staged scenario, more people pushed forward, making the point even stronger than I ever imagined. I had planned this little vignette with as much forethought as possible, hoping all would succeed, but there was more to it.

More than twenty-five-years before, as a new FBI agent-in-training, our instructors emphasized the "Six *P*s." *Prior planning prevents piss-poor performance.* It had become a normal part of the job. This operation, going as smoothly as it had, was one result. But you must always be aware of what might be around the next corner—operationally and administratively—because, sometimes, certain things were just not foreseeable.

Older attendees who knew Polly came over to shake hands or give a hug. There was a moment's chat with each of them, and then we moved on. Anyone who knew who Polly was, but didn't know her personally, would not have made an overture to her. They followed but kept their distance. She was a charter member of the Hollywood in-crowd, and none would be so crass as to shove a screenplay in her face.

Polly told me at our very first meeting that, on her own, she would never attend the American Film Market. It wasn't beneath her—it was just not a place she would ever go.

Many were from the international community trying to find a spot in the American market. While they might be established abroad, making it here, in the actual Hollywood, was the goal of everyone. This film festival could be that path. The locals, American wannabes, were also vying for their start in the industry. Well established, Polly was simply in a different circle, on a higher plane. She explained to me, "For you—and my brother—I will do this."

There was another aspect to Polly's decision to help us that went unstated, but I knew would be telling on her. Decades before, Hollywood A-listers, who had testified before the House Un-American Activities Committee, naming names of communists, did so to the detriment and careers of those individuals. Over the years, the pendulum swung back—and hard. Left-leaning actors now had the upper hand in Hollywood. They were more than dismissive of those who even voiced support for a Republican presidential candidate. Although not entirely blacklisted, once "outed," this minority certainly had difficulty finding decent parts in movies, and weren't invited into certain projects, all because of their "politics."

Polly knew that participating in our scam could potentially end her career. She was helping *the government—the FBI!* I would do everything within my power to keep our connection confidential so none of her peers would ever know what she was doing.

But it wasn't as though she had to hold her nose to be in the limelight. Johnny Carson, longtime host of *The Tonight Show*, said he did it to feel the intoxication of the audience every night. I am sure Polly was surprised at the welcome she received. Ironically, it was happening because this was a place where most true Hollywood insiders would never be, so, in a way, she was elevating the whole festival. The American Film Market owed this one to the FBI.

From the corner of my eye, I saw Ivan watch the gathering around Polly. This was another important block checked.

I thought of all the effort this one scenario had taken. Over a dozen surveillants had flown to Los Angeles to be at the film festival. Their hotels and cars, meals and overtime hours, all had to be justified to FBI Headquarters. That was another headache in the making. And the timing, to have it come together with the precision of a diamond cutter, all for just those few seconds, at that exact moment, was never guaranteed.

You can't worry about such things; rather, just go about doing everything you possibly can so all the pieces fall into place. I knew there was the possibility of a mishap, when everything could fall asunder. I liked to think, *not on my watch!* That's why I spent hours in the planning. It may have looked easy, but as we walked through the atrium doors, a single drop of perspiration rolled from the nape of my neck, inside my shirt, and slowly ran down the center of my back. No one else would be aware of the tension that had built up for the director of even such a small play. You don't try to hide it, you just live with it, part of the job, while the missteps that could spoil it are gnawing in your gut.

But then—*success*!—and the moment was over. We could leave at any time, but Polly was made of more than that. We went on to walk the route through the circus-like atmosphere. I will give her full credit for taking advantage of being there and just seeing what happened. She knew that some of the swirling around her had been a put-on, but she also knew much of it was genuine and she earned it. Working as a producer, director, and stage set designer over her long career, it was as though the Wizardess of Oz had come out from behind her curtain—and was finally revealed.

CHAPTER 7

THE UNLOADED GUN

After a couple of hours at the Loews hotel, I was ready to take Polly home. However, she was much more on solid ground here than I was, and she told me there were other things to do. My brain was still on working the case, but all of our leads for the day had been covered.

The American Film Market commandeered a dozen local theater screens showing films that were part of the festival. Many were foreign made, which was a big deal for those film companies from places like Russia and the Nordic countries, to the Far East and South America. We looked at the list of those to be presented that day and picked out a couple to see.

Polly and I attended one in the cops-and-robbers genre. Approaching the climax of the film, the police were in hot pursuit of the bad guy, who had just committed a violent offense using a handgun. He entered a tenement building and sped his way up several sets of zigzag stairs to the fourth floor, the good guys not far behind. He ran down a hallway and made a quick entry into an apartment on the left. Within seconds, the police charged down the corridor and pulled up, abruptly, before reaching his door.

Now the camera angle came over the shoulder of the lead detective, in street clothes, with the rest of the police in uniforms. This communicated to the audience that the detective was in charge. While the actor was not known to me, he was certainly in the action-hero mode, like Sylvester Stallone and Arnold Schwarzenegger—a square-jawed strongman who would soon save the day.

Now the hero is given his close-up. He looks back at his troops lined up behind him, also with their backs to the hallway wall, guns drawn. He has his 9mm semi-automatic pistol in his hand, and it becomes the focus of the cameraman's attention. The hero grabs the slide on top and racks it back, then shoves it forward. He looks back at his men, his expression saying, "Let's get this *mother fucker*!"

The standing-room-only theater was filled with pin-drop silence as hundreds awaited what was sure to be a quick and violent entry, a shoot-out, and a takedown of the bad guy. You could feel the anticipation in the air.

It was at this point that I simply could not control myself and burst out laughing. It certainly broke the tension in the auditorium, to the dismay of many. Little Polly threw a swift elbow into my ribs with more force than I thought she could have mustered. I let out a muffled *oomph* and sat still.

Then the dynamic scene took place, predictable for all, but no less exciting in the way it was choreographed and the outcome—an exchange of gunfire, the bad guy giving up, then taken away in handcuffs.

When we emerged into the daylight, Polly turned to me and asked, somewhat scornfully, "What was that all about?"

"In this formula for police movies and TV shows," I explained, "there is a moment when the director wants his audience to know there is about to be an action scene. He has the hero-cop hold out his 9mm and rack the slide back. The audience knows the detective *means business* and is ready for a gunfight."

Polly's eyebrows were up, waiting for the rest of my explanation.

"But that's all *bullshit*!" I told her.

"For anyone who ever carried a badge, when he gets up in the morning, there is already a live round in the chamber of his handgun. If not then, for instance, if there are small children in the house and he wants to keep it unloaded at home, before he steps out of the house, he loads his weapon to be ready for duty."

Polly was listening and staring at me, but didn't see my point, so I went on.

"When the hero-cop ran down the hallway with his weapon drawn, then racked back the slide in order to load a cartridge into the chamber, it meant that, up until that moment, *his gun was not loaded*! So, as he ran down the street after the bad guy, climbed all those steps, even chased him down the hallway, his gun was still not loaded, no round in the chamber. Had the bad guy turned around and shot at him, the hero could not have returned fire.

"And, had his gun actually been loaded with a round in the chamber, when he racked it back, a live round would have been ejected, flying out into the air, then bouncing around on the hallway floor. This would really be stupid, and it never happens in real life. For those who have carried a handgun for a living, that scene was absolutely ridiculous."

Polly stood facing me in stunned silence. She finally grasped my point and was thinking how to respond, but there was more.

"What made it worse," I said, "actually another stupid mistake, is after the hero racked back the slide, he shoved it forward, showing his assertiveness. But semi-automatic weapons have a spring inside the slide so when it is racked back, it is intended just to be let go. It slides forward at a very specific speed, which the weapon designers calculated to peel the top round off of the magazine full of cartridges and seat it in the chamber.

"If you shove the slide forward, it will be the wrong speed and the cartridge jams. With the cop's gun jammed, the bad guy can kill him at his leisure."

From the expression on Polly's face, she was no longer stunned, but was a bit angry—although, I am happy to report, not at me.

"Don't the directors know this?" she asked, incredulously.

I told her, "Every cop and FBI agent would laugh out loud, as I did, when this scene takes place. Only the truly uninitiated—those who have never fired a handgun—think racking the slide adds to the tension, instead of telling you how stupid the movie-cop is."

Mentally, I had to cut her some slack, because almost all of her movies were romance comedies with no gunfights, but it was still *her* industry.

Since there were, no doubt, law enforcement consultants on all of these action movies, I could only imagine they would have told the directors not to have the good guy run down the hallway unloaded, but I didn't know how that conversation would end.

Polly was flustered. She said she would have to tell all of her friends, and especially the directors who made action movies. I laughed out loud again, and she just stared at me.

This showed the great chasm between movies and reality, the people in the studio versus the ones out on the street. Ironically, my current undercover role met just about midway between the two, with one foot in each world. Ultimately, I saw it as fitting for these scenes to be in the movies, because they perfectly demonstrate that the movie industry deals in the fantasy world, even if it is intended to appear real.

More importantly, I was giving back to Polly, even if in a small way, for all she was doing for me.

CHAPTER 8

IVAN'S BACKGROUND

To prepare to meet Ivan, I was provided with a copy of his file from the 1980s. I reflected on how much I had changed since then and wondered how the years had worn on him.

Because he had not been an intelligence officer, there were fewer hours dedicated to him by the FBI than there would have been for an active intelligence target. Still, some of the information was very useful.

He had been raised in an all-female household, except for himself. At least no one who the FBI interviewed had ever heard differently. He had a twin sister, and his mother was the controlling figure in the family, a strong-willed woman.

Ivan had come to the US with his wife and their young twin daughters. Everything in the file indicated he had a solid relationship with his spouse. He was a devoted husband and loving father. I thought of the big three questions I had conceived for personality analysis back in 1977: What makes him laugh? What makes him cry? And does he love his wife? From his file I found partial answers, but good ones.

There was something in Ivan's old file about how he received his assignment to Washington. The kindly woman who had lived next door to him in his youth would often look in on him and his sister when his mother was out. She practically doted on him through his growing-up years. Coincidentally, she had influence with a higher-up in the Communist Party. In Russian, this is referred to as *blat.* Her connections were what enabled Ivan to receive a plum posting to the US.

Further, there were times when Ivan might have been disciplined, even sent home to Moscow in disgrace, or to a less desirable location, but this same blat was his saving grace.

Much of my career was made on addressing anomalies in the personalities of my subjects, and Ivan surely had them. I wished I'd had this knowledge when he was assigned to Washington in the 1980s and might have sought to put together an operation to get closer to him—an outsider within the embassy. But that was now mental gymnastics.

There was one memo in the file for which I was grateful, because it filled in a blank.

Ivan was at a gathering in Washington where there were many journalists. He had an encounter with a woman who was later interviewed by the FBI. At the meeting, she seemed to have been suffering from something, emotionally, and Ivan made a soft overture to ask if there was anything he could do for her.

She stifled a sniffle and told him her father had passed away a few days before. She had been very close to him, and it was a crushing blow.

A heretofore unknown aspect of Ivan's past then came to the surface, and he related a story from his youth.

Ivan said he never had a father growing up, but there was a single occasion, when he was around the age of six, that left a huge impression on him.

He was playing in a wooded area behind some of the larger houses on the outskirts of Kiev. An older boy, a teenager, approached him. With no prelude, he asked Ivan if he wanted to meet his father.

This was a shocker, and he looked dumbfounded at the boy, who motioned toward a path through the woods.

Ivan's eyes followed where the older boy had pointed, not sure what to do. After a few moments, he found himself walking cautiously down the trail.

About twenty meters farther, there was a clearing where a man of about thirty was building a chicken coop. He sat on the top, legs spread over both sides of the roof, and was driving nails.

When the man saw young Ivan, he stopped hammering. The two stared at each other, but for only a moment. Then the man said, "What are you looking at, *ty malen'kyy pokd'ku?* Get out of here!"

Ivan paused in telling his story, embarrassed, realizing he had said these words in his native Ukrainian. To the woman, he said, "It means, 'you little bastard.' That is what my own father called me, in the only encounter I ever had with him."

He told the woman she had so many wonderful memories of her father—*they* were what she should focus on. He compared them to his own devastating experience. In kindness, he said he was envious of what she had, and that her fond recollections should comfort her.

This interaction with his father—the man who had not raised him, not loved him, and had not taken on the responsibility of fatherhood—was a verbal slap to the young face of his own progeny. It may have been the genesis for what lowered Ivan's deep-seated feelings about all men, and his reluctance to deal with the ones in positions of authority. But it probably did more than that. It may have had the additional effect of elevating the status of all women, in his mind, especially when there was an option to deal with a woman, instead of a man.

What mark would that have left on any of us? It is hard to tell, but there would assuredly have been something.

It was only because this had been such a revealing personal story that, when interviewed, the woman decided to tell it to the agent. But back then, Ivan was a journalist from the Soviet Union, and not really a *target* of the FBI. Monitoring the activities of such individuals was just about at the edge of the authorization limit of what counterintelligence agents were permitted to do. Approaching a journalist was outside of those bounds.

To add to the long-ago information, I would try to learn as much as possible while Ivan attended the film festival. I wasn't in a position to observe him, so until it was my turn, I would rely on the Gs for updates.

We still needed to learn who he had come with, how many, and where they were staying.

Surveillance said Ivan was seen in the presence of only one person, a woman. They said she was "big," and one compared her with an East German weightlifter from the Cold War.

I laughed and asked, "That big?" They all nodded, with one adding, "and with two-inch heels, she is six feet—taller than Ivan."

One of the Gs had gotten close enough to see her name tag, but it was such an unfamiliar set of letters she couldn't figure it out. Ivan was in nearly constant conversation with the giantess. I asked the female Gs to assess their relationship, and they said it was close, but not intimate, all business.

The woman wore a black pantsuit with silver trim at the collar and down the front by the buttons, then around the bottom of the jacket. Where a husky woman might wear black to make her appear slender, here, the color could do little to disguise the bulky figure beneath the clothing.

She had short black hair in a pageboy, a pale complexion, and wore bright red lipstick. They assessed her as relying on Ivan, but it seemed we were missing something. We needed to know why they had come all this distance—and if anyone else was with them. It seemed so odd to be just the two of them, and how had I not seen her before?

For the overt prong's mission, if Ivan was just one of a traveling band of five, he might be pulled away for a conversation. But if he was attached to this woman all the time, it might be difficult to break them apart so Agents Suchan and Cardillo could make their pitch to him.

For my role, I would have to do something dynamic to get in touch with him and establish a relationship. I told the Gs how much I appreciated all they had done for me that day, knowing it had been a different sort of surveillance for them. Hooker later told me he had taken his colleagues aside and mentioned some of the cases we had worked together in Washington. He said he had warned them to "expect the unexpected when working with Captain Cosmic!"

CHAPTER 9

THE TOUCH

The days of the festival were passing, and it was time to take action.

The Gs told me the target and his "girlfriend" had spent the morning at a table out by the pool. They were there now and had been for over an hour. It was a relaxed setting, but—why were they *really* at the American Film Market?

They hadn't had any meetings and none of the hustle-and-bustle that many exuded. I didn't know if they had appointments, or whether they were the ones others would make appointments with. Those questions could only be answered through personal contact.

I strode through the doors to the pool area and took up a position in a corner with some shade. The California sun was beating down, but it was the beginning of March, and the temperature was just about perfect. Golf, tennis, biking, inline skating, or just strolling on the beach, were calling to any distant visitors in this Eden by the sea. There are few places in the world for weather like coastal Southern California. I could understand someone coming from Russia in February and wanting to soak it all in.

I saw Ivan and his friend sitting leisurely at a round table on the other side of the pool, never even glancing at their watches. The occasional stirrings nearby had no effect on them. He was neat and clean, hair combed with not a lock out of place, and again wearing a white dress shirt, cuffs buttoned.

His colleague, once again, wore her black pantsuit with the silver trim. Her bright red lipstick was set off by her clear white skin and jet-black hair. But what an observer could not miss was that her large frame nearly filled the chair, and Ivan, right beside her, seemed almost small in comparison.

The aroma of barbecue wafted through the air—burgers and ribs. Only an inveterate vegan would not love that smell. Great minds think alike and, in an instant, Ivan and his lady friend got up and walked to the lunch line along with many others.

I took a spot a dozen places back, and the masses continued to form behind me.

Ivan and his friend got their food and went back to where they had been sitting—creatures of habit.

I took my Styrofoam plate, thumb held over a can of soda, with a small bag of chips lying beside my cheeseburger, and slowly picked my way through the tables. I rounded the shallow end of the pool and walked very near the raised tile lip that extended over the edge of the water.

I had been quite athletic in my youth, a gymnast and springboard diver. Our pool in Solana Beach had similar coping to what was at Loews. Often, my two young daughters would play in their flotation devices and "Daddy" would seem to get too close to the edge. I would do a tightrope-balancing act, arms swinging wildly, with appropriate facial contortions, to the giggling and laughter of the little ones. In a swimsuit, I might fall into the pool with a great *ker-splash*. But in clothes, I would seem to catch myself, just before falling in. Little did I know how these antics would come in handy in the ultra-adult world of international intrigue.

Within a few feet of Ivan's table, I stepped sideways to go around a chair at the next one, up close to the edge of the pool. Then I began to *whoa-whoa*, one arm stretched out in the air for balance, the other hand extending the plate over the pool—a catastrophe in the making, right before Ivan's eyes.

I wished I didn't have to depend on his quick thinking and coordination. I hoped he was the good dad who had been described in his file—and that his apparent concern for his lady friend was a valid assessment. I held myself off-balance and flailing for only a second more before Ivan's hand shot out, reaching for my free one. He grabbed it and pulled me to safety.

I am certain I had a look of relief as I moved both feet off the uneven coping and took one step closer to him. Then my expression was surely embarrassment. I thanked him profusely. He offered me a seat at their table, which I could hardly have turned down.

The round table had six chairs, but only two were occupied. I took the one nearest Ivan, with the woman on his other side. We heard several good-natured comments from nearby onlookers about my close encounter with disaster. I expressed gratitude to my unnamed rescuer and shook his hand, profusely, saying, "Thank you…" and raised my eyebrows which, as planned, brought his name to his lips.

"John," he said, and, quickly giving him my name, I said, "Wayne." We both laughed. The combination of these two names, in such close proximity, of the cowboy movie legend—here at a film festival—could not have been missed.

Ivan calling himself "John" was something few Russians with that name ever did. It indicated his effort to make life easier in dealing with Americans.

Almost all Western languages have some derivation of John, extending from John the Baptist, and for Russians, their infamous "Ivan the Terrible." The names include Ian, Ion, Ioan, Jan, Johan, Juan, Jean, Sean, Giovanni, and others. Ordinarily, hearing his accent, I might have called him on it, but here, for the sake of the case, I let it go.

I had studied Spanish in high school and French in college. After a couple of years in the Bureau, I had been transferred to the Defense Language Institute in Monterey, California, to learn Romanian. It was a third romance language for me, and over the next nine months I became a proficient speaker. But that was not something I would share with my new acquaintances. Importantly, I spoke no Russian—probably a good thing for this case. I didn't want to understand words my tablemates exchanged, and Ivan translated for me into English, only for me to mistakenly blurt out a comment in English, meaning I understood what he had said in his native tongue. That would make me the ultimate suspicious person—and would put the kibosh on the entire operation.

Ivan presented his friend as "Anahit."

I was not familiar with the name and squinted at the nametag dangling from her lanyard—but it was facing in. So that, too, had probably caused a problem for the Gs.

Looking down, she turned it over to reveal that she was "Anahit Avakian." With this name-ending she had to be Armenian, but all she had done, thus far, was nod her head and smile.

"And you are from…?" I asked.

Ivan answered for her, "Armenia, and I am from Moscow."

I said I had visited the room with the Gorky Film people and saw the trailer for their version of *Star Wars*. "It was very interesting. Are you with them?"

"No," he told me. The two of them were here independently. Anahit was a film producer in the Armenian capital of Yerevan.

When Anahit heard the name of her city, she brightened up, but it also told me her English was very limited.

I turned to her and asked, "So, how are you enjoying the film festival?"

She looked over at Ivan with an inquiring glance.

In Russian, he translated. This brought a genuine smile and a response, also in Russian.

A good interpreter, Ivan told me her words of praise for all she had seen. Quite simply, there was nothing like it in her country. Well, *duh*, I thought.

I looked around at the glorious day, lifted my palms into the air, and inhaled deeply through my nostrils. I told Ivan we should all take a few minutes to enjoy life here, the beautiful weather, and then go back to whatever had brought us to this wonderful place. Ivan went right back to translating my statement. I was sure he was smart, and he was going strictly by the book: a pure interpreter.

I told them why I had come to the film market. I mentioned working in Washington, DC, then moving to San Diego, and the wealthy clients from Texas who had gotten rich through oil and cattle. They saw the stock market as gambling, as much as the casinos in Las Vegas. They wanted to put some of their money into another form of gambling where the results might bring a feature film to their local theaters. I made the side comment, "You wouldn't be surprised if these rich men did not trust people in Hollywood to tell them the truth?"

Ivan laughed. He said, "I have already seen enough people who would say anything, and do anything, to get their movies made. It is no wonder your clients want someone they can trust to handle their money."

Well said!

We understood we had a mental link, a common bond. For me, it was more blocks checked—truth and honesty.

Then I did something that was also planned, but seemingly so natural. I reached for my wallet and brought out the most recent Christmas photo of my family, with all five children sitting in a semi-circle in front. In each one's lap was a golden retriever puppy.

It was a real winner of a photo from a few months before. Under some circumstances, a photo like this might have been created just for this case, but that wasn't necessary, as my actual family photo perfectly met my needs. I was happy to display it and inwardly thanked Cirus and Haley, our AKC golden retrievers, for their part in supporting this operation.

Happily, it worked its magic. Ivan was smiling from ear to ear. He quickly recomposed himself and held the photo in front of Anahit. She looked at it longingly, like one would hope for from an affectionate person. The photo said so much about me, the family, the camaraderie, and the expressions of the little ones. It was the picture-perfect example of what you would want in your household, and with all of the puppies seeming to cooperate at just the right moment for the photographer.

What a prop!

It had done its job and was put back into my wallet.

Now they knew all about me, and it was their turn. This is a moment when silence is on the side of the undercover agent, when the person across the table feels it is their time to speak. It works almost every time.

Ivan said he worked for a company which owned several media outlets, including radio, TV, and magazines. He was assigned to one of the latter, but his original articles were used for stories in the other areas. This was good for him as the source of the material.

He said he was affiliated with offices in Moscow and London and enjoyed traveling.

I asked if it was difficult on his family.

His eyes moved down and to the left. I could see him watching them in his mind's eye with a look of regret. Finally, he said he did what he had to do. He went on that his twin daughters were doing very well in school, but he had no comparable photo to mine.

I mentioned that with so much of his time away from home, it would be important to have a strong and independent-minded wife.

He thoroughly agreed. Then he said something that was surprising and more personal than anything I thought he would say. He said his children were "born of love," and he could tell from my photo that all five of mine were, too.

That was a special moment I wanted to hold on to, and I think he did, as well.

As he went on further about his family, he repeated much of what I had recently read in his file. I was happy it was consistent, and there appeared to be no deception in telling his story. I made myself look interested—and I was—as though it were all new to me.

So, Dave Cardillo's assessment was on the mark, although Ivan had still returned to the Soviet Union, untouched by an FBI operation in the 1980s.

On my old Eastern Bloc squad, we would have called Ivan a "nice guy" and marked him for further assessment. There had been so many hardline communists back then that Ivan's personality would have been a pleasure to deal with.

As we went back and forth in conversation, Ivan paused every few lines to translate for Anahit, with her nodding as he spoke. She was not participating in the conversation, but he still included her as part of his job and their good relationship.

Then it was Anahit's turn. I asked what brought her to the festival.

Ivan conferred with her, and then went on at some length setting up her background.

Besides being a movie producer in her own right, Anahit's family, including her brothers, owned a film studio where she had an office. Of course, the government owned the land, which it leased to their business, but only Anahit had an actual office on the premises.

This seemed to be an important point, so I smiled and nodded a silent compliment to her as Ivan spoke. I was thinking of Polly's office on the Carsey-Werner lot in Burbank, and perhaps, in some ways, the world is not so different from one side to the other.

One thing was quite clear. Anahit spoke only Armenian and Russian, meaning she was essentially joined at the hip with Ivan for the duration of the conference. How, exactly, that would affect the FBI's overt pitch team was not clear, but it would surely have to be dealt with.

The film Anahit was working to produce was from the time of the genocide in Armenia. In 1915, the Ottoman Empire, the core of which is now geographically Turkey, was Muslim. It annihilated as many as 1.5 million Armenians, mostly Christians. The word *genocide* was coined over twenty-five years later to describe this event. Then in 1944, it was used to refer to the Nazis' murderous reign over the Jews.

There is an enormous amount of historical record surrounding the Armenian genocide, with dozens of books written about it. Perhaps the biggest block from crystallizing its place in history is that many present-day Turks deny it happened. That may have worked before the advent of photography, but not since then. Still, the Turkish government, somewhat the successor to the Ottoman Empire, has steadfastly avoided acknowledging or engaging with something that took place under a whole different government some eighty-five years before. This has been a rallying point for the Armenian people whose national grief will not subside.

Anahit said—through Ivan, of course—her movie would take place during that era, but instead of a documentary, it was a fictional tale. I asked how she planned to do that.

She said it was a romance, where an Ottoman soldier falls in love with a beautiful Armenian girl and must risk his life to save her and her family. She set out many of the scenes to make the plotline work, and it was very interesting.

But standing back, one could see this was Shakespeare's *Romeo and Juliet* all over again—star-crossed lovers. More to the point, just three months before, in December 1997, James Cameron's megahit, *Titanic*, had been released. Earlier that month, it had received a record-tying fourteen Academy Award nominations and would go on to win eleven just three weeks after the festival. If Anahit wanted to produce her own movie with a similar storyline, it was perfectly understandable.

I made the point that, if this was the genre she had chosen, what would make it work, in my view, was not the genocide, but the love story, with the genocide in the background. That is what they did in *Titanic*, where everyone knew how the plotline with the ship ended, but waited on pins and needles for the love story to unfold.

I will have to admit, I liked my own on-the-spot analysis, and so did Ivan and Anahit. I think it even inspired her, but I wanted to shy away from giving her false hope. I told her that, while I had some experience in the film industry, I had a dear friend who was a member of the Academy of Motion Picture Arts and Sciences. I used her as my sounding board if I found a project I considered investing in.

My tablemates could not possibly have had bigger eyes than they did at that moment.

We had become friends in a matter of an hour and a half, but all such meetings must come to an end. It is operationally important for the undercover agent to be the one to break it off and bring it to a close. You simply cannot let your target think you have an unlimited amount of time and an unfounded interest in him. There was a whole film festival surrounding us, and I had to excuse myself, in theory, to make additional contacts. There was much more I could have said, and more to be learned from this traveling duo, but this was enough—for now.

Before leaving, I asked where they were staying. Ivan mentioned a place right down the street and brought out a hotel business card he had picked up in the lobby. He wrote his room number on it and began to hand it to me, but hesitated. He brought out a second business card, this one his own, and handed both to me. He turned to Anahit, but she was ahead of him. From her large handbag she had hauled out a folder which, when opened, showed a set of brochures, each with her business card stapled to it. It was, essentially, advertising for her planned movie.

She slid it over to Ivan for him to pass to me.

Then there was the sound of silence at our table, and I realized it was my turn to produce. How silly of me, my expression seemed to say. I fished out a short stack of business cards from my shirt pocket. It had the perfect logo, the perfect font, and a phone number that would ring the operational telephone in my bedroom in Solana Beach. Should it have rung, my family members were under strict instructions *never* to answer it. The FBI had also provided an answering machine which sat beside the phone. That was my "office," on the surface of the raised marble hearth around the fireplace in my bedroom.

I handed one to each of them and told Ivan that if anyone asked for the information on my business card, please, do not provide it. He indicated he understood.

I was now standing and ready to leave.

"I'll tell you what," I said. "The friend I mentioned was here with me yesterday. I will speak to her about your project, and if she thinks it has merit, perhaps she would be willing to meet with you. Would that be all right?"

From Ivan's expression, I had to think of his long-ago fellow countryman, another Ivan—Pavlov—who elicited conditioned responses from his dog. Now it was the present-day Ivan salivating, almost drooling, every bit as much as Pavlov's dog, at the very thought of dining with a member of the Academy.

Ivan didn't mention that he had seen me with Polly the day before, while I knew he had. So, he was being circumspect, and maybe a little coy. He wouldn't want me to think he had been stalking me at the festival!

It was the great irony of the gameboard. Ivan had checkers, while I had pawns, rooks, knights, bishops, and now Polly, a queen—playing chess. It was another internal laugh-out-loud moment. I told them I would be back in touch, either way.

I walked away from the table and did not look back.

CHAPTER 10

BRIEFING THE OVERT PRONG

After my "accidental" meeting with Anahit and Ivan, I made my way inside and through the crowd, pretending to look for someone or something.

Ivan and Anahit would be watched by the Gs, who would alert me if there was any change in their status. For instance, if Ivan had jumped up after I left and followed me to see where I went and who I met. It didn't happen, but that's why a counter-surveillance operation was put in place—to make sure.

Once certain I was in the clear, it was time to hoof it to the hotel of Special Agents Suchan and Cardillo to brief them.

It should also be noted the SSG maintained surveillance on me from a distance. If anyone else was interested in my movements, they would watch the watchers. That could have included other Russians from Moscow attending the festival, or anyone at all, not previously known to us. We had absolutely no reason to suspect this, but comprehensive coverage is the norm. However, my trail was clean, and I had a green light from the Gs.

I imagine the dinner conversation one of the Gs might have with their spouse.

"What did you do today, honey?"

"Well, I was watching a guy who was with another guy who I was also watching. When the first guy left, I watched to see if the second guy took off after him, and also if anyone else was watching the first guy. Oh, and the second guy could not become aware I was watching him, or that would have been a problem. But no one was watching anyone, except my team, so it was a good day."

Suchan and Cardillo were still in the planning stages. The SSG's updates on Ivan's current location, and my information on his plans for the next few days, were crucial for how they would proceed.

Ivan and Anahit wanted to take the Universal Studios tour, but they had no reservations and no idea how they would get there. It was twenty miles away, but in Los Angeles traffic, who knew how long that would take?

They didn't know the options of a taxi or shuttle bus, or the costs, and they seemed short of cash after the big expenditures of airfare, hotel, and the entry fees for the festival. As the Gs reported, and I verified, the pair set up shop out by the pool and were taking in the California sun. That was certainly not a place to make an overt approach.

I informed the agents where Anahit and Ivan were staying and that they were not connected with other Russians. With Anahit's need for an interpreter, Ivan would almost never leave her side. This meant their approach would have a very narrow window. And a Universal Studios tour would cut out a full day from their options.

I also told them of my plans to meet Polly, and my belief that she would come out to dinner for a foursome. That might give the agents a time when Ivan would be alone in his hotel room beforehand and, depending on how long the dinner lasted, possibly afterwards. Certainly, there would be more personality assessment gained during dinner.

While I took my assigned role as support for the overt approach seriously, I had been relegated to the bench—second string.

However, my money was still on the covert prong, if there would be success in our future. The more I learned about Ivan's personality, the better would be my chances. All through our conversations, he would have no idea he was being assessed, at least not with the goal I had in mind. He might think I was gauging him, but mostly Anahit, for credibility and competence to produce a movie in Armenia, which my ostensible clients might finance, but that was all a feint. Every new piece of information about him would be integrated and constantly modify my views of his personality for the scenario I hoped would play out.

There comes a time in every undercover operation when the next step is the great leap, when the target becomes aware he is a target. In intelligence circles, this is known as "dropping the fig leaf," homage to ancient Greek statues of male nudes whose private parts were later covered up by a fig leaf to suit a Victorian sense of modesty.

For me, the irony was significant, if not somewhat humorous. Most of the subjects I had encountered while undercover would have sworn up and down that I was exactly what I originally said I was. There were just too many details to prove it, whether I presented myself as from a conservative Political Action Committee, a lobbyist for General Aviation, an attorney from Philadelphia, or an agent working on behalf of wealthy Texas businessmen to finance independent films—and with photos of my different families to match!

The problem with sewing up a legend so tightly is, if it comes time to reveal who you really are, it may be almost impossible to convince your target that you *are* an FBI agent. If he finally integrates this information into his brain cells, there are two possible outcomes. He may see you as a dear and close friend, who he will continue to rely on for advice, or he might take it completely the other way, which would be very bad. In this scenario, everything you have said to him is seen as a gross insult. You were lying every minute you were with him, from the instant you met until the present. Sometimes it matters that "you even lied to my wife!"

It all boils down to the issue of trust. As with any marriage or close business relationship, once it is lost, getting it back is nearly impossible. So, trying to keep the undercover operation undisclosed to the target is the best chance of not having all the work you put into it blow up in your face. You would also have wasted a great amount of time and Uncle Sam's resources, something to be avoided at all costs.

Better, I have found, is to keep the close friendship and monitor the subject while other events are going on in his life—for instance, being pitched by the overt prong.

I was getting close enough to Ivan that he might confide in me if he had a crisis, one he wanted help dealing with. Alternatively, he might think highly enough of our relationship that he would not want to involve me in his personal problems.

Here is the scenario I like to use to get past this tricky situation:

"Ivan, I was approached yesterday by two men from the US government who are aware of our relationship. They spoke with me for quite a while. They were very friendly and courteous and seemed to know a lot about you. I have nothing to hide about our relationship, and I don't think you do either. They asked if I thought you would agree to meet with them, at least to hear whatever it is they have to say. I don't know what this is all about, but they seemed to be decent people. I told them I would be glad to speak with you. If you don't want to, that's fine with me, and I will tell them. But if you would agree to speak with them, they told me how to put you in touch with them. They also said they wouldn't take too much of your time. What do you think?"

This tactic preserves the undercover role, gives an impression of *us* (Ivan and me) versus *them*, and avoids the issue that he has been lied to all along. It also enables feedback to a friend.

Is it deceptive? Of course. Everything going on was deceptive, but it is part of the job description. Here, it was the crux of the matter—enable an approach to a viable target.

After the pitch is made, which might not be successful, there is still the option of a continuing relationship, seemingly unconnected with the US government. The target can be monitored for his reaction and any statements he might make about *his* next steps.

All of this, I am sorry to say, was seen as my mental gymnastics, not relevant by the overt pitch team. They had their script and didn't need a setup from me, just a window of opportunity with Ivan. The cold-pitch approach was their plan, but—had it ever worked?

In my years in foreign counterintelligence in the FBI, counting recruitments-in-place and defectors, I had met and debriefed a total of twenty-five individuals, likely a record that will stand for decades. Yet, there was not one of them who had taken the biggest step in his life because he had been offered a suitcase full of money. It may go without saying, but none of them had ever asked for money, either.

True, there are significant costs to resettle a defector in the US, but that is not figured in when it comes to the value of giving up intelligence information.

I had never seen a cold pitch work. In fact, that had even been the premise when it was used in the clever Pitch-A-Bum-A-Month scenario against Soviet military officers in the 1980s.

I started to tell Suchan and Cardillo about my developing assessment of Ivan, but a few sentences into my spiel, I realized they were not listening. In fact, we were not on the same page. Granted, they had a great deal on their minds, but I didn't think that should preclude them from hearing the information I had learned just that morning.

No matter. They had their marching orders—the cold pitch—and they had their suitcase full of money. Nothing I could say would alter their plan, and that was that.

Last, I told the agents I would write up notes from my meetings with Ivan and Anahit. It was important while it was still fresh in my mind, but even this didn't register with them.

I had always come away from undercover meetings with intelligence targets where, during the contact, I could not make enough mental notes as the evening progressed. Sometimes, I thought my brain would explode while waiting to write it all down—new information, vignettes, facial expressions, segues in conversation—always hoping I could later mentally retrieve everything in a coherent and chronological fashion for a comprehensive memo.

During one long meeting in a restaurant with a Hungarian target, I went to the restroom and into a stall. I took out a piece of paper and began making notes, one-liners, and individual words that would bring back different stories I had heard, thus far, from the evening. But then it occurred to me, what if my target should somehow see these notes later in the evening? How could I possibly explain away why I had made them?

I flushed them down the toilet and hoped I had enough of a steel-trap mind to remember everything that was important. But in these intelligence operations, *everything* is important, or might be, so you really don't want to miss, or leave out, anything. It was normal for me to produce a twenty-page memo, written that same night, until late, and added to the next morning—all part of the job.

But, again, why would Suchan and Cardillo care about this? If their prong worked and they got what the FBI needed, in short order, I would be packing my bags, thanking Polly for her patriotism, and driving back to San Diego. But, if the overt prong did not work, the ball would be back in my court—at least, that is what I believed—so, I had better take the necessary steps to commit everything to paper. Wasn't that what the director of the FBI was paying me to do?

I left the agents and called Polly.

CHAPTER 11

PREP FOR DINNER

Polly Platt had a quaint house on Carroll Canal in Venice, three miles south of Santa Monica. Surrounded by the cacophony of Los Angeles, this was an oasis of silence, a Shangri-La unto itself.

Four parallel canals, a few hundred yards long, came to *T*s at the ends with connecting canals. Lining the water's edge were magnificent homes, some large, some cottages, some modern, and others like fairytale gingerbread houses. Rainbow-shaped wooden footbridges brought you to the next string of homes, each exuding the personality of its owner.

Polly's schedule was hectic every day of her life. She was one of the first women to crash through the glass ceiling in her industry, paving the way for so many to follow. The peacefulness of her home, the calm you felt inside, was a world apart from the hustle-and-bustle of sprawling Los Angeles. Polly needed this each evening and richly deserved it.

We had only met in her producer's office, and I now understood her better. Home was where she caught her breath. When she left it, even for a dinner with me, she would glance over her shoulder after locking up, a touch of regret at leaving behind its tranquility, even for a few hours.

We went to one of the finest restaurants in the area, Shutters on the Beach, at One Pico Boulevard. True to its name, it was dramatically right on the beach. An enclosed walkway, bridged over Appian Way, connected to a five-story hotel across the street. In a city which cherishes prime locations, you always hear the question, "Where's the view?" Well, this one was obvious!

Continuing to build our relationship, I updated Polly on events thus far. Now I needed to check out a restaurant for dinner with our target.

So close to her home, Polly would be recognized, not just by the waitstaff, but by other patrons. I had to be conscious of how I acted.

We were given a table with an ocean view and privacy away from listening ears. If Polly had a new project, even a rumored one, it could make *Variety*, the Hollywood trade magazine. That kind of publicity I did not need in my undercover capacity.

I told Polly what I had learned about Ivan and Anahit, and that they had a film in the making. I wanted to invite them for dinner with her.

She took this request seriously and said she would be glad to help their project along. At least, she could provide some consulting, which might be the incentive for them to get it moving. She made several comments on worldwide film markets, information I was sure would greatly interest Anahit and Ivan.

I showed her the Armenian's brochure and Polly looked at it askance. She said the English was stilted. If the screenplay was in the same style, it would not bode well.

When I said the film would be in Armenian, her eyebrows shot up. "Not if they expect it to have legs," she told me. Polly realized she would have to cover the very basics over dinner of how to produce a movie with more than the hometown crowd in mind.

Until I had met Ivan and Anahit, face-to-face, we had no idea why they were attending the film market. Now it was a catch-up game for my backstopping to fit their needs in order to stay in touch. There is nothing like an Academy member in your corner when discussing the film industry, so thanks again, Gene McClelland and Jack Platt!

For a couple of hours, Polly and I went over the conversation we planned to have with the Russian and the Armenian. I didn't want to seem like too much of a doofus, but how could I disguise that all of my knowledge was newly learned?

When Academy Award winner Richard Dreyfuss had the title role in the 1995 movie *Mr. Holland's Opus*, he played a high-school music teacher and was incredibly convincing with his ability at the piano. When asked on a late-night talk show about his musical training, and how many years he had been playing, he revealed that he did not play the piano—not one note! Astounded, the host asked how he had played the role so well. Dreyfuss calmly said, "That's why they call it *acting*!"

So that is what I would have to do—and be a quick study.

Another point to keep in mind was that Polly was completely in the dark: not just about the overall objective of why we wanted to get close to Ivan, but also that there was another team of FBI agents planning to make an overt pitch. Of course, she didn't "need to know" any of this. It demonstrated how one must keep all of the moving parts compartmentalized for what exactly each person knows, and how their piece of the puzzle fits into the overall picture. Like a juggler's balls, everything seemed to be circulating in the air, high above me.

Invitation to Dinner

In the morning, the next step was to find Ivan and Anahit and invite them to dinner.

Before entering the Loews hotel, I touched base with Hooker to verify that everything was normal with the surveillance. His team was spread around the area, two of them with eyes on the couple at their usual spot by the pool. If they were waiting for something to happen, it was better than being inside, surrounded by the bedlam of Hollywood wannabes.

I went out to the pool and directly to their table. I watched their faces for their reactions to assess where I stood in their minds. I was pleased that they both smiled right away.

I sat down across from Ivan but made sure to face Anahit. I gave her the attention she was due, even if she would not understand a word I said.

I told them I had met with Polly Platt the night before and she had agreed to meet with them. The plan was to have dinner and discuss their movie project.

Before these last words were out of my mouth, Ivan began translating. He was keen enough to translate what I had already said, and also to hear what I was saying at the same time. This was an extraordinary talent.

Anahit was overjoyed at the news and extended both her hands across the table to me, palms up. I extended my own and, grasping hers, accepted this as a sign of gratitude. I spoke directly to her, now with Ivan off to the right, simultaneously translating every word.

"But there is one condition for all of us to have dinner together," I said.

With this, I paused, so Ivan would have to pause, too, and hear my next words without interruption. Actually, it was a bit humorous, placing a pregnant pause in a conversation to force the translator to listen, not to the words, but to the content. He did, and I had their attention—and their concern—which showed on their faces.

I said, "The condition is you must be my guests for dinner."

With no facial reaction, Ivan translated this immediately for Anahit. It was only when she grasped the meaning of the words, and had her reaction, that Ivan permitted himself to have a similar one. It was relief and happiness, as I intended.

I was amazed that Ivan's brain had been on hold while he translated. He did not seem to comprehend the content of the words until after Anahit had heard them in Russian. So, was that normal for a translator, or was it a show of respect for the Armenian movie producer?

I smiled broadly, and so did they. Our dinner date was agreed upon.

We discussed when they would be free, and it was more complicated than I would have liked.

Ivan mentioned the tour of Universal Studios, again, and that they had not yet managed to make reservations for transportation. I told him of a shuttle service for fifty-five dollars in a van, and that was the total price, no matter how many it carried.

This brought more smiles and renewed their desire to take the tour. Of course, my ulterior motive was to learn their schedule to tell Suchan and Cardillo. How anyone could imagine this information might have been collected through surveillance was beyond me.

One important fact Ivan added was that they would not be staying until the end of the festival but would leave a day early.

Uh-oh, I thought, bad news for the overt boys.

I told Anahit and Ivan more about Polly. I said I was not *promoting* her, and for most in the film industry in America, she would not need an introduction. I mentioned her involvement with Barbra Streisand movies and award nominations for *Broadcast News*. I asked if they knew the name Brooke Shields. At the end of Ivan's translation, Anahit nodded vigorously. It seemed that even in faraway Armenia, Ms. Shields was a hit.

I said it was Polly who had discovered her and put her in the title role in *Pretty Baby*. She also wrote the screenplay and was the associate producer twenty years ago.

All of Polly's accolades were not necessary for them to hear, but I did not want to lay out any of this in front of Polly in the restaurant. It was worth making sure the visitors knew they would be in the presence of Hollywood royalty.

By the time I finished, they were duly impressed.

Then we discussed the best time for dinner. I tried to follow my philosophy of sooner-is-better-than-later, but it was really their convenience I had to work with.

Meanwhile, I thought Polly was an absolute dream for putting up with all of this. But I had to believe she found more entertainment than aggravation in this caper. I think part of her enjoyment was, finally, peering into a small slice of the life her brother had lived in the CIA.

The Armenian TV Interview

Ivan glanced at his watch and said something to Anahit. It seemed they did have something scheduled, and he apologized in excusing themselves.

That was fine with me. I was glad they were doing something else at the festival, and it would give the Gs something to do.

I told them I had to go, too, and we filed into the atrium. They walked to the area where Lea Thompson had been interviewed a few days before. Lights were set up, focused on a long table with several chairs on one side. It seemed like the makings of a panel discussion.

Standing back, I saw the cameramen and someone directing people to seats. An elderly man, with a hint of Attila the Hun's DNA in his eyes, sat beside Anahit, with Ivan on her other side. Two more individuals were on the other side of the older gentleman.

I asked someone nearby what was going on. It was to be a live interview, beamed all the way back to Armenia. I was impressed and learned this had been done for other attendees where their presence at the film festival would be broadcast in their homelands. Television coverage promoted the producers and their films, as well as the foreign-film aspect of the eight-day film market. It was thoroughly organized, but something else interested me.

Even though the older man garnered respect from those on the platform, Ivan's attention never wavered from Anahit. It was not romantic or brotherly, but almost a kowtowing to her needs, which I was sure was not part of his job description. It is simply how Ivan was.

Anahit had a strong presence, physically, but she also had a forceful personality. She held a unique position in the film industry in Armenia. It was only diminished here by her inability to express herself in English.

Ivan seemed, strictly speaking, subservient to her. This was not merely as a translator, always on her arm, but psychologically and, seemingly, in every circumstance. I wondered how this would play out with Polly, who had a decorated resume of her own.

CHAPTER 12

DINNER WITH POLLY

Finally, it was time for dinner with Anahit and Ivan. I picked up Polly in Venice, briefed her, and profusely thanked her again for her help.

Polly was a charm to work with. She extended her hand over to my arm as I drove and said, "I have to eat sometime. Now is as good a time as any."

I burst out laughing. She surpassed my expectations for mental preparedness. She was not stressed in anticipation of "meeting a spy" and was ready to give counsel to someone in need. Perhaps being a good undercover operative is in one's DNA, because I knew, beyond doubt, her brother, a longtime CIA operative, had it.

We pulled up to the hotel to pick up our guests, who were waiting for us under the portico. We got out and I made the introductions, with Ivan translating.

Anahit was wearing the same black pantsuit ensemble as when I first met them. It must have been her nicest outfit, worn now for a special occasion.

When we drove through the latticework of the restaurant's courtyard, I glimpsed at the expressions on our guests' faces. Seeing their wide eyes was enough to get the point. I was glad I had made the invitation conditional on my paying, because they would have been in shock with what this would cost.

We were seated in the lavish setting at a prime table. Now our conversation would not be confidential. To the contrary, it would be good for our guests to be seen with Polly and feel her Hollywood aura, with those nearby trying to listen in.

Polly graciously thanked them for coming to dinner. It was all Ivan could do not to fall all over his words, trying to turn the tables in thanking her for letting *us* join *you*.

My role had been relegated many steps downward. Had I not been the one secretly running this show, I could have felt really diminished. But this was great! I was getting good assessment and could sit back and watch the magic.

There was small talk about the festival and what had brought the visitors to our shores. Ivan had spent three months in Yerevan shadowing Anahit on producing and developing a film.

In one of my rare interruptions, I asked Ivan if his family had been with him in Armenia. No, they remained in Moscow. His facial expression said he regretted it, but his wife was strong and could do what was necessary to take care of their daughters. He missed them very much, but this was his job. I had heard this before, but I wanted Polly to hear it from Ivan.

Anahit was not married, but I wanted to make a point about Polly. I said she had two children and was also very close to her two step-children from an earlier marriage. I knew her own children were "born of love," as Ivan had said, but she felt just as close to the children she had gained through marriage. This really presented Polly in a very personable light, separate from the hard-headedness of a Hollywood mover and shaker.

Polly expressed interest in Anahit's project and asked her to lay it out for her.

Anahit went into the Ottoman Empire's 1915 genocide of a 1.5 million Armenians: pretty astounding, as Armenia is only about the size of Maryland. She went into the love story between the soldier and the Armenian girl who was trying to save her family.

Polly immediately compared this dramatic moment in history with what James Cameron incorporated as the love story in *Titanic.* I had made the identical assessment that first day at the table by the pool. But when the words came from Polly, a true authority, Anahit's facial reaction, when Ivan finished translating, was over the top with excitement, and so was Ivan's—bordering on ecstasy!

Anahit brought out her brochure with her business card attached and presented it to Polly. Ivan quickly brought out his own card and handed it to her. I was surprised when Polly withdrew a little gold case from her purse containing her cards and gave out two of them.

I could not object, but this had not been part of my plan. In fact, Polly no longer needed to carry business cards. If you didn't know who she was, then why were you talking to her? And how had you gotten beyond the buffers Hollywood puts up to get into her inner sanctum?

No matter; now her cards were in the foreigners' hands.

Polly glanced at me, knowing she had crossed a boundary. I raised my eyebrows. She turned to our guests, who held her cards tightly.

She said, "Of course, please make sure that you reach me through Wayne, and you already have his card."

Dutifully, Ivan and Anahit reached for them, Ivan in his wallet, and Anahit, in her purse, and produced them.

Inside, I smiled. They had kept them safe—and I still had 498 left!

With their nods, they confirmed they would go through me. Polly would not say how overworked she was, but if Anahit thought the movie industry was busy in Armenia, she could only imagine what Polly went through every day in Burbank.

Polly added that if she wanted to speak with either of them, I would handle it.

More dutiful nods came from across the table, another big block checked for me.

In looking at Ivan's card, I decided to make a point—actually, a gambit. His name was Ivan Fyodorovich Kurylenko, yet he went by John.

Referring to his other two names, I said, offhandedly, "Then your initials are JFK!"

Happily, he got the joke and smiled. So did Polly, but it was lost on Anahit.

What it told me was that he knew who JFK was, just from the initials, and didn't mind being compared with the American president, as a person. Many of my hardline targets from a couple of decades before would never have had that reaction.

In response to my humor, Ivan told a joke.

There had been news from the Russian Mir Space Station, where cosmonauts were recently joined by an American astronaut. Ivan said the astronaut and a cosmonaut were looking at the earth through a new strong telescope. The American was surprised to see all of the people in Moscow looking back up through their own telescopes. No, the cosmonaut explained, they were just drinking vodka and trying to get the last drops out of their bottles!

Polly laughed, and so did I, and then he translated the joke for Anahit. But what did the joke say about Ivan? He had no problem telling a self-effacing story about his own people, knowing the world picks on them for their alcoholism. Ivan was less of a nationalist than when he was under the authority of the Soviet Union.

It made me think of the file from his assignment in the US. He didn't get along with the intelligence people, who saw him as an outsider. Good to know, and it would play into any further assessment.

Of course, I could not let this go by without telling a joke in return.

"One evening, a Hindu, a Jew, and a lawyer were driving down a country road when their car broke down. They walked to a nearby farmhouse and knocked on the door. The farmer answered it. They asked if they could stay the night and get their car repaired the next day.

"The farmer agreed, but he only had two extra beds. One of them would have to stay in the barn.

"The Hindu volunteered, and they all went to bed.

"A few minutes later there was a knock on the door, and the farmer answered it. It was the Hindu, who said there was a cow in the barn. His religion did not allow him to sleep where there was a cow.

"They looked amongst themselves, and the Jew volunteered to sleep in the barn.

"A few minutes later there was another knock on the door, and the farmer answered it. It was the Jew, who said there was a pig in the barn. His religion did not allow him to sleep where there was a pig.

"Only the lawyer was left, so he went out to the barn.

"A few minutes later, there was yet another knock on the door, and the farmer answered it. Standing at the door were the pig and the cow!"

Polly laughed out loud, covering her mouth with her hand.

Ivan had been translating, line-by-line, for Anahit, and when I said the punchline, he did not flinch at all until Anahit heard it translated. Then she laughed and so did he.

This was my turn, with all of them knowing my background as an attorney, to be self-effacing, at least of my chosen profession. But it was interesting how well Ivan held his reaction to the punchline until he could laugh at it with Anahit. Just as when I extended the dinner invitation, conditioned on me paying, Ivan had kept his emotions in check.

Having heard the plotline of Anahit's proposed movie, Polly took the floor. She said she had produced many romance comedies, "rom-coms," a term Ivan had a problem translating. It was clear that Anahit's project was definitely not a rom-com. So, while Polly might be able to give some advice for Anahit's monumental movie, it was not something she would personally be involved in. That being said, she discussed the concept of "legs," and the movie's potential for audiences in countries other than Armenia. Polly added, this would also move it into a position to be judged for international awards, if the quality of the product held up.

While Anahit may have considered this, Polly brought her up to speed on what she had to know, and do, to make that happen.

How many screens were there in Armenia, or even just in the capital of Yerevan? Anahit had no idea.

How much money was made, on average, in each theater, on each evening's showing of a movie? What was their seating capacity? There should be a list, but Anahit did not know.

Polly referred to the brochure. She said the English was not well presented, and it would be important to have it as perfect as possible. Polly suggested that Ivan, whose English she acknowledged was excellent, be the one to edit it.

I once had an English professor at Penn State, Dr. John Sutherland, who was considered an expert on Australian literature. I had to ask him what made him an expert, and his response was memorable.

"The farther you are from the point of origin, the easier it is to be an expert!"

The concept played out here, in that anyone with the ability to translate the brochure into English was an expert by Armenian standards, but that didn't make it so. In the real world, where millions of dollars would be spent bringing a project to fruition, the very best presentation was an absolute necessity.

Polly looked over to me, and I nodded. After all, I was the one who represented investors.

Polly asked about the screenplay, but Anahit didn't have it. Polly asked her to send a copy, which was followed by silence after Ivan translated.

Anahit was embarrassed that, right now, it was only in Armenian. She said it would be translated into Russian, but she didn't understand this would not help in the Western market.

Ivan added that even since the collapse of the Soviet Union, eight years before, politics continued to be involved in such a project. People who should not have a say in Anahit's story wanted to add their two rubles. This hindered the writing process, caused many revisions, and delayed the authority to move forward.

Polly put her foot down and said, "It *must* be translated into English." She also wanted to make sure that if Ivan didn't do the translation, he would have to review the best product Anahit could come up with so he could put the finishing touches on it. Then it would be ready for others to judge on its merits.

Polly went into how the movie should be presented. She asked about Anahit's plans. I didn't know how she would answer, but Polly did. Anahit said it would be filmed in Armenian, with Russian or English subtitles.

Well, that would never do, and Polly's frown said as much.

While Anahit was a large woman and had a commanding presence when she had points to make, right now, diminutive Polly had center stage and was driving the conversation. She was running circles around a senior producer from Armenia. Polly was getting down to business, and her ideas kept gushing out.

She explained that the cost to make the film could not be recovered only from Armenian screens. Neighboring Turkey, the geographic location of the former Ottoman Empire, would not have people coming in droves to see how their forefathers nearly exterminated a whole population. The bet Anahit had to make was that the rest of the world would want to see this story. For that, the movie would have to be filmed in English and dubbed in whatever languages they wanted or have subtitles. Armenians would be accustomed to that because it was almost all they ever saw in their theaters.

Further, the lead roles would have to be actual stars and not Armenian actors. Of course, the movie would be filmed there, with its dramatic mountain backdrops and historic landmarks. But only the secondary actors could be from Armenia. While the Armenian population would like to see their fellow countrymen on the big screen, people in China and France, and especially the

English-speaking markets of the US, UK, Canada, and Australia, and all the international film festivals, would require well-known actors. Polly's point was that if the film was worth making, and the story worth telling, and if Anahit wanted her secondary message of the horrors of war and the evil deeds of the Ottoman Empire to draw the attention of a worldwide audience, it could only happen by taking these steps.

Anahit was nearly dumbfounded and had a great deal of homework to do. She had not known before this fine meal that, compared to Professor Polly, she was still in kindergarten in her industry. But she picked herself right up and addressed some of Polly's points.

All the while Ivan was the middleman, sending the information back and forth between these two impressive women.

As an observer of the human condition—as my father used to describe himself—I was entertained more than the others could have imagined. I was seeing something special in Ivan. He was reveling in this: not the movie-making talk, but being in the presence of these two women of power and authority. They knew what they wanted and got right down to business. Meanwhile, in Ivan's eyes, I may as well not have been there.

The check arrived. I let it sit on the table until I was sure Ivan saw it out of the corner of his eye. It was around $300, a tidy sum in 1998. He went quite pale. He and Anahit said this was the most wonderful meal, and company, and setting, in which they had ever dined. Their gratitude was genuine, almost overwhelming.

I asked about their travel plans. While Anahit would return to Armenia soon, Ivan would be back in London, then Moscow. Both expected to be in Cannes later in the spring. She would attend the festival for films, while he planned on the one for television awards, which was two weeks later. Anahit might have to find another translator for her trip to France.

Ivan said he had been quite successful in gaining advertising for a magazine. Much of his success he attributed to Anahit, with her influence in the film industry in Armenia. All of this was good to know.

However, I had learned, just a few minutes before picking up Polly, that Agents Suchan and Cardillo had found Ivan alone in his hotel room before our dinner outing. They had made their overture to him, and it had not gone well—quite the opposite.

Yet Ivan had passed the entire evening, four hours, and never mentioned a single word about it. He said nothing to the group and didn't pull me away to discuss it privately. So, if there were emotions running wild in his mind, from his easygoing demeanor, you would never know he was contemplating anything beyond his newfound friend in the movie business.

CHAPTER 13

THE OVERT PITCH—PICKING UP THE PIECES

Only a few minutes before we gathered to drive to Shutters on the Beach, I was told the Washington agents, Suchan and Cardillo, had just made their overt pitch. I wasn't given the full details, but Ivan had not been happy about it.

My new assignment was to see if that short meeting had a noticeable effect on him. It was possible that he might confide in me, maybe even ask for advice. None of that happened.

Because of the intelligence gathered by the Special Surveillance Group and me, a window had been identified in Ivan's movements when the two agents could approach him.

An on-the-street effort was ruled out since it was likely his non-English-speaking movie producer from Armenia would be with him. They waited until Anahit was elsewhere and found Ivan in his room.

So, how did it go? It could not be described in a positive light. Picture this....

After a long day at the film festival, Ivan returned to his room. The FBI agents walked up to his door and knocked.

How were they dressed? Would it make a difference? Should they have worn suits, white shirts, and ties? Or should they have appeared more relaxed to match the Santa Monica atmosphere? Would it have mattered to Ivan?

When Ivan answered the door—fully clothed, I am happy to say—what should their first words have been? Certainly, they were planned, but this was a never-happened-before moment for all three of them—the pitchers and the pitchee!

Maybe something like, "Mr. Kurylenko, we are in the FBI and would like to speak with you for a few minutes. Could we step inside to talk?"

That would be a good start, but it would take your breath away if you called Moscow "home." Through all his years assigned to Washington, the FBI had *never* come knocking.

They had to be up front, businesslike and, at the same time, exude personability.

Did they do that? I know both of them and hope they did. Was this part of their script, which was more written than interpretive? To me, the psychological part is very important, but not for every agent.

They had to explain why they were there. Chit-chatting about how nice it was that Ivan was attending the film festival, or asking how he was enjoying his time in Santa Monica, could not possibly minimize what would be looming in Ivan's mind: *Why the hell are you guys here?*

So, their mission was difficult from the moment they knocked on Ivan's door.

I imagine they told him he had acquired knowledge when he was in Washington, DC, now about fifteen years ago, which they wanted to ask about.

This would certainly start his brain puzzling for what *he* could possibly know that *they* would want to know. Why ask now, and not way back then?

He was here at the film festival in his new, post-the-supposed-fall-of-communism life. Why couldn't they just leave him alone? It wasn't as though this was a chummy circumstance and they could all sit around drinking beer, discussing whatever they came to talk about. *Comfortable* could not describe any of what was going on.

The agents had a folder of photographs to show him, but it never got that far. Ivan voiced his objection and did not want the conversation to continue. Suchan suggested Ivan might want to hold off until he could confer with his family.

This is something you want to incorporate into your strategy, but not to be said out loud. Ivan knew how he made his life decisions, and this would clearly be one of them. But to have a complete stranger—an FBI agent—say something so personal to him came off as insulting, even if it were absolutely true. It would have been better left for Ivan to figure out without the FBI's help.

How Ivan felt about this aspect of the overture became crystal clear when he uttered the now-infamous words: "*I will tell them on my deathbed!*"

Ouch!

This left little room to negotiate. Whatever further efforts the agents made, Ivan was not interested, so they left.

It was my greatest hope, despite whatever else might have happened, that they maintained proper decorum, and that Ivan would remember their behavior as professional and acceptable. Despite the message, I hoped Ivan would not hold ill feelings against the messengers.

It was not clear to me if there had been an offer made of money for information, but I don't think so. Straight arrows like Ivan act based on principle, not because they are paid to compromise their principles.

Because Ivan and the FBI agents would be in town another couple of days, it would be worth another shot to ask him to reconsider. However, Ivan had an all-day tour of Universal Studios planned with Anahit. He would also be leaving one day before the festival officially ended and had a prepaid flight reservation. He may even have stayed in the company of others to insulate himself from another approach from the FBI. Either way, with the two-prong approach—overt and covert—in an effort to recruit Ivan, this attempt had been a disaster.

Picking Up the Pieces

After the big dinner, my part in this scenario was over. I had supported the overt prong, which went well enough to the extent that they met with Ivan securely, as planned. But I could only set the match near the fuse. It was theirs to touch the flame to the rocket, win or lose.

The next morning, it was natural for me to touch base with our traveling Russian and Armenian. Most important was to monitor Ivan, should he make a comment about his encounter with the FBI, even though he hadn't done so the night before. You never know what might happen when there is a potential crisis and a person has the opportunity to sleep on it.

It was perfectly natural for my undercover character to ask for feedback from their dinner with Polly, and for me to make comments to Ivan and Anahit, as well. Also, more was still needed on Ivan's travel plans. That would be useful for senior decision-makers who might want the FBI to have another go at him. I fell back onto things my mother taught me: be a good person, and follow up with the relationship.

Like clockwork, they were out by the pool—same table, same everything.

Both had expressions of happiness when they saw me—still a good sign. Anahit began to speak. Ivan started his one-sentence-behind translation, which I continued to marvel at.

She said the dinner with "Polly-the-Legend" was "the greatest event of the film festival." They would be "forever grateful" for her having them to dinner.

It is times like these, when the deep-seated humor of who actually put the occasion together and paid for their meal, makes me feel all warm and fuzzy. They were, of course, hosted by Uncle Sam.

Anahit said she would have her script translated as soon as possible from Armenian to Russian, and then into English. As requested, Ivan would add the finishing touches so it would be acceptable to Polly.

That was well and good, but further efforts by Polly would never happen, unless she took it up on her own time. That was unlikely, as the Ottoman genocide—even viewed behind a love story—was just too far outside of Polly's comfort zone.

I did feel bad that they might have been lured away from other potential prospects at the film festival, who might actually have worked on getting Anahit's movie made. But I thought this was highly unlikely, given the attending population I had met.

At the very least, Anahit and Ivan learned more from Polly than they ever would have elsewhere at the festival about the actual filmmaking process—thanks, again, to Uncle Sam.

Then I had a thought I wanted to kick out of my head the moment it occurred to me. If there were a renewed mandate to stay in touch with Ivan and have him come back to the United States, it might be accomplished only if we actually made Anahit's movie. That could take an initial million bucks, but it would almost certainly get him back on American soil.

It wasn't my money to spend, but the FBI had spent millions on this overall project already. Could it include actually making a movie to get their answer?

It would depend on how much need was seen for Ivan to return. I wanted to push the thought from my mind. You never break your arrows over your knee—just remove them from your quiver for a time and keep them handy.

Ivan explained that Anahit could communicate through email, which seemed like a big deal to them. Their point was, in 1998, the capital of Armenia actually had email service. This would not have been a given, so they made no small point that her small country—landlocked, and surrounded by the likes of Azerbaijan, Iran, Turkey, and Georgia—could communicate on the internet. They may not have been cosmopolitan, but it was a step in the right direction.

For the purpose of receiving the screenplay, however, I said we would want it sent in hard copy, rather than have Polly try to download and print it out. Regular mail from Armenia was another story, but we figured they could get it to LA, somehow.

For the greater communication effort, we would use the telephone, only with Ivan and through me. I would speak with Polly about whatever they needed.

Besides Cannes, Ivan said he might also attend a television convention in New Orleans, but it wasn't definite. That seemed to be wishful thinking on his part, as there would be no Anahit to pitch in and pay for that trip, so all of his future travel plans were iffy.

Even if he did travel, what would it mean to the FBI? Who from the Bureau would go there, and what would the effort be like? Would it be more of the same from the overt-prong boys? Would they choose different people? What would convince Ivan to help the FBI?

Trying to get authorization for me to travel to Cannes would cause a huge bureaucratic fight with FBIHQ managers, who would see it as a "Barnes boondoggle." They would write "not appropriate for this UC operation," but what would I be trying to accomplish, really? We had plenty of personality assessment and potential meeting locations, should a brilliant plan arise.

At the table by the pool—a place I knew they would miss—Ivan reiterated something he had said during dinner. It was how proud he was at the amount of advertising for which he was responsible for his magazine.

Not baiting him, but more like testing him, I said how great it was to be recognized by his employer.

I paused—now for the test.

I added that on the way to her home, Polly also referred to this accomplishment and had been very impressed by it.

With this, Ivan's face lit up, much more than from my compliment for the very same thing. That further clarified what was going on in his mind.

Ivan lamented that he had wanted to interview Polly. I explained that she had other matters to attend to and would not be back at the film festival. He asked how he might source the material he had learned from her. I told him he should refer to Polly as a "Hollywood insider."

This put another big smile on his face, enthralled that such a description would appear in an article he wrote. He would feel like he was having a conversation with Polly, but through me.

Ivan mentioned he sometimes takes extended trips, like the one to Armenia to shadow Anahit. Surely there were movie producers in Yerevan who were men. I wondered if he would have made the same sort of trip with one of them.

Anahit started to speak, and Ivan picked up the translation. She wanted to invite Polly to attend next year's Armenian Film Festival in Yerevan. They said they wanted me there, too, but, clearly, Polly was the apple of their eye.

However, Polly would never make such a trip. She was supporting our operation with her brother in mind and a sense of patriotic duty, although she *would* admit she was having fun.

Here she was, in the middle of an enormous international intelligence case, deeply involved in an FBI undercover operation against a Russian, of all things, living through stuff her movie-making colleagues could only dream about.

I kept my response as neutral as possible, not wanting them to set their hopes too high.

Ivan reminded me of their early departure from the festival. He even thumped his jacket over his left pocket which held his plane ticket.

It probably didn't make any difference now, as another overt contact by the FBI would just piss him off even more.

With all of my preparation to play the role of an independent film financer, and sell my cover to the target, I realized I had accomplished what I set out to do. In fact, now it would be difficult to convince Ivan I was anything else. Should I have shown him my FBI credentials, he would have thought they were just a prop from a movie set!

It was time to stuff this persona into my undercover closet, where it might be taken out, dusted off, and used again another day.

Back at the San Diego FBI

One aspect of having been in Santa Monica for all those days is where I was not. I was not working my healthcare-fraud cases in San Diego, which were crying out for me to return.

During this time, no one in the field office knew where I had been or what I had been doing. To this day, they do not know. It really was the first time I had a case where no one else had a need-to-know. Back in the office, I had to operate as though it wasn't going on behind the scenes, and there was some other reason I had been out of town.

It was more difficult to hide the true explanation from my colleagues than it had been to hide my true identity from Ivan. They were closer and knew more about me.

Ivan knew only what I revealed to him. I just had to keep my legend memorized. But from my San Diego colleagues I was asked, "Where the hell were you? Vacation? Death in the family? A special assignment?"

My supervisor had been given strict instructions to remain mum: not asking me, and not inquiring officially—perhaps not on pain of death, but something close to it, administratively.

To my squadmates who knew me best, this was not typical. As well as my FBI work, I had five children to raise, so perhaps somewhere in there, my absence was not completely unexpected. Out of respect for what I had done for over twenty-five years, if I wanted my friends to know, or if I could tell them, they knew I would.

Perspective on the Film Festival Outcome

As for Suchan and Cardillo, they were fine agents, but their pitch had been cold, dead on arrival, as far as I was concerned, almost always with a result you don't want to report. They had been declared the first string, while I was backup.

I had learned a unique set of facts about Ivan's personality. His relationship with his family, women in general, some women in particular, and his lack of relationships with men, said much about what made him tick.

What makes him laugh? What makes him cry? And does he love his wife?

I tossed over these old counterintelligence questions about Ivan. It was all about women—wife, mother, a kindly neighbor, daughters, a movie producer from Armenia, and now one in Los Angeles—who had his respect, admiration, and his strong desire to please them.

How could I use this to our advantage?

CHAPTER 14

WHY IVAN KURYLENKO?

I was working on the understanding that Ivan was one of the few Soviets who might be able to identify the ultimate unknown subject—a spy working for Russia in the FBI, who had been, and still was, compromising US Intelligence. Three senior agents had flown across the country two months before to ask me to work the undercover case, meet Polly Platt, attend additional training, create backstopping, and spend hundreds of hours in preparation. This is to say nothing of what the FBI invested in surveillance and the two overt-prong agents, Suchan and Cardillo—flights, hotels, food, and the like—plus a myriad of other logistics to make this case work.

But at some point, one must ask, "Why Ivan Kurylenko?"

I was not told why it was believed Ivan had information the FBI wanted to know.

It was clear he was not an intelligence officer, based on his past assignment in the US and what he had done since the Berlin Wall came down in 1989.

The vocations of most former KGB officers followed certain patterns—in security work and with import-export companies—but Ivan's did not. He was strictly a journalist, and a good one. So, this was a real poser for a guy like me.

The powers that be had decided my piece of the puzzle was to support the overt prong, and, only secondarily, to recruit the man—if the opportunity arose. I was not to wonder why.

It felt like I was in Alfred, Lord Tennyson's 1854 epic poem, "The Charge of the Light Brigade," about the six hundred soldiers who went into battle in the Crimean War, almost all of whom perished:

Theirs not to make reply,
Theirs not to reason why,
Theirs but to do and die....

I had an uneasy feeling in the pit of my stomach when I thought about all this effort, based on something of which I was not aware. One thing FBI agents simply hate is to be told to do something, but not why. We are not a squad of privates first class—maybe more like lieutenant colonels, who do not expect to be coddled but do want, at least, to be informed.

The military has a necessary and appropriate chain of command. But the FBI is a civilian organization that takes great pains to hire the best and brightest so it can trailblaze in every aspect of investigations. It is a bad decision to keep street agents out of the loop. They have greater initiative if they know why they are doing what they've been told to do.

A close friend, Jon Siverling, was a captain in the US Army Special Forces before becoming an FBI agent and my partner in San Diego. He once told me he could tell I had never been in the military. That small bit of profiling came because I carried my briefcase with my right hand. No one in the military would ever do that. They keep that hand free to salute a senior officer.

True enough, I had entered on duty in the FBI several months after graduating from law school. I wondered if left-handed agents carried their briefcases with their right hands so they could quickly access their holstered handgun when the need arose. No, the vestiges of their military experience—keeping the saluting hand free—would be the controlling factor.

With this vignette, Jon also said it is probably good the FBI has people who don't have a thought process in military lock-step—and don't all carry their briefcases with the same hand. That is the tip of the iceberg for what this profile actually means.

Loosely described, it is thinking outside the box, and the FBI is an organization that prides itself in hiring outside-the-box thinkers. To be outside of even *that* box is rare, but it is where I usually found myself. My personnel file indicated this was not always a good thing.

I recall my transfer luncheon, after seventeen years in the Washington Field Office, to San Diego in 1990. Jim Stassinos, my former supervisor, introduced seven of his fellow GS-14 supervisors from the dais to the attendees, numbering over 250 in the Great Hall at Fort McNair. He said, "These are the supervisors at WFO who *thought* they could supervise Wayne." Laughs all around.

In 1998, I had absolutely no idea why the agents, who did have a need to know, thought Ivan knew anything the FBI would be interested in. At least, I saw nothing which would support the mammoth effort to get close to him and finesse the overt prong into having even a few minutes with him on the narrowest of topics. It bothered me, because I had never before gone into an investigation blindfolded. But I took all of my years of experience and did my best to accomplish what I was asked to do. I truly did feel like one of Tennyson's six hundred, marching forward into the blazing cannons—but march I did.

Only much later did I learn why Ivan Kurylenko merited so damned much attention.

CHAPTER 15

THIS IS WHY IVAN KURYLENKO!

If you were an American with a top-secret clearance during the Cold War and wanted to sell secrets to the Russians, how would you do it? If you never thought about this, that is a good thing. But if you have, I would hope it would be in a theoretical way, maybe because you worked counterintelligence in the FBI. But that has not been the case with everyone.

If you were a defense contractor's employee working on a new bomber wing, you certainly never met a Russian. You might not have received your security clearance if you had. You don't even know where the Soviet Embassy is in Washington, DC. But that could be remedied easily enough from a telephone book and then driving right to it.

You locate a few vehicles parked on Sixteenth Street, with diplomatic license plates, right across from the Soviet Embassy, five blocks north of the White House. If your timing is good, you drive down the street and chance to see a Russian getting out of his car. You decide he looks like a spy. Then you drive a few blocks away and wait.

You don't know where the diplomats live, so you come back around 5:30 PM. You drive down the street slowly, looking for someone approaching one of those cars.

After a few minutes, you are rewarded. The same man walks across the street, gets in his car, and starts driving. You assume Russians are used to being followed, but hope the FBI is not watching this man. You must be very careful, but the Washington rush hour is your saving grace. Traffic crawls across the Fourteenth Street Bridge to Northern Virginia, and down I-95 to King Street, where the Russian exits the interstate.

He drives a few more blocks, then turns into a garden-apartment community. You follow to see where he parks and watch him walk to his building.

To avoid being seen loitering, you drive to a nearby Denny's restaurant for dinner.

A couple of hours later, when it is dark, you drive back to the complex, park out of the way, and walk through the lot. Others are there, so you try to look inconspicuous.

On the way to his car, your nerves are on edge and you finger a plastic envelope in your coat pocket. Approaching the Russian's car, you scan the area to make sure no one is watching. You take out the envelope. In a second plastic envelope, which you have not touched, inside of the one you hold, is your note. Wearing gloves, you slip it out of the envelope and slide it under the Russian's windshield wiper. You walk away, not the same way you came, then circle back to your car. When you get home, you go to the bathroom and throw up, with the heart-pounding realization that you have begun to commit espionage.

The note reads that you have US secrets to sell to the Russians. You have designated a park in Fairfax County, and a particular bench, where you will meet with a Russian on Saturday at 6:00 PM. He is to bring $10,000 with him, in cash, in exchange for your secrets. Sounds simple enough.

This method of making secure contact with a Soviet intelligence officer has been done on many occasions. The problem for the man making the overture is that, while he thinks the deal will be done quickly, he doesn't have the KGB's playbook, but they know his. Their objective is to get the American on the hook, so he will come back, again and again, with more secrets.

The KGB will conduct an analysis of the note, its credibility, level of sophistication, what it promises, and make a decision. Almost every time, they go through with the meeting. If there is an ongoing summit between the Soviet Union and the US, with the fear that this might be a ploy—a *gambit*, in their beloved chess terms—the KGB would reject the overture to avoid a possible international incident.

That administrative decision was the result of the Russians shooting down Francis Gary Powers, in his U-2 spy plane in 1960, when President Dwight D. Eisenhower and Soviet leader Nikita Khrushchev were soon to have a summit meeting, which was then cancelled.

Barring any of that, it will be a go.

They will certainly record the moments on the park bench, audio and video, and those before and after, using a car with tinted windows conveniently parked a short distance away. They want to identify the new traitor.

When the Russian approaches the man on the bench, he will be personable. There will be chitchat, and if the American has written a script—a parole—they will exchange those words.

Usually this means the American has been watching too many spy movies.

The Russian will want to see the documents, and the American will want to see the money. He will be told they must first see the documents and assess their value, not wanting to be confused with a Soviet bank for anyone promising to provide valuable information.

They eventually depart, with the American quite dissatisfied, although a follow-up meeting will have been arranged. The Russian would not look at the documents during this meeting because it would not be secure. He would not understand the contents, anyway, because he is a professional spy at the tradecraft of espionage. Someone else in his embassy with technical knowledge would have to evaluate them.

All of this makes for an American who will come back for a second meeting. There, he will be told the Soviets appreciated what he gave them, although it was only worth $5,000. If he wants the other $5,000, he must return with more documents.

Then he is in their spider's web from which there is no escape. He has committed espionage, the only crime singled out in the US Constitution as punishable by death. The Soviets can dangle him any way they like to squeeze more out of him. This is accompanied by sleepless nights, weight loss, and no explanation to his wife as to why he is so irritable. There is also no possible justification for, "Where has all this money come from?"

There is always the danger, the American believes, the Soviets will turn him in if he doesn't continue to cooperate. But that never happens. If they did, any information they might receive in the future would dry up, which would be counterproductive to the KGB's mission. It is the threat of such an action which usually works. Also, it would open up a beehive of what the turncoat had already furnished to the KGB, something they would never want revealed. In spite of this reasoning, of which the naïve American is not aware, he is certain he has opened himself to extortion.

My friends, former FBI agents, who have reviewed these pages, suggest I should not be giving lessons in How to Become a Spy for the hapless beginner with a security clearance. But this vignette, or a close variation, has taken place enough times that these pages should not be considered a revelation. And relaying this scenario is only the setup for the one that follows below. This windshield-wiper overture is to be compared with one divined by a man who was far from hapless. In fact, he was one of the most dangerous and despicable spies who ever worked for—actually, *against*—the US government.

In this second scenario, it was an intelligence professional who decided how he would make his approach to the Russians, at the time and place of his choosing. He did this by walking right through their front door.

In the early 1980s, as the history of this case reads, a US Intelligence official walked into one of the many Soviet establishments in Washington, DC. Most nations with representation in the capital have an embassy, an ambassador's residence, and sometimes a separate consular location. But during the Cold War, the Soviets had more than a dozen locations in Washington, some quite small, the size of a wooden duplex house with three steps up to a porch, a wooden railing, and a screen door.

He would choose a day when it was raining so he could hide his face with an umbrella. Marching up the steps and into the front door would alert absolutely no one from US counterintelligence.

To the person at the reception desk, not far inside the front door, the American would ask to speak with someone in the KGB. The man would give him the pro forma response that there was no such person there. The American would tell the man to walk to the back offices and find someone who handled intelligence matters.

This would cause a long stare by the man at the desk. Finally, he would walk to the back.

In a few minutes, another man would return and usher the visitor around a partition and into his office. They would sit down across from each other.

The American would say he had a position in US Intelligence and was willing to provide sensitive information to the KGB. He would use nomenclature indicating he lived in the world of intelligence and spoke that language.

He would bring a set of documents, examples of what he could provide in the future, and hand them to the Soviet. He would not need a *quid pro quo* but would leave them with the Russian to establish his bona fides. He would also not ask for money at this first, and only, face-to-face meeting, because he knew the value of what he was providing. But, for the Russians to receive more, he must be paid. In this scenario, the shoe was on the other foot—the American's.

He would have written down instructions of how and where the next contact would take place. It would be in a way to further indicate he knew what he was doing. He would not say his real name but would use an obvious alias.

His instructions would include non-personal communication—a dead-drop—with which the KGB officer would be very familiar. After all, that had been at the heart of some of the classes he would have gone through in the KGB training school.

Because the visitor had planned carefully when choosing this Soviet establishment, he knew when it was safe to enter, and he might even have known the identity of this intelligence officer, maybe even his rank in the KGB.

This would knock the socks off the Russian, who would hope he recovered his composure quickly. But when his surprised reaction became the cat that was already out of the bag, he would have no option but to just sit and listen to what his visitor had to say.

Since this visit was completely unexpected, the Russian was not prepared to take surreptitious photos or make audio or video recordings.

The American would have told the KGB man that his documents were not mundane, like ones they might receive from a defense contractor. Rather, they were of higher quality—from the US Intelligence Community.

The lump in the Russian's throat would seem to block his airway. It would have taken all of his professionalism to recover and do what he was trained to do. But the visitor would need nothing from the man, for he would have made plans of his own.

They would walk down the stairs to the building's small garage. The American would get into the trunk of the Russian's car. The KGB man would open the garage door and drive out. He would clean himself off, using a classic surveillance detection route, and finally arrive at a county park in Fairfax, Virginia.

At a secluded location, chosen by the American, the Russian would stop the car, open the trunk, and the man would get out. Then the Russian would drive away.

The American would walk to a vehicle he had parked not far away.

The Russian would return to his embassy and be an immediate hero, although not entirely. He would not know who the American was: not his actual name or the agency he worked for. And, unlike anything that had happened before to the KGB, it would be their new American spy who controlled everything—meeting sites, times, frequency, and whether he would continue to do this.

Senior KGB officials at Dzerzhinsky Square in Moscow would not have been happy about that part, but they would be overjoyed that this *walk-in* had chosen to do so. Vetting his information would be a pro forma matter, because it was so unique, exceptional, and of such high quality. Champagne corks were popping that evening in the KGB *rezidentura* in Washington, as they would be the next at KGB Headquarters in Moscow.

And by the way, Ivan Fyodorovich Kurylenko had, coincidentally, been in that same small official Soviet facility on the afternoon when the American walked in—and saw his face.

You might inquire, much as I did, how all of this was learned.

During the early 1980s, there were two KGB officers recruited by US Intelligence in Washington, DC: Valery Martynov and Sergei Motorin. They were humorously referred to, by those with inside knowledge, as "M&M." During FBI debriefings, one of them furnished the details of the most extraordinary above scenario.

In the same timeframe, an American, working on behalf of Soviet Intelligence, provided the Russians with the identities of the two KGB officers, M&M, who had been recruited by the FBI. But the KGB was never quick to accept accusations about one of their own and had to conduct an internal investigation to verify the information. During that passage of time was when one of the FBI's sources in the KGB provided the information about the American walk-in at the small Russian establishment on that rainy day. That is what spurred the current investigation in which I was the key player.

An irony, greater than most would ever know, was that these two men, one Russian and one American, were in something like a death struggle, where each one, living as a turncoat in his own intelligence service, was undone by the other.

CHAPTER 16

OFF TO EUROPE

US government employees, including FBI agents, acquire annual leave each pay period. As a long-tenured agent, I received eight hours every two weeks. Some eat them up right away, using them as soon as they are earned. But the more patient, those of us who plan ahead, accumulate the leave and build up the hours to do something memorable, often far from home. But one should not think the mind of an FBI agent is ever far removed from his life's work.

In the summer of 1998, a few months after the American Film Market in Santa Monica, my wife and I took a trip to Spain. She wanted to attend an International Urban Planning Conference in Madrid.

Being away from our five children for three weeks would be a first, and the logistics were daunting. My young daughters, seven and nine, flew with us to the East Coast to stay with grandparents. We flew on to Madrid.

The boys, ages fourteen, sixteen, and eighteen, would be left to their own devices in San Diego. Well, almost, for friends and neighbors would be looking in, to say nothing of my FBI colleagues who respond to emergencies for a living.

The conference hotel in Madrid would be our home base. From there, you can drive an hour or two to visit several walled cities with ancient fortresses and castles. This was special to me, a lifelong fan of Prince Valiant and days of yore.

We traveled to Toledo, Segovia, Ávila, and Salamanca. There is nothing like it for a student of history—treading foot on all of those stone-carved stairways. This was topped off with a visit to El Escorial, the centuries-long residence of the king of Spain, and the nearby Valley of the Fallen, with massive memorials commemorating their civil war in the 1930s.

Halfway through our trek around this rugged terrain, my pants had taken a beating. The next morning, we went to El Corte Inglés, a major department-store chain.

The men's department was a few floors up, and I picked several pants off a rack to try on. As an FBI agent, I was pretty athletic and healthy, but I did not have the slender form of the classic continental man. I would need to see what fit.

There was no salesperson in the department and no other customers. I walked toward the changing rooms and pulled back the curtain closing off the entrance. I chose the left side and a booth three down the row. I had given my wallet and FBI credentials to my wife to hold in her purse: a normal security precaution for someone who carries a badge.

I took off my trousers and placed the belted waistband over a large hook at the top of the six-foot partition. I tried on one pair, then another, proof that I did *not* have a Spanish man's body shape!

The third was a charm. I exited the booth, leaving my pants on the hook. I walked past the two vacant stalls and went right, out to seek my wife's view of my fashion choice.

As I left the changing area, a man passed me going in. He was tall and slender, much more the continental body shape. He had about an inch on me in height, something fairly rare in Spain, and a complexion that would have been a quality suntan in Southern California. Out of the corner of my eye, I saw him make a left in the changing area.

As I walked through the carousels of hanging pants, a thought occurred to me. I quickly spun around and darted back to the changing rooms. I entered and looked left, just in time to see the man in my booth, his hand high in the air, and his fingers reaching into the left rear pocket of my pants. That is where I kept my wallet. Fortunately, it wasn't there, but that did not change his intent.

In a loud voice I called out, "*Hey, ladrón*!" This means *thief* in Spanish, and that was what he was about to be, if he'd had his way. But with my outburst, he pulled his hand back and started shaking his head, saying, "No, no, no *ladrón*!"

I held my ground as he left the booth and darted toward me, but not at me. He slid past quickly, then continued to the other end of the changing aisle, entering the last stall, three down. I remained near the portal entrance. There was silence.

Stepping out into the sales area to look for assistance, there were still no store employees to be found.

My wife was walking toward me.

"A guy just tried to steal my wallet, and we need to call security."

A phone was on the counter near the cash register. I picked it up and clicked the button in the cradle. A female voice came on.

In high-school Spanish I said I needed "*Securidad, rápidamente, en el departamento de pantalones, porque hay un ladrón aquí.*"

In a few moments, two large men came trotting toward us.

They were there to help. But after a moment of telling my story, their expressions indicated they were not sure it reached a level of attention for them to take action. Then I added something important.

The man had not brought any pants in with him to try on. That is, his sole reason for entering the changing area was to steal my wallet. I motioned to the changing doorway and suggested they see for themselves. He seemed to be hiding, waiting for me to go away.

This did pique their interest, and the senior man gave me an appreciative nod. The two went through the opening, then turned right. There, in the last booth, they found the *ladrón* seated, seemingly patiently, but not really waiting for *them*.

After a couple of minutes, the three came out. The two security guards had the thief's hands cuffed behind him. Each held one of his arms, two-handed, above and below the elbows.

The one in charge asked us to wait. Another security man would be there shortly.

I quickly changed back into my own pants and returned to the sales area.

True to their word, a third security guy appeared walking briskly through the store. He introduced himself and asked us to follow him.

We wound our way through several departments, then to the right and into an employees-only door, down a corridor, and out an exit door to a metal fire escape, where we zigzagged up a couple of floors. An impressive view of Madrid surrounded us. Then it was back in through another door, and down more corridors to a door labeled Head of Security. We were ushered past a secretary and into the top man's office. I had begun to wonder if I was under suspicion.

The *jefe* (chief) came from around his large desk and we shook hands. We all sat down, and he opened his palms to me, essentially asking what had happened.

As though on a witness stand, a place I am familiar with and actually enjoy, I briefly laid out our travels and the need for pants.

I described the visit to the men's department and the fellow who seemed to have observed me going into the changing rooms, then entered just as I was leaving. I quickly returned to witness him reaching for my wallet.

No, he hadn't gotten it because it wasn't there. My wife had been holding it.

The chief's eyebrows went up. He agreed that had been a wise precaution, but it also meant no crime had been committed.

I mentioned that the man had entered the changing area with no pants to try on, which had been suspicious to me. Again, the security chief's eyebrows went up.

It was time to explain to him what I was, which was really behind all of this.

I told him I was an *Agente Especial en el Effay-Bay-Eee, en los Estados Unidos*.

I brought out my FBI credentials with the small gold badge inset on the front of the black leather case. I handed them to the security head.

He looked them over carefully. His head slowly began to nod, lips puffing out. Now he understood my motivation. He returned the credentials, leaned far back in his chair, and smiled.

He explained that a man matching the description of the one detained had been making a menace of himself in several of their stores over the last eighteen months. His *modus operandi* was stealing wallets from men's changing rooms, while unsuspecting customers were looking for more pants or conferring with their wives. None, however, had caught him in the act. Today, the thief's luck had run out.

In my mind, I questioned his use of the term "luck," but let it go.

He added that the perpetrator would be transferred to police custody. He had already confessed to other thefts, so it was clear he was their long-sought *ladrón*.

Knowing we had a travel schedule, the chief said that because of the evidence they had, he would not ask me to return to Spain for the trial.

That made me feel good. I had been away from work long enough and didn't know how the Bureau would deal with the administrative leave necessary to make another trip to Spain to testify. Besides, somebody at FBIHQ would have seen it as just another Barnes boondoggle.

I was almost beside myself that I had been able to assist local law enforcement while on vacation. Then it occurred to me—that was exactly the point!

A vacation, for the likes of me, is not sunning myself on a Mediterranean beach, or climbing through the Valley of the Fallen and around stone staircases in half a dozen castles. On my own time, and my own dime, it is catching a bad guy seven thousand miles from home. It was like a vignette from *Fantasy Island*, but on the European continent. *That* was my idea of a badge-carrier's perfect vacation!

Epiphany in Madrid

We left the security chief, accepting his overflowing appreciation, and went back to buy a couple of pairs of pants. It wasn't until the next day, on the way to another walled city, that I contemplated the previous day's events. What I had done actually *was* working, and it felt good.

Then I pondered something I had been pushing for several weeks after the Santa Monica film festival, with the continuing objective of getting Ivan back to the US. It was for me to take a trip to London. I wanted to meet with his boss in the hopes of finessing his assistance for Ivan to return.

Ivan had made the point that all of his business travel had to be approved by this man, so greasing the skids seemed like a good idea. There is nothing quite like an in-person visit to show how much you care and, here, how much Ivan was respected.

Not surprisingly, the Bureau flat-out turned it down. The justification was the cost of the plane ticket, and the belief that the results would not contribute to the overall case, not to mention that they saw me as a street agent who liked to work with a very long leash. They wouldn't buy my argument. I strongly took issue, but there was nothing I could do.

Then the thief in El Corte Inglés changed my perspective and what I realized could be accomplished in a distant land. It inspired me to call Red Pop.

I explained to Gene where I was and what had happened the day before. After hearing my story, he laughed so hard I thought he would hurt himself, saying, "Only *you*!" But I was sure many FBI agents would have done exactly the same thing—well, maybe.

Then I told him my epiphany. The Bureau had given me an out in the reason it denied my travel request to London—the cost! I said I would be glad to fork out the cash for the shuttle from Madrid to London, but would rather the Bureau pick up the tab. After all, it would be on company time and for an FBI case.

Gene said he'd make a quick call and get back. He realized this would mean a couple of days taken from my vacation in Spain, and I only had a few left.

Later, the same day, Gene called. Happily, he announced, it was a go.

Working in London

Two days later, we were on a morning flight to London. Because this opportunity had knocked, we would spend a couple of days there. In the event that Ivan's business was not open when I visited, I would have a fallback day to try again.

We stayed at a hotel near Victoria Station, and I took a taxi to my destination.

If I had the money, I would love to own a London cab: shiny, black, old, and boxy, driven on the London streets by the thousands. I could picture myself with several children, driving one in Solana Beach, its backseat filled with groceries, running errands, and having a jolly good time.

Ivan's company was in the East End, where almost all the newspaper and magazine businesses were based. The building was not at all what I had pictured, nothing like the headquarters for *The Washington Post* or *San Diego Union-Tribune*. It was quite a few steps sideways and down from there, and in a desolate neighborhood.

It was a four-story commercial structure. The way up to the unit number was another zig-zagging set of fire-escape stairs on the outside of the building, similar to El Corte Inglés.

On the fourth floor, a note was taped to the door with the name of the company in bold handwriting. Coming up the stairs behind me was a postman. I could not imagine a US letter carrier going through this same process every day.

I stepped aside and followed him in. He was a known quantity, and I stood there after he left, in the open lobby area.

There were eight desks, arranged in two rows of four, in the twenty-foot-by-fifty-foot room, with long wooden floorboards that creaked when you walked on them. Fluorescent lighting made it as bright as daylight. While the space was smaller than I might have expected, it was clearly a professionally set up business, clean, neat, and efficient. I also knew they had many journalists, like Ivan, spread around the world. So, while their headquarters wasn't that large, their tentacles stretched far and wide.

I asked the receptionist for the man in charge, and she motioned in his direction.

Conferring near one of the desks was an older, slender man—my target audience.

I was wearing a navy-blue blazer and tie, which seemed out of place in the relaxed atmosphere. But it brought my presence to the attention of Ivan's boss.

As I walked toward him, he approached me. He had wavy salt-and-pepper hair and a lined face with character. I liked him immediately. But I was not Wayne Barnes. I had to rewire my brain in the taxi, and while trudging up the steps, that I was Wayne Johnson, again.

The business card I handed him was only the third one I had given out. I introduced myself.

I said, "I have been traveling in Spain and England for a few days and wanted to take the opportunity to stop by your office. At the American Film Market in Los Angeles, a few months ago,

I had the pleasure of meeting Ivan Kurylenko and the Armenian producer he accompanied there. He made such a positive impression on me and others that, even if he is not here, I wanted to tell his boss how highly regarded he is."

Nigel Aynsley produced his card.

"Ivan is in Moscow, where he spends most of his time, for which I am very glad." He added, "He is very good at what he does."

Chiming in, I said, "Yes, I agree. I found him to be both knowledgeable and gracious, and he was the perfect gentleman with Anahit Avakian. We also had the opportunity to have dinner for four with my dear friend and Academy member Polly Platt."

Aynsley smiled. "I gather Ms. Platt might be the 'Hollywood insider' mentioned in Ivan's articles." I confirmed she was.

I explained my ostensible role of independent film financer, working on behalf of a set of wealthy clients. I added that I appreciated Ivan's knowledge of the film industry, so his meeting with Polly had not been all one-sided. Well, actually, it had been, but I had an objective.

I could not have endeared myself any better to Mr. Nigel Aynsley.

He invited me to tour the office and showed me how their system operated. Most of the staff was in London, with others spread around the world, many in Europe. Of course, Ivan covered Russia and the former Soviet Republics, including Armenia.

I asked about Ivan's travels and learned he had been to both Cannes festivals—film and television. He had no set plans for future travel, not to the rest of Europe, and certainly not back to the US. He wasn't prevented from going, it just wasn't his territory. Another man covered America. The trip with Anahit had been a special deal.

With the difference in time zones, I said staying in touch with Ivan was difficult.

With that, their commercial director, at a nearby desk, set up a link for me to send Ivan a message.

I wrote about my travels and stopping by in London. I had met Mr. Aynsley and was glad to have come to see the company he worked for. I asked him to give me a call when I would be back in San Diego the following week, then closed with best regards from Polly.

The message was everything it should have been—for Ivan to receive, and for his boss to see in what esteem he was held, even by an Academy member. The Brits have their comparable BAFTA awards, but they hold the Oscars in high regard.

Ivan would receive the message in Moscow when he next logged in.

Just before leaving, I asked Aynsley if he wouldn't mind my taking a few photos of their offices "for the investors back home."

He was glad to oblige and provided me with some of their recent publications.

From the street, I took a few more pictures outside the building. This was for FBIHQ.

It had been years since Ronald Reagan's comments about dealing with the Soviets, using the phrase, "Trust, but verify." That also encapsulated the philosophy of FBI management throughout the history of the Bureau. These photos would preempt anyone from questioning whether I had actually been in London.

Ivan's boss seemed to have been taken by my trip to his office, even if in a vain attempt to visit Ivan. The extra details of how and why I had arrived, and the friendship and value of Ivan to me and others, were not lost on him. It was all done to enhance Ivan in Aynsley's eyes, but mostly to begin to pry him out of Moscow for a trip back to the USA.

For me, it was just another rock turned over in the stream.

CHAPTER 17

POLLY TO THE RESCUE

After Ivan and Anahit returned home, there were several reasons to remain in touch. It was still the position of the Bureau to make another approach to Ivan, although under what circumstances was not clear. The link to him was my role.

Many more conversations took place with Ivan than have been written about here.

If you ever heard a recording of an undercover meeting with an intelligence target, besides all of the restaurant background noise, there are trivial things that are minimally discussed, topics that would not grab the attention of tape monitors.

None of the meetings with Ivan in Santa Monica, or any of the phone calls, had been recorded, but some salient points should be noted. One aspect of conversations-in-passing was to sow the seeds for future contacts. Even if this did not mean in-person, face-to-face meetings, at least we could speak through emails or on the phone.

The eleven-hour time difference between Moscow and San Diego was a logistical nightmare. In addition, the phone number on my business card was the only one Ivan could use to reach me. That instrument sat in my bedroom in Solana Beach. But I was almost never there to answer it during the day, still a full-time FBI agent working healthcare fraud. On evenings and weekends, it would be pure happenstance for me to hear the phone ring and answer it.

The FBI answering machine was essential to maintain communications with Ivan. My family abided by the sign I had taped to the top: "Dad's Work Phone—Do Not Touch!"

Imagine if Ivan called, only to hear a young boy's voice, and he asked to speak with "Mr. Johnson." There could be no good outcome.

During a poolside conversation in Santa Monica with Ivan and Anahit, I had described the beloved American film *It's a Wonderful Life*, the 1946 Christmastime movie. Jimmy Stewart, as George Bailey, lived in a small town surrounded by good friends and family. He became so depressed, one day, that he said he wished he had never been born.

For the rest of the movie, his own personal angel, Clarence, walked him through what it would have been like for those whose lives he had touched if he hadn't been born. Pointing out all the good he had done makes the hero see the folly of his earlier position. The ending is truly heartwarming, particularly so because it took place on Christmas Eve. This made the movie nearly required viewing for millions of Americans annually, and one of the most popular of all time. But Anahit and Ivan had never heard of it.

I agreed to send them a copy.

In return, there was a Russian movie Ivan and Anahit spoke of highly, which was also required annual viewing in their countries: *The Irony of Fate*, from 1976.

Its plot begins with several men enjoying an annual tradition of a public steam bath on New Year's Eve in Moscow. They are also celebrating the impending marriage of one of them, Zhenya. After multiple toasts, they all become drunk.

One is to fly to Leningrad that evening, but the friends get confused and put Zhenya, the wrong man, on the flight.

A fellow passenger, realizing his drunken status, helps Zhenya off the plane and leaves him in the Leningrad airport.

Because Soviet-era architecture had so many buildings that appeared almost identical, when Zhenya wakes up, he doesn't realize he is not in Moscow. He gives the address of his fiancée to a taxi driver. Also, because of the street names in Soviet cities, there *is* such an address (3rd Builders' Street), but this one is in Leningrad.

Once at the apartment, another poke is made at Soviet-era construction, and Zhenya's key from Moscow even opens the lock. The furniture inside is so similar to his fiancée's, he does not know he is in the wrong apartment and collapses on the bed.

When the real tenant, Nadya, returns home and finds Zhenya in her bed, she is furious.

When her boyfriend shows up, he, too, becomes furious and more comedic action ensues.

Finally, Nadya believes Zhenya's wild story, but he must return to Moscow where his fiancée is furious with him as well.

It takes another day for Zhenya to get a flight, and the hours spent with Nadya develop into their own love story.

In the end, Zhenya returns to Moscow, but Nadya sees their meeting as fate, something she should not pass up. She takes a flight to Moscow to find true love with Zhenya, hence the title.

With all of its fun-poking at the Soviet system, it is amazing that this movie was made under the scrutiny of a communist government overseer.

Ivan agreed to send me a copy as a continuing part of our long-distance relationship.

There were other factors that merited further contacts.

Polly had set out blocks for Anahit to check in having her screenplay translated from Armenian to Russian, and then into English, and more.

Then came consideration for the actors, especially the western stars, but also secondary characters from Russia and Armenia.

I had many calls with Ivan, but he always wanted to speak directly with Polly. He had a positive attitude and was good-natured, but on the occasions when he did speak with her, he blossomed—perhaps *gushed* better describes it.

She was used to being kowtowed to by many, but with Ivan, this took on another dimension. He was not like a lapdog, but he was clearly in the mix with Anahit's project and would do anything to make it happen. Polly came to understand that Ivan had this attitude because it was for *her*, as well as Anahit.

All of this took place because the Bureau—at least that small body of decision-makers on the Graysuit case—wanted to get access to Ivan again, preferably in the United States.

Our only known avenue to do that would involve Anahit's project. Perhaps they could both be brought to Los Angeles, but I was reluctant to push that on Polly. Her view was that the movie would never be made, at least, not with her involvement. She simply had other projects she was committed to. As Polly reiterated, "I don't do epic movies!"

One evening on the phone, Ivan announced what he called "enormous news." Anahit had received $6 million to make her movie. This had simply never been done before. Now Ivan and Anahit thought it was a go, and that "we" could begin to move forward.

Talk between FBIHQ and the field continued to revolve around getting Ivan back. Then someone came up with an idea, beset with either genius or venality, maybe both.

The plan involved bringing Anahit and Ivan to the States. While it would appear the movie project was advancing nicely, there would be a moment when "the government" would step in. Certain bureaucratic requirements had to be met. It could have been some sort of taxes, or permissions triggered by the foreign aspect of the production, perhaps involving Anahit and Ivan's visas. The details were not clear to me, but the ultimate description would be something close to extortion.

Anahit would be told that in order to receive all the necessary permissions to make the film, Ivan would have to agree to speak with US government representatives. The theory was she would be so completely dedicated to her movie that she would not let some little thing like a conversation between Ivan and government representatives spoil the opportunity to get it made.

I hoped Ivan would not see this effort as revolving around him alone, but rather as part of the bigger picture of Anahit's grand project.

In Anahit's experience, a glitch involving *any* government would not be unheard of, because she had lived under the communist system with its incomprehensible requirements.

In America, this is not how movies are made, but Ivan and Anahit wouldn't know that.

I understood this was for the greater good, to identify Graysuit, but it simply did not seem workable. This scam, for Anahit to convince Ivan to speak with the FBI, would still have no guarantee that he would divulge what he knew.

Another downside was that, instead of complying, Ivan might see this for what it was and realize that, once he gave up his information, the plug would be pulled on Anahit's movie. Then her dreams would swirl around her as they rushed down the drain. She would realize she had been duped, all because of Ivan, which would be crushing to him.

All of this was a significant quandary. It included the logistics of bringing the Russian and the Armenian to America, what to do with them, where they would stay, for how long, and the fine-point details of what the heck they would be doing when Ivan was *not* meeting with the FBI. This would all fall on my shoulders!

I wouldn't rely on Polly to do any of it. I could not possibly make that kind of demand on her time and her mental state. But we could come up with no other plan to finesse Ivan's return to the US.

In the late 1970s, in the FBI's Washington Field Office, Assistant Special Agent-in-Charge Cornelius ("Neal") G. Sullivan made a comment to me I will never forget. "The problem with having secrets is you have to tell *someone*."

Secrets cannot simply be hoarded but must be used to your advantage. They are no good locked in a safe. The greater question is whom you tell, and how much you tell them, to accomplish what you need to do.

Now, twenty years later, I was faced with this issue. Polly was in the loop regarding our operation, but only so much. She had met a Russian who US Intelligence wanted to get close to, or it might have also been the Armenian producer, but she had no idea why this operation had been set in motion.

Importantly, she was not aware of the bigger issue—trying to identify, then catch in the act and arrest, the most damaging spy in our midst. Polly knew all she needed to know. Even her brother had agreed with that.

And then it changed.

I was almost beside myself with the idea of bringing Anahit and Ivan back to the US, biting off far more than I could chew. While investigating my healthcare-fraud cases in San Diego, continuing contacts with Ivan now seemed like just an extra bit of work. But they were linked to the seven-hundred-pound gorilla over in the corner—the whole rest of the Graysuit effort. Still, no one in the field office knew anything about it, including my supervisor.

I spoke with Ivan at least every couple of weeks, then reported to Washington.

Reflecting on all of the wrangling and angling surrounding Ivan and Anahit, I feared the moment when a long, sharp pin would be raised to pierce the enormous bubble which we were—but mostly *I* was—creating, with a resounding *pop*! The remnants of the proposed Armenian saga of a love story during a genocide would fall, completely deflated, over all of us.

That really didn't matter, as long as we got the information we needed—*right?* And that piece seemed so small, so teensy-weensy in comparison, actually only one sentence, with Ivan's finger pointing at a single photograph, that one would have to wonder if it was worth this supreme effort. Well, of course it was, but *Jeezus*, look at all it was taking!

One day I let down a little of the fig leaf when I lamented to Polly that it was really only Ivan we wanted back in the States.

Up to that point, he and Anahit had seemed inseparable in our operation. Polly had thought they would have to return together.

I didn't tell her why, and she wouldn't have asked, but she gave me a look of, *why didn't you tell me this sooner?*

Then she made a game-changing suggestion.

Five years before, Polly had founded a film festival in Austin, Texas. While I had heard of the ones in Colorado, New York City, and Toronto, I had never heard of this one. She was interested in supporting the writers of screenplays, and not the films, their directors, producers, or actors. Her position was that so much is based upon the work of screenplay writers—her specialty—who, as a group, receive so little credit, she wanted to hold a festival just for them.

She was right, of course. Without a screenplay, there is nothing for producers to produce, directors to direct, or actors to act in, to make the magic that is the cinema. It really does all boil down to the creative juices of someone who sits down and begins with "Act One, Scene One" at the top of the page.

Polly and I discussed this at length. It was one of the best sessions I ever had the pleasure to experience, with all of our creative juices flowing.

The festival in Austin would have nine thousand attendees—far larger than I had imagined and more than three times the size of the one in Santa Monica.

She had first-rate actors, directors, and producers coming and, of course, scads and scads of screenwriters, from neophytes to Oscar winners. There were also premier showings of movies which would be serious contenders for major awards. *Pleasantville* was a standout that year. The lead actors were a young Tobey Maguire, long before he would swing through skyscrapers as Spiderman and ride to victory on Seabiscuit, and a young Ms. Reese

Witherspoon, half a dozen years before she would Walk the Line as Mrs. Johnny Cash and walk off with an Oscar.

It was Polly's status in Hollywood which enabled quality motion pictures to be shown at her film festival.

But what would be the justification for getting Ivan there? The festival would clearly be in his American colleague's assigned territory, so what were we to do?

Polly had the answer. She said Ivan could be a "special invitee" of the festival. He could participate as one of three members in a breakout session on International Film.

I asked who had been on the panel before, who Ivan would replace from last year.

"Oh," she explained, "I have never had a panel for International Film. I just made it up!"

I had to laugh out loud. But who would she have on the panel?

Polly thought about it for a few minutes and came up with two individuals. One actually had a good deal of international film experience. The other, she said, was such an egomaniac he would gladly sit on the panel, whether or not he would know what he was talking about. But he was well known among the film community. Hundreds of people attending that session would assume he knew his stuff simply because he had been chosen for the panel!

Polly said Ivan would be sent an official letter from the Austin Film Festival. His plane tickets, first class from Moscow, with a $7,000 price tag, hotel room, and a stipend for spending money, would be paid for "by the festival"—but actually Uncle Sam.

This special invitation was just for panel discussion participants. Anahit might have to be let down gently, because she would not be invited. I felt genuinely relieved that I would not be an international babysitter for her.

We still had to run this by FBIHQ, and the very small cadre of senior-level people working behind a double set of cypher-lock doors, who would make this decision. But the upside was, if Ivan would not be in the presence of an Armenian producer, and would have no translation duties, no ball and chain around his ankle for as many days as he would be in Texas, it would give us our best-case scenario for another shot at him. What a relief for me!

While there was less of the venal factor involved with this new scenario, there was still some. There would be nothing I could do to lift the spirits of both Ivan and Anahit about her well-intended efforts to produce such an ambitious film. There would be heart-wrenching deflation when her movie-making process (the American aspect, anyway) would come, hopefully gently, but more likely *screeching*, to a halt.

The Austin scenario was much easier to swallow, operationally, in terms of a narrower scope. Ivan would be within our grasp for whatever he might agree to tell the US government.

CHAPTER 18
UNIQUE

Grammarians tell us there should be no modifier with the word "unique." No *sort of* unique, *very* unique, *especially* unique, or even *astoundingly* unique. No, just *unique* will do.

In the FBI, when working foreign counterintelligence cases, there was a great deal of variety for how each one might be approached. Among the most complex are when an undercover operation is in play. The facts are dealt with as they come, sometimes at a moderate pace, but often, seemingly flying at you through the air. You feel like you are in the middle of the circle in a high-school game of dodgeball.

What separated this case with Ivan Kurylenko from the rest was a fact pattern that had never occurred before—fortunately—and, it was hoped, never would again.

There were very few FBI agents who had gone wayward before. For short lengths of time, they provided minimally sensitive documents to the Russians. In 1984, Richard Miller was the first special agent arrested for espionage. He had been assigned to Los Angeles and, pre-computers, had little access to highly classified information.

Earl Edwin Pitts, arrested in 1996, had initially been thought to be our unsub, but he simply did not have access to the most sensitive documents the Russians were receiving. There had been nothing like our current unsub, a senior person in the Bureau who, for two decades, provided highly classified intelligence from within the FBI's system to the enemy.

With the advent of computers and the remaking of the FBI's paperwork with FOIMS, the Field Office Information Management System, around 1988, access through computers to our internal documents became immediate and far-flung, if you wanted to do that. Most agents did their jobs and were satisfied to add information to their files, one memo at a time, and did not meander through the system. Apparently, that was not the case for our current unsub.

The biggest problem confronting those managing the case was that it was believed—assumed, actually—the unsub could monitor thousands of FBI cases to find one that zeroed in on him. He could easily search his name, or the general organization of a case that would be looking for him. Some very serious steps were taken to avoid this possibility.

Foreseeing this as a potential weakness in the investigation, it was an easy decision—although not easy to implement—that there should be no paper trail to reflect the massive effort. I did not have access to this, nor did I need to know exactly how it was done. It could have been written up as some sort of organized crime case or even used alias names, where only the intended participants would be aware of the true names behind them. However it was done, my part was made all the more difficult because of this no-paperwork-in-FOIMS parameter.

The evening after my first meeting with Ivan and Anahit, I wrote a comprehensive memo in my hotel room with as many details as I could recall, typed on my personal laptop. (At the time, only new FBI agents had Bureau laptops, which were issued during training.)

I printed the memo in the hotel business office and was careful not to leave any pages behind, also making sure the document was not saved in the printer.

The next morning, I went to a FedEx office and, in a sealed envelope, within another, mailed the hardcopy report to Gene McClelland at his home in Alexandria, Virginia.

The next day, when he received it, he drove it into the FBI office where the small cadre of agents working on the case read it. I did this for each encounter with Ivan.

The details were not readily reportable in a telephone conversation, only a summary of the basics, but the full contact had to be committed to paper. As far as I know, those memos remained in a sensitive area of the squad in Washington. They were not scanned into the FBI's computer system, at least, not while the case was ongoing. They were, therefore, protected from the unsub's eyes. But it also made sharing the information cumbersome, rather cavemanish, compared with how the rest of the FBI was transmitting information—at the speed of light. But, for certain, if you were not working on our case—were not "read into it"—you could not possibly have access to the status of our operation…or know the next steps we were taking.

I have said that no one else, none of my colleagues, were aware of this operation. That is to say, in the San Diego Division, not one other agent, supervisor, or anyone in senior management knew what I was doing. The few agents back in Washington with an extraordinary amount of authority to do almost anything that was needed for this case made arrangements to cover my tracks with paperwork from FBIHQ. Besides having been the only San Diego agent at the Undercover Training prior to the film festival, there were several other aspects that could have been glitches, which were planned to be headed off in advance.

My then-supervisor, Eric Birnbaum, was a very decent fellow who would go on to become a Special Agent-in-Charge. He had read my personnel file and knew what kind of a long-leash agent I was, mostly through my reputation after working decades of foreign counterintelligence. He would just have to deal with me. He only knew, on a vague administrative basis, that something was afoot, but had to stay, operationally, in the dark as to what was going on. He had certainly been warned away from making any inquiries of me, or anyone else, about what I was doing.

It occurred to me that someday I would want to apologize to him for all of this spy-versus-spy stuff taking place underneath the radar on his healthcare-fraud squad. At the time, it simply wasn't my place to say a word. The nature of the case demanded it.

Our squad, investigating healthcare fraud, was so distant from counterintelligence work that my current activities of trying to find a spy in the FBI should not have occurred to anyone. Still, some of my colleagues who had also transferred from Washington to San Diego in the mid-1990s had no hesitation in telling their new colleagues, "Back in WFO, Wayne was Mr. Foreign Counterintelligence!"

Then an anomaly occurred which, depending on your sense of humor, might have seemed funny, or potentially disastrous, but at least ironic.

I managed to get into administrative trouble, quite unintentionally, when I invited my son to come and watch a day of firearms training. He had recently been a summer intern in the field office and was good friends with many agents.

Back in Washington, it was nothing to have a teenage child in a Bureau car, driven by an agent-parent, to go to the firearms range at Quantico, Virginia, and the FBI Academy, forty miles south of the Capitol. But a new San Diego Special Agent-in-Charge seemed to want to make a point: that he was the New Sheriff-in-Town. He was looking for someone to discipline, to make an example of. My arrival at the range with my son, in far-from-Quantico, San Diego, was what he picked to be his "example."

My defense was that this was the norm back in Washington, and all those who had been assigned there knew it. At the end of a daily shooting session, the head firearms instructor would even take two or three visiting teenagers downrange to give them a few minutes of proper weapons instruction and a safety briefing, all part of the FBI-family thing. But that didn't matter to the new boss in San Diego. They waved the flag of the Bureau's potential liability, should there be a traffic accident. But this seemingly normal practice had been going on for as long as I could remember—back east.

I received a letter of censure, which included verbal and paperwork reprimands for my infraction. Fortunately, I was not suspended and didn't have to go without salary for a pay period or two—a saving grace with five children. I was far along in my career and could have had a certain *attitude*, as do many senior agents, which is: you can take just about anything they throw at you and still do the job—until you don't. The attitude is called "KMA."

If you have twenty years in, and are over fifty years old, you can retire at any time. Most agents mark a calendar with their

KMA-Day, and it usually affects their personality. If they were given an assignment which they felt was not exactly beneath them, but certainly something they did not want to do, they would have words with their supervisor. In the back-and-forth, the last ones out of the agent's mouth might be, "...well, you can *kiss my ass*."

While I had plenty of time in, and was past fifty, I could not imagine objecting to something I was told to do, especially if it was part of the job as an FBI agent. My current big case, I hoped, would be the icing on the cake of my FBI career. So, I did not have the KMA attitude. But many others who saw what was happening to me—and as a senior agent, who was being made an example of—shared their thoughts with me, emphasizing that I *was* "KMA."

Now take this entire catastrophic, bureaucratic situation, and lay it over the operation where I was doing everything I could to recruit Ivan Kurylenko. None of my senior administrative detractors were aware of what my *real* priority was in my day-to-day FBI work.

Even in this situation, I could not "break cover." The office management in San Diego clearly knew something was going on behind the scenes with me. They might have suffered administrative angst about it, having been warned away from raising the issue of the mysteriousness of my work schedule and unexplained travel away from the office.

While it was a bit painful to me, I could lean back, psychologically, and see this was really people in positions of authority—deservedly or not—who were administratively getting back at me for a situation in which they had no right to be involved, no *need to know*. That didn't stop the SAC from simmering about it and taking whatever administrative steps he could, sort of an *I'll show you*, for not including him in the *big secret*.

With hindsight, I really can't blame him. He wanted to be in control—or at least appear to be—over all of his agents. I don't know what I would have done, had I been in his shoes. But in my life, I had chosen not to take the administrative path in the Bureau and would happily remain a street agent for my entire career—the position where you get the job done.

Sadly, I had to suffer his wrath, and there was nothing I, or my Washington colleagues, could do about it. I was not in a position to yell back, "Hey, I am the UC agent in the most important case in the FBI, and you are about to screw it up!" No, not my personality. Everything that made me who I was would not let that happen, even if it were true. I didn't need to lower my opinion of management any further, but those above me weren't making it easy for me not to.

What a mess!

All of this is just to mention other aspects of my life when the great middle of the Ivan Kurylenko case was upon me. I had to ignore—push into the background—all the crapola of office intrigue and concentrate on the matter at hand.

Still keeping up my regular contacts with Ivan, security-wise, it was the same as before. After a call, write a memo on my laptop at home, print it out, then FedEx it to Gene. All of these continuing security steps were unheard of—before this case or since. Having had a very long career in the FBI, there had never been anything like these precautions: not for other spy cases, the mafia, top-ten fugitives, serial killers, or even terrorists.

So, yes, even among all of the unique cases in the FBI, this one unequivocally stood out!

***

There is one other point to make on this issue, which I would never have thought of while the case was ongoing.

When the FBI Prepublication Review Unit granted approval for this book to be published in 2023, I was required to reach out to all those named for permission to use their names, then twenty-five years after the fact.

Philip Jing was the agent in the Los Angeles Division who I met, for only a few moments, before I went off to the film festival. When I finally located him in his retirement, he did not recall me at all, but did remember agents Suchan and Cardillo, the "overt prong" team, who had been slated to cold-pitch Ivan.

Jing said he drove them around Santa Monica, and they had some connection to the film festival. He asked them why they needed him, instead of driving themselves. They said it was because they had a large sum of money and wanted to have an agent with them who was armed. When he asked what this was about, they told him, "We could tell you, but you would have to take a polygraph."

Jing bowed out of that option and was never told any more about the operation.

For me, this confirmed that their cold pitch *was* backed up with a "large amount of money," which was intended to entice Ivan to agree to look at the array of photos of possible traitors in the FBI. So even the agents in the Los Angeles Division, with the action in the case all around them, had no idea what was really going on in the search for the traitor among us.

CHAPTER 19

PULP FICTION AND THE HORODINCA EFFECT

We were now at a long hiatus of many months. Ivan was deep in Moscow, and every effort was being made to get him back again. But even if he did return, what would we do with him? How could we approach him differently in order to have a different, and almost certainly better, result? Again, all of this fell onto my shoulders.

In the small cadre of agents involved in the Graysuit case, almost all of them had worked against only Russian targets. My experience covered a much wider span, because I had also worked Romanians, Czechs, Poles, and Hungarians, and then Russians for nine years. There were dozens of different fact patterns to draw from with so many cases in FBI history.

Ivan had a unique personality, not necessarily aberrant, but just not the norm for a Russian officially assigned to the US. How could we conceive of something which would be far afield from the last approach—two male agents making a cold pitch—but rather something specific, crafted just for Ivan?

For all of this, the most nitty-gritty of intelligence matters, there is no Intelligence School to learn from. So, I dug back through scores of cases with which I was familiar for any that hit on major points aligning with Ivan's personality. I hoped something from the past could shed light on what my next move might be.

I found two.

Pulp Fiction

Under FBI Supervisor Don Gruentzel, in the 1970s, we had a creative set of agents working on the Eastern European Bloc counterintelligence squad, CI-6, in the Washington Field Office. With thirty-nine agents, almost all of whom spoke a language of Eastern Europe, either from youth in their émigré families, or immersion language-school training, we handled the intelligence services of Bulgaria, Czechoslovakia, Hungary, Poland, Romania, and Yugoslavia. Something agents did in working one country could easily be applied to another.

This was so when Special Agent Ed Appel had a case against a Czech journalist.

Before his time in the Bureau, Eddie had been a stringer, writing articles for various newspapers and magazines. Then as an agent, he parlayed that position into an undercover role in order to meet journalists from the Soviet Bloc embassies. Some were intelligence officers and others were merely co-optees of their country's intelligence services. When he wanted to get close to one of them, Eddie went into that role and established a relationship to discuss the broad spectrum of "international affairs."

This would be the beginning of personality assessment, with the goal of recruitment.

Sitting beside Eddie's desk, he was patient as I laid out the story of one of my Romanian subjects. In a few minutes, he was all in.

Mihai Iaşi (MEE-high Yash) was a journalist, known throughout Romania for his reports from abroad. Although Mihai resided in the Washington area, he traveled to the United Nations in New York for each fall's General Assembly sessions. He wrote about them and transmitted his stories to Agerpres, the Romanian news agency in Bucharest.

These jaunts to New York City gave the appearance that Mihai had freedom to travel, but that was fantasy. He was just as much controlled as the rest of the official Romanian population.

There was a press officer in the Romanian Embassy who was Mihai's primary contact. Of course, the man was an officer in the Romanian Intelligence Service, the DIE, while Mihai was a co-optee of the service and was required to do their bidding. Living under the rule of Dictator-for-Life Nicolae Ceauşescu, you did exactly as you were told.

Mihai lived with his wife and teenage daughter in a high-rise in Rockville, Maryland, and was relatively independent. He was a little guy, just over five feet tall in his shoes, but he was fit and trim. The power of his pen, however, was pretty exceptional. Millions in Romania gave credence to whatever he wrote, in spite of knowing that much of the news they were fed from the West was tainted, if not completely rewritten by the government that controlled their lives. Emigres described Mihai as "the Romanian Walter Cronkite!"

At the time, Cronkite was considered to be "the most trusted man in America." That said a lot about Mihai, but it did not make him interesting, intelligence-wise, until something else happened.

Information received from within the Intelligence Community, as well as a very good live source, helped with the rest of Mihai's story.

One day in March, the embassy press officer phoned Mihai to say he was very sorry to tell him his father had died.

Mihai was devastated and broke down on the phone, enough so the embassy man had to wait a few moments for him to compose himself. Mihai said he had to travel to Romania, right away, to take care of the funeral and be with his family.

Mihai was told he would have to speak with Counselor Anghelescu about any trip.

Just as we in the FBI were aware, Mihai knew Anghelescu used his senior embassy cover position of counselor to maintain high contacts in the US government. He was actually one-star *General* Gheorghe Anghelescu, in charge of Western Hemisphere intelligence operations for the Romanian Intelligence Service.

Anghelescu, in Romanian, means "the son of an angel," but most of us thought this was a misnomer. It would have been more accurate to call him *Draculescu*, "son of the devil," considering his reputation. Once, when someone happened to observe him walking out of the embassy and down the cement path to Massachusetts Avenue, a little white dog veered into his path. Without missing a step, he punted the dog into the base of a sycamore tree a dozen feet away, then kept on walking.

Anghelescu was the epitome of a smooth-talking, convincing communist. He wore expensive business suits, had swept-back gray hair, and eyebrows configured in a way that he seemed to question everything within his field of vision. We called him "The Silver Fox."

When Mihai was told that he would have to speak with Counselor Anghelescu, I am sure he just heard "The General" and must have grimaced. Still, he would drive to the embassy, straight away.

We had no knowledge of what happened in the embassy in real time, but the anomaly of the death of the journalist's father was worth monitoring in the hopes of learning more.

Later that day, one of our sources received a call from Mihai. He was sad on the phone and asked to come by to see the man. They had been close friends for years.

When the source called me to say he had heard from Mihai, I didn't tell him what we already knew. He had to be genuinely surprised when he learned about the death of Mihai's father—presumably, the reason for meeting.

The next day I was in my source's office to discuss his visit from the Romanian journalist. He seemed almost as shaken as Mihai had been the day before.

Mihai told the source what I already knew, but I had to play dumb about that part. It is all part of the game.

Then he got to the part I didn't know, the kernel that moved Mihai up from merely *of interest*, to *a target* of an intelligence operation.

The chair where Mihai had sat was immediately to the left of the source's desk, on which his elbow had rested for support. The source said his face had been swollen and he looked harrowed. He seemed to be a different man, even before he told his story.

The source let the scene play out at whatever pace his old friend needed.

Mihai told him of the phone call when he learned, so abruptly, about his father's death, and that he was told he would have to speak with the General. He even used that title, which the source also knew meant Anghelescu.

When Mihai finally sat across from Anghelescu in his small office on the third floor of the embassy, "up under the eaves," as they describe it, of the mansard roof, he said he felt as frightened as he ever had. That was before the General uttered a word.

Mihai gathered the courage to tell Anghelescu that he had to return home immediately to support his mother and his family. As the oldest sibling, they would look to him to fulfill that role. It was imperative!

Mihai described Anghelescu's expression—his *countenance*—when he said there was no reason for him to travel to Romania. His father had died last September: *six months ago*!

Mihai had been taken aback and was nearly overcome in just repeating to the source what Anghelescu had said. He stammered as he had when he sat in the hard wooden chair across from "that horrible man."

The source was beside himself, feeling for his friend. He did not understand the delay in telling the journalist of his father's death.

Mihai explained that President Nicolae Ceaușescu *personally* read and enjoyed his reports from the fall sessions at the United Nations. Had Mihai been told of his father's death back then, he would have demanded to return to Romania.

But Anghelescu needed him to write the UN reports to please their president, so he made the decision not to tell Mihai of his father's death until the session was over.

Mihai had wanted to protest. It had now been months ago, so why was there a further delay in telling him? But those are not words you speak to General Anghelescu. It was a crushing moment for Mihai. His journalistic skill had indirectly brought about this terrible tragedy.

Nothing more could be said to the General. There would be no trip to Romania.

Then Mihai told the source something else. He was staring at a spot high up on the wall, over the source's head, and saw a terrible moment clearly.

At Christmastime, he had called his parents to pass on season's greetings. The official Romanian community was not allowed to phone Romania whenever they wanted. The government strictly controlled such calls and scheduled them.

Now Mihai was mouthing the words to his old friend.

His mother had answered the phone. She seemed to be her typically pleasant self, and he spoke with each of his siblings. His father, he was told, was not there. He had to run an errand but asked his family to send his Christmas greetings to his son.

Mihai stopped speaking. He had a glazed look and continued to stare high up on the wall. He now saw that scene in a completely different way.

For his family not to have informed him of the death of his father in September was beyond understanding. On the phone at Christmas, Mihai pictured a Kalashnikov rifle in the hands of a Romanian Securitate officer, pointed at his siblings as his mother spoke, and then right in the ear of his mother, while his siblings each spoke to him, so none of them would mention the passing of their father. The secret also had to be kept from all of the members of the Romanian diplomatic community, including those on home leave, so they would not tell him.

Mihai had lowered his head onto his arm on the source's desk and cried, his entire body trembling for several minutes.

In the springtime there were less-compelling stories to write about at the United Nations. When Mihai would go on official home leave in the summer, he would learn the truth. To head off that surprise, the General decided it was finally time to advise him of his father's death.

In counterintelligence, an anomaly like this is an opportunity to recruit a person in a key position. If this sounds harsh, I wouldn't jump to that conclusion too quickly. I had met many such people who had been treated so horribly that they were looking to do something about it. They needed an outlet to enable them to feel like they were fighting back. Often, it was the FBI that stepped in at that moment.

When I relayed all of this to Eddie, he, too, saw it as an opportunity. He agreed it was time for his journalist persona to cross paths with Mihai Iaşi. FBIHQ quickly gave the go-ahead for their first meeting, assigning the codename Pulp Fiction.

The first meeting went smoothly, as did the next. Eddie's assessment added to what we knew of Mihai's psychological devastation, so it was time to make an overture. He would be in New York City for several days before leaving for Bucharest. FBI Headquarters agreed that the pitch could be made in New York.

Eddie called Mihai to arrange to meet at his hotel room.

Their rapport went a long way to making this smoother than if it had been a cold pitch. Even if Eddie broke cover, we saw no real downside, like the Romanians lodging a protest with the Department of State.

We had high hopes, not merely because of how Anghelescu treated Mihai, but because the Romanian government caused outrages like this one to occur.

A week later, Eddie and I flew on the Eastern Airlines shuttle to LaGuardia and took a cab to midtown Manhattan. We entered the hotel right on time.

The good spirits Mihai displayed at greeting Eddie were followed by a surprised look when he saw me in the doorway.

It was most important not to have Mihai think we had leveraged his grief to make this overture. Well, that is exactly what we did, but that is only one way of looking at it. It really did boil down to the changed relationship he had with his government, a mental metamorphosis, which we believed gave him a different set of eyes with which to see it. His entire life, from the cradle until the present, had been in the hands of, and at the mercy of, the Romanian government. But this was the first time he personally felt the enormous hammer of communism crushing down on him.

However, that was not the face he would show us. Rather, he would be the upstanding journalist of integrity, "the most trusted man in Romania."

We expected him to act that part, at least initially.

Eddie opened the conversation, getting to our reason for being there right away. He apologized that we were meeting him under some level of false pretenses, but it was well intended, which we believed was for Mihai's own good.

He introduced me in true name—important to be honest at this crucial point. I told Mihai I was an FBI agent. It was never stated that Eddie was, too, only that we had been friends for years. Eddie's backstopping was solid and would have held up under scrutiny, but the conversation never got that far. Mihai's focus was on me.

I consoled him with what Anghelescu had done, never mentioning the source of the information. The implication was that his story was widely known. Who wouldn't feel compassion?

For years, assets had advised the FBI of similar heartbreaking stories about people who had left Romania, most *escaping*. Mihai, however, was still a respected member of Romanian society, yet look at how even he was treated!

I told him we knew he was not an intelligence officer. It would never have occurred to Mihai to think he would be accused of that. But I wanted to establish my own rapport—and make plain a common ground on which we could base a future meeting.

I will give Mihai credit for listening, at least initially, to me. Because of his angst about Anghelescu, I told him the FBI knew all about the General and his many intelligence officers in the embassy.

This brought a faint smile to Mihai's face, as the General's minions saw him as something of an Intelligence Deity, all-powerful and unmerciful. This information dropped the General down a peg or two for Mihai.

I explained to him that I wanted just to talk about whatever was going on in the Romanian community—the official community—as well as assignments he might be given beyond his ordinary reporting. That would be, unstated, intelligence activities as a co-optee of the Romanian Intelligence Service.

I saw Mihai as a nationalist and a patriot, in spite of what had happened, so there was never a thought of offering him money for his cooperation. The harshness of the General had pushed him to the edge. I was reaching a hand out to save him from that.

After a few minutes, Mihai's face turned red, seemingly in the realization that he had been hoodwinked. He was having none of it!

He didn't yell and scream, but he was not calm and contemplative, either. His voice rose, which came off more amusing than serious, considering that he was a foot shorter than me.

This kind of offer was not intended to force or cajole him into our way of thinking. Defectors and recruitments have to make such decisions themselves. They need to know that options exist, and that there will be arms waiting to catch them if they decide to jump to the West, physically or mentally.

Finally, Mihai finished berating us and we were no closer to success.

We would like to have ended with a follow-up meeting arranged, but that wouldn't happen.

We did not leave his hotel room with our tails between our legs, but Eddie and I had a long discussion on the flight back to Washington. We did not want to paint this as a complete and utter failure, which we feared many of the naysayers at FBIHQ would, but we had to admit it did not go as we had hoped.

We wondered where we had gone wrong.

Our analysis of Mihai's psyche, crushed by an Anghelescu tsunami and now little more than flotsam, should have brought about a different result.

We finally agreed on how to describe the result of our pitch to Mihai Iaşi: *While the overture made to Pulp Fiction was not immediately successful, it is believed there will be a positive result in the future.*

I don't think there could have been a more optimistic assessment.

Fortunately, we were not reamed out over what had happened. We could almost feel the powers that be holding their cumulative breath, waiting for an official protest that never came.

Mihai's not reporting our overture was not a certainty. But it would have required him to walk back into Anghelescu's office and sit in that wooden chair across from his desk, which we were sure he never wanted to do again.

A couple of months later I received a secure phone call from a contact in the CIA. A few days before, Mihai had walked into the US Embassy in Athens, identified himself, and asked to speak with someone in the CIA.

When he finally sat down with an appropriate person, he referred to our hotel meeting in New York, which the interviewing officer knew nothing about. Mihai even mentioned my name. He said he had changed his mind and wanted to do business with the US.

Further conversation, including lengthy debriefings, revealed that Mihai did receive assignments from Romanian Intelligence. He confirmed that he was not an officer, but information from the normal course of his journalist business was valuable to them. He was aware of Romanian intelligence interests, which made him valuable to the US government.

What had changed his mind?

The answer was simple—but had been unknown to us.

In spite of his nationwide recognition in Romania, and his authoritative voice in the journalist community, psychologically, Mihai was completely dominated by his wife.

When he returned to Bucharest several days after our hotel meeting, and joined his wife on their home-leave, he told her what had happened.

We did not get the details of the give-and-take from that moment, but learned that she had berated him, using words like "How could you have been so stupid not to accept an overture from the FBI?" and "How can you get back in touch with them?"

Of course, Mrs. Iaşi had lived in the US for several years and had become used to American conveniences—but was now back in Bucharest. This overture she likely saw as a path to get back to them.

I am certain she was more assertive with her husband than he had been with us, and to greater effect. When he was not sure what to say to us, he did the only thing he could, which he had been trained to do, even if it appeared to be bluster. But the dominance of his wife, to her submissive husband, changed all of that, for the better—for them and us.

His next assignment outside of Romania was Greece, where he had found his way to the US Embassy and followed through on his wife's edict.

Summing up: Mihai Iaşi had to ask his wife's permission to work with the FBI.

It was a poser as to whether Ivan Kurylenko had a similar situation at home in Moscow. More information was needed to see if there was a match.

The second case was quite different.

The Horodinca Effect

When it comes to discussions between husbands and wives who live under a dictatorship, the oppressiveness of the government often controls the outcome.

In the late 1970s, a Romanian ship captain defected to the United States. I flew to Wilmington, North Carolina, to debrief him. His comprehensive knowledge of shipping and maritime technology was valuable intelligence.

While it is never asked first, an important issue is the motivation for their defection—not to question it but to understand it.

The captain had contemplated this step for years. Unlike 99 percent of Romanians, he had seen the world. He knew how far behind Romania and the entire Eastern Bloc were, not just in shipping but everything about their economics, so they could not grow or prosper.

As to his final steps before defecting, I asked him, "What went into that?"

This was a sad moment for him, and he told his story.

A few weeks earlier, there had been big news in Romania when Nicolae Horodinca, a third secretary in the Romanian Embassy in Washington, defected to the US. I had intimate knowledge of the case as I was one of several agents who dealt with his defection under Supervisor Ted Booth.

Horodinca had many contacts on Capitol Hill and could have approached any of them. We would rather have had him just speak to one of those friends—many were our sources—and remain in place, working for the FBI while still at the embassy. However, he chose to defect by driving right up to the gates of another government agency.

Also, Horodinca was a captain in Romanian Intelligence. It would have been good to debrief him quietly while General Anghelescu was still in the dark. Instead, it became a splash in the news with embarrassment all around.

So, what had been Horodinca's motivation?

There had been an edict sent from Bucharest with a new dollar limit on how much intelligence officers could spend on meals with Americans. It was an austerity measure.

The new limit would be enforced retroactively, meaning the money a dozen-plus officers had already spent the previous month above that limit would have to be returned to the coffers of the intelligence service.

Horodinca had already spent his limit and more. This is where the devastating effect of having General Anghelescu in charge came into play.

Horodinca, as did all the other officers, feared him, but had no means to repay the amount in question—a mere $620. He simply could not face his intelligence nemesis. Instead, he drove to another government agency and requested political asylum.

We wanted to "turn him around," have him go back to his embassy with the $620 we would give him, and work for us. But that was not possible.

The evening before, he had gone up to General Anghelescu's office and slipped a nasty note under the door. It set out what he was doing, and what he thought of the General.

Horodinca was given defector status, and it caused a blot on the relationship between our two countries.

You never know what might come from any single intelligence situation, however, and one of the positive results of Horodinca's defection could not have been foreseen.

The ship captain I was debriefing had been assigned as the military attaché at the Romanian Embassy in Sofia, Bulgaria, accompanied by his wife and eight-year-old son.

One evening, the couple sat in their living room listening to Radio Free Europe. News from the West was always of interest to anyone from behind the Iron Curtain. No matter how strongly they might approve of their communist regime, they knew the news their government provided was not to be believed. This was no less so in Bulgaria, so almost everyone listened to Radio Free Europe for *real* news.

The captain sat in an easy chair several feet from his wife. The broadcast turned to events in Washington, with coverage of Horodinca's defection. They both listened intently.

The captain had his own stirrings of leaving and settling in the West, but his relationship with his wife was never so comfortable that he felt he could broach the subject with her. When the Horodinca story was concluded, the captain gathered himself together and turned to his wife.

"This Horodinca fellow…what do you think about him?"

Her response was short and unequivocal. "He should be shot!"

The captain nodded, making mental plans that would not include her.

That night, at two in the morning, he gently shook his young son awake, told him to keep quiet, and said they were going fishing. He had the rods and other fishing equipment.

The boy dressed quickly, wondering why they would leave so early. The two got into the captain's car and drove nine hours, straight to Athens, leaving his wife behind—forever. He was the second Romanian to walk into the US Embassy in Athens with intelligence information.

Now go back to those three important personality assessment questions: What makes him laugh? What makes him cry? And does he love his wife?

The last one is more complex than the first two, and follow-up issues reveal more about each individual who is under the microscope. It was his son who the ship captain loved more than his wife—and also the yearning for freedom.

No matter what the analysis, and how you use this information, it is better than simply going with the decision to cold-pitch your target and offer a suitcase full of money.

For our approach to Ivan Kurylenko, his relationship with his wife was definitely an issue. But we had no way to know if it was a determining factor for how he had reacted, or how he might react if approached a second time. Still, all of this had to be considered.

CHAPTER 20

PROFILING IVAN

While FBI agents hate to reinvent the wheel, there is something they hate more—banging their heads against the wall!

I had already visited Ivan's boss in London. We believed it was a near certainty that, if invited, Ivan would come to the Austin Film Festival in September. Most important was how to finesse re-pitching him.

Red Pop and I discussed it on the phone. We had nothing personal against the agents who had pitched him before, but we didn't see the potential for them to have greater success a second time.

And I was supposed to put together this grand scenario—for *what*? The same result?

The powers that be at FBIHQ had given their official blessing to the project as it was, but I was not happy about our prospects.

Immediately after Santa Monica, I had written a two-dozen-page memo covering everything that had taken place. There were vignettes about Ivan, his personality, his family, and the influences in his life. Combining this with his old file, it was a lot of information. I read and reread it.

In the mid-1970s, I had participated in what we called "brain trust" discussions. The group included the most active among us working foreign counterintelligence against the Eastern Bloc nations in the Washington Field Office. This was before the word "profiling" was coined for what we did.

Most investigations are deductive—find fingerprints, or maybe a license plate leaving a crime scene—while the new profiling was inductive. It would identify a personality type, which was not a lead coming directly from a crime scene.

There were two personality types we wanted to look at—and look *for*—which we thought would help us do our job.

The first was, "What is the profile of a Soviet official who can be recruited?"

The second was, "What is the profile of an American with a Top Secret clearance—for example, working on the design of the new B-2 Bomber wing—who makes covert contact with a Soviet official in order to sell secrets?"

These two personalities might seem to be diametrically different, but they turned out to have something very important in common. Almost everyone who fit into these categories had a crisis in his life. It would convert him from the loyal person he had always been…to what would seem to be a turncoat.

I was familiar with almost all the scenarios involving anyone who had ever been in the KGB in the United States, and what they thought of the opposite sex. Women were something to sleep with. Not one Soviet intelligence officer had ever taken a woman seriously. They had wives, but they were not part of the workplace environment.

Ivan had not been in the KGB and was further from that personality type than the uninitiated could ever know. He thought very highly of women, and the strongest and most assertive among them were sitting atop a lofty pedestal Ivan had mentally created just for them.

With this analytical history in mind, I set out to figure a different way to approach Ivan Fyodorovich Kurylenko. It boiled down to the question: *What makes Ivan tick?* He was clearly different than most people, Russians in particular, so I reviewed everything we had. The effort was to find a psychological chink in his armor, and Ivan's would be the ultimate profile.

How important women were in Ivan's life could not be understated. This was not the normal situation where men merely like women, date, love, and marry them, then have children with them, and live their lives with them. For Ivan, this took on another dimension. I pictured a throne-like setting in a vast room with rays of light shining down where, seemingly, the essence of the entire female gender was seated in grandeur, held in the highest esteem—in Ivan's mind.

This was countered by his thoughts about men, almost certainly starting with that long-ago vignette, the one time in his life when he was face-to-face with his father—and what a devastating moment it was!

Other than this revealing blurb, the column in Ivan's life chart regarding men was completely blank.

In today's terms, Ivan's mother might have been called a single mom, but that was certainly not a Russian term in the 1950s. Every piece of information indicated she was a strong woman.

He had sisters. Although we were not aware of how many, or their ages, there was no indication he had conflicts with any of them. While "strong" might be a word to describe his siblings, he certainly had good feelings for them: his only known relationships with children around his own age.

When Ivan finally married, and the details leading up to it were not known, his wife was, unequivocally, another strong woman. It was not an issue in Ivan's mind as to whether she dominated him, but of the two, Ivan was clearly the submissive. This was seen as a psychological and not a sexual description. The submissive aspect of Ivan's personality, vis-à-vis women, was like a blanket over his life.

To top this off, Ivan's nearby neighbor, who so doted on him in his childhood, continued with their relationship into his adulthood. She had an assertive personality, enough to have influence with a senior member of the Communist Party. Her *blat* had resulted in Ivan's assignment to the US, which gave Ivan's entire family the opportunity to live in America.

On more than one occasion, Ivan had done something to displease his superiors, and there had been talk of his being returned to Moscow, but it never happened.

Colleagues in the embassy thought it was curious, even mysterious. But it turned out that this same woman—seemingly, a fairy godmother—saved the day, again, and Ivan's career.

Another factor was that Ivan and his wife had two children: twin girls! There was no denying that twins were hereditary in his family. Everything indicated he loved them very much and was a wonderful father.

What the picture of his personality would have looked like if he had a father figure, or a father-in-law, who was the one with the *blat*, or even if a son had been born, instead of daughters, will never be known. We dealt with what we had. Ivan may be one of the few men on the planet, in all of his years growing up, who never had the influence, or presence, of even one man, with the most devastating introduction to an authoritative man at the tender age of six years old.

In his work in Moscow, Ivan didn't have close colleagues, and most of the time he worked from home, thereby having the daily, reinforced influence of females.

Then the major movie project, where he was authorized to shadow Anahit Avakian for months and months, was led, not just by a woman, but another very strong woman. She even had the added factor—not to be unkind—of a weightlifter's physique. But she would also get her way through the force of her personality.

At the American Film Market in Los Angeles, wonder of wonders, the person I set Ivan up with was yet another extremely strong woman. Polly Platt was diminutive in size, which only tended to emphasize how much she'd had to have overcome to get where she was. The true strength of her personality had enabled her to crash through Hollywood's glass ceiling to become a major movie producer.

Imagine what a group photo would look like where Ivan Kurylenko sat in the very middle, surrounded by all of the influential women in his life, the ones who, psychologically, had made him the man he was. Ivan could probably picture this image, but never would on his own, because he saw each of them as individuals, so personal and meaningful to him.

You could take this surrounded-by-women fact pattern with a different man, who might not particularly like all of these women. He might see himself as dominated by them, or he could be the ultimate wimp, just going along to get along. For someone else, the reaction might be to despise them, seethe about his misfortune, and go on to avoid women at all costs.

But Ivan was not like this. He admired women and was constantly attracted to them. Was he henpecked? Maybe to an outside observer, but Ivan would not see himself that way. He was too busy reveling in the milieu of women and trying to please them.

Ivan favored women for everything. Any circumstance where he could be in contact with another person, it would be a woman, and not just any woman, but a woman of consequence!

When Polly came into our scenario it was completely fortuitous, because she was Jack Platt's only sibling in Hollywood. But the coincidence certainly played out well. With perspective, our scam probably would not have worked at all if the person who agreed to help us get close to Ivan had not been a woman, and not one with Polly's mettle.

This analysis of Ivan's personality could never have come about, had we not made our way through Ivan's psychological open door with Polly, and we would not have known why it was working. I was pretty happy how things were turning out with Polly on our team.

Another important factor about Ivan was that he loved his work and was proud of what he did. I couldn't distinguish whether this was simply an aspect of his life that he enjoyed, or if it was because it enabled him to be in touch with strong women. At the very least, the two dovetailed nicely. He would have a great story to write about the movie-making process, which now involved not one, but two strong women. So, this was the answer to "What makes him laugh?" Essentially, "What makes him happy?"

"What makes him cry?" translates into "What makes him sad?" That would seem to be anything that did not have to do with women, and especially not authoritative ones.

Picture a man with Ivan's background and psyche now surrounded completely by men—not a good feeling for him, one where he might even cringe. It is not what he was familiar with or used to. Imagine Ivan forced to be surrounded in his Soviet Embassy assignment, not just by men, but strong and assertive ones—as are most KGB officers—and a complete absence of women as colleagues in the office.

You don't have to put yourself in Ivan's skin to realize the feeling he would have. Men were simply not on Ivan's radar. He would never have preferred any man over any woman.

So, how did *I* fit into Ivan's profile?

I had, literally, forced my way into his life: friendly, outgoing, and entertaining with him and Anahit, for sure—all part of the operation. Others at the film market had their own agendas, but Ivan and Anahit were mine. I later realized that only because I was good for Anahit was Ivan interested in me at all.

Had I been Ivan, I think I would have been suspicious of me, but why? What could I possibly have to gain? I had a pile of money to finance films. There was certainly nothing from the Soviet era that he could ever think would cause an operation to be mounted against him.

Therefore, the *Wayne factor*, as Ivan experienced it, may have seemed a little anomalous, but I was just another player in the Hollywood milieu out to find a film worth financing.

Then Polly entered the picture, first seen by Ivan from a distance. She was surrounded by admirers in the massive atrium of the Loews Santa Monica Beach Hotel, and he may not even have seen me with her. Our earlier ploy to make sure Ivan had seen me before we ostensibly met for the first time, with hindsight, had played out as intended. But I never knew if my presence in that made-up scenario, with the SSGs pitching movie ideas to me as Ivan walked by, ever registered with him. Still, it had all been part of the game—preparation for what was to come.

Later, when I met him and spoke about Polly, she became real to him, three-dimensional.

Finally, when I introduced her, it was a moment of supreme elation, as much as one could imagine for the psyche that was Ivan. It was an incredibly wonderful feeling which completely overtook him. For Ivan, it could not get better than that!

I pondered all of this. I thought back to when I had sat across the desk from early FBI profiler Pat Mullany, in the mid-1970s, deep in a subbasement at Quantico in the Behavioral Sciences Unit. I would pour out stories of my dozens of hours of contacts with a now long-gone Hungarian intelligence target, and he would figure how best to use the information.

The California caper to recruit Ivan came back into focus.

Ted Suchan and Dave Cardillo, who made the cold pitch, were fine agents. Ted was the stronger of the two, and had advanced further, administratively. Dave was good with paperwork and certainly knew the rules. But there was nothing either of them could do to make Ivan interested in talking to them, to say nothing of agreeing to whatever they proposed to him.

Despite their valiant efforts, they could not have gotten Ivan's attention. Their overture had been DOA—dead on arrival!

The solution for Ivan to hear words spoken to him was to have them uttered by someone he *would* listen to.

It finally dawned on me: *It has to be a woman, stupid!*

CHAPTER 21
CREATING THE PERFECT WOMAN

Without knowing all of the above, one could never have understood Ivan's innermost thoughts. We needed to mount an operation where he would be a willing participant.

I had written reports about Ivan and Anahit from the film festival, and also from the months of phone calls, some an hour long. It was not clear who in the small cadre authorized to read them back in Washington actually *was* reading them. I hoped someone in charge was examining the information closely, but I could not imagine they would draw the same conclusion I did.

Picturing in my mind's eye—actually, trying to view through Ivan's eyes—I wondered what would be the best-case scenario for a woman to approach him. Certainly, someone he had never seen before and knew nothing about. Her personal presentation would have to be quickly summed up into what she looked like, how she acted, and what she would say.

For what she looked like, this would be about the individual herself, but also the clothes she wore, how her hair was done, and her makeup, if any, but much more.

Was she tall and lean? What color hair might work best in Ivan's mind?

Would she dress *chic*—feminine-fashionable or businesslike, or some combination?

Her words would be of critical importance, but that would come later, after her initial impact on Ivan. First, she would have to get into his head so he would *hear* the words she spoke.

I pictured a woman who, if not as tall as Ivan, was around 5′9″ at least, so when wearing heels, she would be taller than him. This is significant, psychologically, but there is something else we could use besides just her height.

When you look at someone, eye-to-eye, you look up to see the top of their head. You don't always have to be taller to give the impression of superior height. Women have much greater flexibility with the varying height of the heels they can wear and how they fix their hair. Here, any height factor at or above Ivan's would be in our favor.

Most female FBI agents are trim and fit, more than just healthy looking, because they had to meet strenuous physical requirements before receiving their appointments. Then they went through the rigorous fifteen-week training at the FBI Academy which added to their fitness.

While there is a lot of paperwork and sitting at a desk on the job, I never met an FBI agent who joined the Bureau to do that. The very active aspect of the work of an agent is the drawing card, and staying in tip-top shape is part of the job. I hoped any female agent would be very fit and, as a group, they were taller than the average height of women in America.

Most of them were also quite assertive. It seems to be a job requirement. There are few, if any, who are shrinking violets. The battery of pre-hire psychological exams weeds them out.

I felt good about the pool of agents from which our "perfect woman" would be chosen.

Now for her clothes—not really mine to choose, but it was mine to ponder, on behalf of Ivan. A combination of businesslike and sensual would be nice, and pulling that off would include how she carried herself, her facial expressions, and demeanor.

I pictured a straight pencil skirt, charcoal to black, just above the knees, still businesslike, not revealing or high enough to be trashy, and a sheen would be good, leather would work fine.

I saw the blouse as white and maybe diaphanous, just clingy enough to be feminine, yet still in the category of businesslike, with long sleeves and French cuffs. There would be a collar, but stylish. There could also be a jacket matching the skirt, not in the form of a man's suit jacket, maybe cropped, styled for a woman—a serious one who didn't take crap from anybody.

And for the heels, of course, three inches would do, and black pumps, to match the rest. Maybe dark, opaque hose would add an extra touch.

Picturing what I had painted in my mind, thus far, I smiled, thinking she would not need a dominatrix's whip, but, psychologically, one wouldn't be far offstage.

I once saw an interview with a group of Victoria's Secret models, the group who wore the angel wings on the runway, and little more, who were looking at a photo of a woman who was not a model. They were fawning over it and exclaiming how beautiful she was.

The male interviewer was in stark surprise, as the photo was being observed by what some would consider among the most beautiful women in the world.

"Oh, no," they said, "anyone can look good in makeup, but just look at her bone structure and her face without makeup!"

That was an eye-opener for me, and I realized our as-yet-unchosen female agent could work magic, or not, based on her makeup choice. I had confidence that she would look…not stark, or too overdone, but just right.

A wise agent, Carolyn Weber, once told me of her grandfather's admonition, "Moderation in all things, including moderation." I thoroughly agreed and hoped the female agent would figure out this part of the plan.

I wouldn't want anyone to change her hair color just for this role, and Ivan seemed to have no particular preference. Anahit's was dyed black, while Polly had her blond pageboy. But for the business quality, I was thinking a French twist would look professional and nice. I also thought of the option for a stylish hair clasp, which would mean longer hair was folded in. Ivan could imagine it flowing over her shoulders. That would have been more sensual—but not now. This was all business!

Next was the issue of how to find such an agent—a woman of strength. You might think there would be something akin to a massive database, where the names and information about all eleven thousand FBI agents could be reviewed and sifted through to find just the right one. She would match the appearance and personality of the female I was looking for—age, height, interests, and a whole psychological profile. If you thought that, you would be very disappointed.

Back in the 1970s, there was a need for a male agent to work in an undercover operation against the secretary of the ambassador of an Eastern European Bloc nation. The opportunity emerged through a source who was willing to introduce one of our agents to his next-door neighbor. They could go on a double date.

Even with thirty-nine agents on the squad, where the ins and outs of all of our lives were pretty well known, you still had to ask, "How do you pick an undercover agent?"

On Don Gruentzel's CI-6 squad in 1977, the case agent for that planned operation had been Doug Gregory. One day he simply stood up in the center of the squadroom and called out, "Anybody want to work an undercover case?"

He received a lot of blank stares.

At the time there were very few agents in undercover roles, most preferring sources for contacts with our targets.

Of the three dozen–plus agents, none of the married guys would go for this, and only two were single. One was Wayne Copple, and the other was me. The other Wayne was on vacation, so Doug and his partner, Bobby Howen, came over to me. Doug gave me the basics, and, after a few minutes, I was in.

So much for fine-tuning, matching-personality analysis, and sifting through a massive database to find the perfect operative!

Over the next several months, that caper turned into an incredibly successful operation. But its inception had been anything but what you would have wanted when planning to put two people together from different sides of the world in an undercover FBI case.

One would have hoped that twenty years later, there would be a better way to choose an agent for an operation. Little did I know it was still unscientific, confined to a small pool of only so many people, and only a few were female agents. And there was still no database to find an agent who would match what I thought was needed.

I called Gene McClelland and told him my thoughts. This was after my in-depth analysis of what we had, what I clearly thought would *not* work again, and what I thought *might* work, even if more-senior people would say it was contrary to well-established, standard operating procedures.

I had spent much of my career contradicting accepted practices, actually made a name for myself doing it, something managers frowned on. A selling point for me was this was completely different and dynamic, but maybe that would not be seen the same way by the bureaucrats at headquarters who relied on the tried-and-true.

Gene always had an open mind, and I was grateful for that. But even he gave me the accepted psychology of KGB officers and, seemingly, all Soviet men regarding women.

I asked him—not quite pleading—to take a look at the analysis I was sending and give it a chance. I would fax it that afternoon and stressed that repeating the overt-prong maneuver would be banging our heads against the wall.

Gene finally agreed to take a look.

I sent off my analysis and unique request, hoping it would not fall on deaf ears.

Just as there was a Soviet KGB full of individuals whose minds seemed to be already decided on certain topics, this was also the case with many senior people in the FBI.

Gene was one of the best agents I knew, well-respected by all, and if anyone could pull this off, three thousand miles away, it would be him.

CHAPTER 22

CASCADING OVER SHARP ROCKS IN THE STREAM

During the six-month period between the American Film Market in Santa Monica and the Austin Film Festival at the end of September, I had more time to spend at home. I had five children, eighteen down to seven, each one in a different school, with the oldest at the University of California, Riverside. Family was my first priority.

Sebastian, at Torrey Pines High School, was a miler on the track team with a meet every Wednesday afternoon. The timing of all the races was so organized that the mile would begin, like clockwork, at 5:18 PM.

I would make sure that no matter where I was in San Diego, I would drive whatever distance was necessary to get to the meet within ten minutes of the starting time.

The Torrey Pines High grounds, a few miles east of the famous PGA golf course of the same name, looked more like a college campus. I thought of my inner-city beginnings, hemmed in by working-class housing in Philadelphia, with not a blade of grass to spare. I was happy to provide more for my children than what I'd had.

I would arrive at the stadium, always in a suit jacket, with my 9mm Sig Sauer, extra magazines, and handcuffs on my belt. I would bound down the steps to meet my son on the lower landing of the long stairs to wish him well. I'd give him a hug and he would be off.

Months later, the mother of one of my son's friends presented me with a photo she had taken of the moment of the hug. She admired it, knowing what it must have taken each successive week for me to be there. I will treasure that photo forever.

In less than six minutes, the race would be over. I would wave to my son, gallop back up the steps, return to the parking lot to mount my Bureau steed, and take off in a cloud of dust to continue catching bad guys.

I found that raising children was a combination of "Do as I say," *and* "Do as I do," a lesson I learned from my father.

Never miss a track meet, soccer match, swim meet, back-to-school night, school play, talent show—never miss anything that makes a difference in your children's lives. You may not remember that you attended all of them, but your children will. You can never rewind history and go back to do it later.

With perspective, it was not that the combination of these family-oriented events took up so much of my time, for they were what I was supposed to be doing.

The other big part of my life was devoted to my career in San Diego. Just then, it included the massive healthcare-fraud investigation of Dr. Herman Eric Wetsman, a cheating ear, nose, and throat doctor.

He had added $500 to each patient's bill and saw as many as thirty a day. On a daily basis, he was overcharging up to $15,000 to Medicare—$75,000 a week. In ten years of this fraud, we calculated he had overbilled around $18 million!

I put this case together from scratch, and there was even a good doctor who I had convinced to help out, Dr. Terry Davidson, head of the ENT program at the University of California San Diego. He said he had wanted to do his part in "cleaning up my own community."

I had miraculously received authority to use three undercover operatives—a retired FBI agent, a female support employee, and a California State law-enforcement officer, who was also working on Medicaid fraud cases—to make a total of two dozen visits to Dr. Wetsman. All of them were surreptitiously filmed with a video camera concealed in a handbag, a briefcase, or a sports bag, carried during their visits to show what Wetsman did, *and did not do*, with his patients.

We later compared the video with his billing, and they were nothing alike.

Our squad had investigated cheating labs and corruption in major healthcare-related companies, but this was the first doctor who had been a billing terrorist, and worth the effort to take him down, individually.

He was one of the few doctors who not only had to return millions of dollars to the federal government, but he was also given a six-month jail sentence. This last was almost never a sanction for doctors. But because he had been so unforthcoming in his allocution—when he was required to admit to the judge, in detail, the crimes he had committed, as part of his plea agreement—the judge threw in the jail time.

The logistics of keeping this case going were staggering. And behind all of this, I was dealing with the ins and outs of what no one else in the San Diego FBI had any idea was going on—Graysuit!

I had two main concerns with the case with Ivan.

I had to tell him about the Austin Film Festival and that he was invited to be a member of the International Film panel. With that came benefits—travel paid, stipend, invitations to various events for the ten days, and he would be treated as an "authority." Hell, he would be a star!

The downside was I had to break it to him that Anahit would not be there. At least, I hoped she wouldn't. I would do everything within reason to make it that way. We needed Ivan unhampered by her presence. Nipping this in the bud would be a crushing blow to his psyche.

The other issue brewing was who, exactly, would make the approach to Ivan—the *new-prong* approach—to learn his sole valuable piece of intelligence information.

My sentiments were so strong about using a female agent, I couldn't imagine why anyone would think the same old, unsuccessful scenario might work if we tried it again.

Sounds simple: (1) Get Ivan to Texas, and (2) have an appropriate female agent make the approach. It should not have been difficult to arrange. But if you thought that, you would be terribly wrong.

I have often said that, in the FBI, by the time you finally succeed in dealing with the bureaucracy, catching the bad guys seems like a piece of cake.

Unbeknownst to me, I was in the midst of one of the greatest bureaucratic nightmares I could ever imagine—and on both issues.

Ivan Sans Anahit

After several tries, and leaving messages, I finally got through to Ivan. I had not wanted to tell him the good news in a voice mail or email, because I wanted to gauge his reaction and handle his questions.

As hoped, he was surprised and very pleased, because this was an invitation *from Polly*.

After a few minutes of explaining it was his years of writing and interviewing so many people, attending so many films, and just being in the milieu of international film, that Polly realized he should be part of the International Film panel discussion.

I could almost feel his chest bursting with pride. No one likes to take advantage of someone when he is feeling a moment of ego, but it was just part of the case.

Who was I to argue with Polly and her superior knowledge of who she wanted at the Austin Film Festival? Of course, none of this would be happening if it weren't for our case, but Ivan would never know that.

I explained that it was *her* festival, one she had founded five years before. Again, Ivan's joy and enthusiasm came blasting through the telephone line.

When he calmed down, I wanted to address the next part before he brought it up. This was a special invitation for him, and him alone. Anahit was not part of it. She might want to attend the festival, but she would need to bring someone else as her interpreter. All of his time would be taken up with his "special status."

This was an up-and-down moment for the man in Moscow. While he felt allegiance to Anahit, he could not turn down such an invitation. He could already see himself as the center of attention in faraway Texas.

The clash was clearly pulling him apart, as we had foreseen. He made the push to have Anahit come, thinking he could still deal with her. But no, I said, it was more complex than that.

He would have his way paid, also his hotel, meals, and he would have, to a certain extent, formatted days. Because of his important status, there would be discussions to have, soirees to attend, the Governor's Barbeque at his Austin mansion, and many people to meet and greet.

He would owe it to Polly to have his schedule open in Texas. Further, if Anahit wanted to travel on her own, she would need to make her own arrangements.

I didn't want to sound too harsh, but I fear that is what Ivan heard, and maybe I was. At one point he said, "Now you are scaring me," with me sounding like I wanted to leave Anahit out in the cold.

I did what I could to soften the blow, but I also didn't want him to think there was room to negotiate. I listened to him speak of the wonderful new contacts Anahit could make in Austin. But put simply, I told him he could not, and would not, have time to be part of that.

He finally said, "Well, she is a big girl."

He could now worry about his own obstacles to overcome, and there were many. One of them was the question about any travel by Ivan to the US, because his company already had a man there, permanently. His own travel to Los Angeles had required special permission from Nigel Aynsley, his boss in London, to accompany Anahit. But that had been a special circumstance and wasn't likely to be repeated.

However, Ivan made the point that, when he spoke with Mr. Aynsley about traveling to the Austin film festival, the man in London commented very positively on my own trip to their office, and how impressed "the American" had been with Ivan. In no small part, it seemed that little outside junket from my vacation in Spain did contribute to Ivan receiving permission to travel back to the US.

I was above telling FBIHQ, "I told you so!" But I did think it.

In the next few days, we sent the original, engraved invitation to Ivan. When he received it, he said it also had it to be sent to the Consular Office in the US Embassy in Moscow in order for him to secure a visa to travel.

Several days later, after the American Consul received it, Ivan called to say they needed a letter to accompany the invitation with all of his identifying information, including his Russian passport number, which we did not have. Well, the FBI had it, but *we* didn't.

There were more days of waiting, which took another go-around before it worked.

At one point, we faxed the information to the consulate, but they did not accept it.

On the phone, Ivan made the point that the Americans seemed to think Russians could somehow fax a letter from a building right next to the American Embassy with the appearance that it had come from California. He said, "They think we can actually do that, and that we *would* do that!"

This seemed preposterous to me, especially when all of this pertained to a solitary Russian attending a ten-day film festival in Texas. Suspicions on both sides made it problematic.

The Russian security service wanted to make sure that, if Ivan did receive a visa to travel, he would be compelled to return to the homeland when the festival was over.

An interesting point is that, if anyone thought the collapse of the Berlin Wall in 1989 changed the security measures in what was once again Russia, there was absolutely no change in the government's dictatorial control over its own people's ability to travel abroad.

Because he had traveled to Los Angeles, London, France, and Armenia, and had a wife and children in Moscow, one would think the Russian security service would believe he would return. But they inherently doubted their citizens' loyalty after seeing the wonders abroad.

Finally, with all of the correct information in hand at the American Embassy, which took the passage of several weeks, Ivan received a verdict on his visa.

His request was rejected!

Our frustration was worsened by having to deal with the eleven-hour time difference and both of our busy schedules.

I called Gene McClelland to tell him the bad news. We discussed having a higher-up in the FBI call the American Consul, maybe even the US ambassador, to ask for some quick dispensation. But that could have alerted anyone listening that *there was something going on with Ivan Kurylenko*. So that option was unacceptable.

It was the same for the FBI legal attaché in Moscow, who could try to make an overture, or even someone from the CIA station. But no one could be allowed into this loop, especially someone assigned to Moscow.

At one point in this process, it was so frustrating, I decided to go right to the top. I wanted senior administrative help with this whole visa thing for Ivan.

Mike Rochford was the man I spoke with, for perhaps the first time since he and the two other agents had flown to San Diego to pitch me to take on this assignment. He told me he had, personally, "worked on it." However, we could not call the consulate "*as the FBI*, due to past problems" with them.

I thought the gravity of this case should have trumped all other bureaucratic issues but, no, Mike explained, he could give me no help, even with his level of authority.

Finally, there emerged an interesting analysis of why this problem had surfaced. This is where the nooks and alcoves and meandering hallways of government puzzle palaces amaze me.

When the FBI agents working the Graysuit investigation had assembled a list of who had been assigned to the Soviet Embassy in Washington, DC, in the 1980s, and who might be able to identify our ultimate unsub, those names were red-flagged. This was to alert those working the case of any scheduled travel abroad by those Russians, especially to the United States. As it turned out, these red flags had remained in place for all of those men.

Someone at the Department of State had misinterpreted this information from "notice" of travel to "rejection" upon a travel request. Those so designated would now be denied permission to come to the US. The tactic, which had so efficiently been used to learn of Ivan's travel to Los Angeles, was now preventing him from receiving permission to come back to our open arms so we could pitch him again!

I am sure there were guttural sounds, gnashing teeth, and strong expletives when this was finally realized at FBI Headquarters. But how to repair the damage? Simply removing the red flag from Ivan's name could not reverse what had already been decided. It could show our hand if anyone—specifically our unsub—was monitoring all of this.

What a mess!

Have I mentioned that, even if Anahit would be completely on her own, she had decided she would come to Austin? Within a few weeks of the start of the festival she asked me, through Ivan, to assist her in receiving a visa. It had to be granted by the US Embassy in Yerevan. They needed a letter from the festival showing she was an invitee.

Of course, no one but the special guests could receive such an invitation. The mere existence of a film festival in Austin, that an Armenian producer wanted to attend, was not enough. Again, so much for the Berlin Wall being down and any changes in Armenia.

I could not do anything to help Anahit, stuck in Yerevan, and had too many other matters to address. But this issue was the deathblow for Anahit's dream of coming to Austin.

Our timeframe to accomplish what was needed had shrunk from several weeks to only several days until the Austin festival would begin. I would soon have to get myself to Texas and hope all of this would be sorted out.

Everything seemed set for the panel discussion, its scheduled time and place, but it could *not* go on without the reason the International Film panel had been created.

Ivan made further overtures with the appropriate Russian ministry, presuming they had to be behind this roadblock, but he was wrong. Even if they wanted to intervene, they could not have resolved this problem.

Ivan was becoming very upset. He saw this wonderful opportunity slipping between his fingers and out of his grasp. Finally, he realized the issue was not really their decision. He would have to go to the US Embassy to resolve the problem.

Think about this for a moment. How could Ivan convince the American consulate that he should be allowed to travel to the US? What words could he use to tell them he really, really had to be on a panel discussing international film in Austin, Texas? They could not tell him he was on some sort of pre-9/11 version of a no-fly list, which he knew nothing about. What would their reaction be when he told them this was all a big mistake? And, actually, it was.

Again, what a mess!

A Midnight Call to the State Department

We were at loggerheads. The only one who could fix it, if it were possible—was me!

It was the last evening before I would fly to Texas, and Ivan still had no visa. The festival would go on with its nine thousand attendees, but it might be without Ivan.

At 11:00 PM, I picked up the undercover telephone in my bedroom in San Diego and started making calls to the State Department. If you think it is hard to get a decision-maker on the phone in a bureaucracy in the daytime, try it in the wee hours of the morning, but I was desperate.

Remember, I was not calling as Wayne Barnes, special agent in the FBI, supporting a counterintelligence operation to have Ivan fly to the US. Now I was Wayne Johnson, agent for wealthy movie-financing wannabes, working to get a Russian to come to a film festival in Austin, Texas.

Does that sound like something a senior night-desk person at the State Department would give a flying f*** about?

Right, it didn't to me, either. But maybe a call in the middle of the night would be exactly what was needed—a sense of urgency that just the right person would appreciate.

It seemed like a dalliance going on in the world outside of the State Department. But I still had to try—to urge *someone* that this was important. Ivan's participation was essential for this important international event to take place.

I recalled when I ruled the Washington Field Office night shift for six months in 1986 and was every bit the decision-maker, even if I was only a lowly street agent. I hoped I could locate a counterpart to that position at the State Department.

That I was able to get through the outgoing message systems and reach a human was just shy of magical. Then I was transferred here and there. My story would not interest many people, and I had to go through much of the tale before the listener could decide whether this was something he or she cared about, or could make a decision about, and would transfer my call.

Finally, I was kicked upstairs to someone in authority who would make or break it.

The man sounded around fifty, with a gruffness which meant he had seen an awful lot of the world. There seemed to be no issue he could not figure out and deal with. It didn't matter who was on the other end of the phone or what the problem was. He *was* the "night desk" at USDS, and he was there for a reason.

I liked him right away and read into his mind in just a few moments. But that is not something I could say—perhaps *reveal* is a better word. After all, I had been doing this sort of thing for over a quarter of a century. Interviewing people and reading them was my stock in trade. But the tricks of the trade are learned only by a very narrow segment of the population, and they were not part of my made-up movie-financer persona.

The beauty of this was I had someone on the other end of the line who was just like me, although he did not know this fascinating coincidence. It went much deeper than reading people.

I assessed him as former military, a no-nonsense person. He could have been working the night desk at the Pentagon. State was lucky to have him.

He would need to hear the absolute truth, stated with sincerity. I would have to make him part of *my* picture, and how it could not become a finished product without *him*.

I told him of the first film festival in Los Angeles and Ivan meeting Academy member Polly Platt. Their relationship and his "special invitee" status to the Austin event naturally followed. It was important to this new and expanded portion of the festival, which, without Ivan, would all be for naught.

The wording I used, and the sound in my voice, were intentionally *not* Hollywood's. It was more official in vocabulary and emphasis. What others describe as my "FBI voice" came into play, but as a tool, with no mention of those special letters.

He kept me doing most of the talking, but he was clearly listening. He was not watching television or doing a crossword puzzle in whatever little room he was sitting.

He came back with some questions to clarify the sequence of events, and he understood the festival would begin the very next day, with Ivan still trapped in the former Soviet Union.

The man searched his State Department computer, and I was pretty sure he found the red flag I knew was there. I was glad he was a person who had access to that very specific information. The slight hesitation of his breath told me what he had just seen.

He could not know that I knew what he saw on his monitor. At the same time, he needed to know we were a pair—on the same team. He could not think he would be doing a favor for a movie mogul in Southern California, but rather for the person who was on the other end of the line with him.

Speaking as Polly Platt's emissary, I said I had been chosen for my part, in the event that there was a problem exactly like this one, where I would need the help of a reasonable person in authority at the State Department.

I told him I knew he was such a man, and the knowledge and authority he wielded had not been given to him lightly. These were words, I was sure, he had never heard from a nighttime caller, and I knew it intrigued him.

Still, I was only talking about a glorified film critic, and who cares about some damned unfamiliar film festival taking place in the middle of nowhere?

He didn't use those exact words, but they were behind the ones he did.

I assessed his words as more of a way to judge me, rather than to evaluate my request.

Of course, I could not mention the red flag on his screen, tell him why it was there, and that it had been the stopping block causing this whole complicated midnight scenario to come about. It was preventing the path to potential success for one of the most sensitive operations the FBI had ever mounted. While I couldn't mention any of that, I did want to imply it—all of it!

I had his full attention, made certain he realized I was *not* from the "Hollywood left," and was not doing their bidding, even if my overt words were trying to pry this particular Russian out of Moscow for a film festival.

I told him, in so many words, "You hear what I am saying, what I am asking of you, and I have the impression you understand there is something more, a larger picture, something behind this which is a cause worth supporting. But right now, it is a single piece of that picture which is needed so the entire puzzle can be completed. It is on your shoulders as to whether it will have the chance to succeed."

At a measured pace I said, "Please, listen to my voice and you may hear there *is* something behind this that you want to say yes to, and only you can do it. And, yes," I told him, "I *am* calling on behalf of the Austin Film Festival, but you know that is not all, and there is nothing I can further clarify for you as to what that might be. I am not asking you to trust me, but to hear my voice, what I have said, and then assess me with the knowledge and insight you have gained in your experience over so many years. Then trust your judgment."

The line was silent for more than a moment. Then I heard sounds of motion on the other end: clicks on a keyboard and papers shuffling.

I remembered the legislative assistants on Capitol Hill who would speak with the FBI, but only when they knew they were one of many contacts of a Soviet official. If the entire burden of an intelligence case would rest on their shoulders alone, they would not help.

My current nocturnal conversation was the opposite. I had a man on the phone who was placed in that very position *because*, daily, he took the weight of the world upon his shoulders. He was hearing from a man he had never met and would never know, but who he had to assess, using all of his experience, and make a decision: the kind he was paid to make.

And then he did.

His voice came back on the line.

"I have just sent a message to the consulate in Moscow authorizing the visa for your man. He can pick it up this morning and make his flight this afternoon. Will that be all?"

"Yes sir," I told him. "And thank you very much."

His last words were, "And good luck with it!"

Two pros had met in the middle of the night and never mentioned what was really going on, but both had come to understand and trust the other. It was a unique conversation which I wish had been recorded for posterity—maybe it was.

My next call was to Ivan with the good news. Then he was off to the US Embassy.

Gene and Sheila

One of my favorite axioms from my years in the FBI is: Recruit everybody, every day. Sometimes it is doing unasked-for favors or being thoughtful with a compliment. It is especially applicable in the FBI working foreign counterintelligence.

Included with this axiom are a couple of postulates. One is that a person may be recruited to do what you have asked, and he may do it just fine. But he might only be going through the motions. It is something else entirely if he not only endeavors to fulfill the task, but puts his heart and soul into it. The latter you can hardly ask for, but it *is* what you want.

Gene McClelland took my words to heart about using a female agent to approach Ivan.

He first discussed this with his colleagues on the squad dealing with Graysuit. The agents there thought they knew not just what was best, but the *only* way this would work—which, of course, was with a man, maybe two. Any additional reasoning had no effect on their tried-and-true game plan, despite the blatant recent track record of no success.

Knowing that would not do, Gene—good egg and good agent—decided to jump a few steps up the chain of command.

He went directly to the Special Agent-in-Charge of Foreign Counterintelligence in the Washington Field Office. Fortunately, that was Sheila Horan, one of the earliest female agents.

We had both known Sheila when she was a Supervisory Special Agent in Washington Field directing CI-5, the squad handling the KGB's line for scientific and technical intelligence. She was highly respected. We all cheered when she was promoted to a headquarters position, and even more when she had been elevated to be very near the top of the pile of SES (senior executive service) positions in the Intelligence Division.

Because it was necessary to have the right clearances to be read into the Graysuit case, it was a very small club. All the members knew each other. Gene knew Sheila much better than I did, so I was glad he would be the one to speak with her for what had to happen next.

One of the thirty-two FBI agents who had died in the line of duty, as of 1998, was Richard Purcell Horan, in 1957. I was among many who thought Sheila had been related to him. It was normal for the child of a deceased agent to want to fill the shoes of the father, but that was not the case here. Having the same last name was just a coincidence. Sheila was not his relation.

So, there had been no administrative sentiment in Sheila's favor in her being hired. It also meant that she got where she did because she was a hard-charging agent. Only because of their past together did Gene take the step to approach her personally.

Sheila was always glad to see a colleague with long experience and would do what she could to help. That was unlike many administrators who often seemed to stand in the way of progress. A bureaucracy can make people that way, but it didn't to Sheila.

She realized Gene was jumping the Graysuit chain of command. He readily laid his cards on the table, setting out the current status of the undercover operation and what had been proposed for the next approach to Ivan: same as before. Then he set out my profile of Ivan and why we needed to have a female play that role.

Sheila knew my experience and reputation, that I had done all of this before, perhaps more times than any other agent. But in my view, neither I, nor any other male agent, would be right for the approach with these facts. What was important was Ivan's psyche—*his* mindset.

Sheila concurred with the rest of her peers in saying that KGB officers would never accept a woman for this sort of thing.

Gene detailed the points I had made about Ivan having been raised by a mother and grandmother, with no father or any other man in his life, and always his need for the involvement of a strong female. The fortuitous circumstance of Polly Platt entering our picture crystallized the analysis of what would be the very best-case scenario for what, not *we*, but *Ivan*, needed for this to work.

Others in the chain of command had heard all of this. It wasn't working with Sheila, either.

Then Gene had a flash of inspiration and changed his approach. He stepped away from the we-need-a-female-agent-for-this-role card and hit her with something more meaningful to her personally.

He told Sheila, forcefully, that *she*, of all people in the FBI, should be the one, not just agreeing with the idea of a pitch-woman, but recommending it. She was the greatest feminist in the FBI and should be *pushing* for a woman to make this pitch.

Sheila countered, again, that all of the FBI's experience said it wouldn't work.

Gene countered, "How many times have you said women in the FBI are not given the opportunity to show what they can do, and—here it is!"

When Gene later told me about this, I was dumbstruck. He was getting to my bottom line, but by such a circuitous path.

I would hate to have the normal KGB-man fact pattern and have someone push for a female agent to approach a hardline KGB officer, who would laugh at the "foolish Americans for sending a woman to do a man's job." But here, it was perfect, and Gene was so close.

He could see Sheila's concentration and imagined the wheels in her mind turning the idea over and over.

Finally, she relented—sadly, that is the appropriate word—and agreed to give a female agent a shot at Ivan.

So, while the motive may not have been on point, the results of Gene and Sheila's hard-fought back-and-forth were exactly what I wanted.

CHAPTER 23

THE AUSTIN FILM FESTIVAL

It was a wonderful autumn day in Austin, Texas. The sky was crystal blue with puffy cotton-ball clouds tossed here and there. Texas was all around you, not just going on for miles in all directions, but its history, our only republic before it was a state, and still the Wild West.

The Hill Country was named for its rolling hills, cut through by meandering creeks that cinched up to craggy outcroppings, and plateaus sprinkled with prairie grasses. There are trees: blackjack oak, American smoke, and western soapberry, along with cedar, persimmon and prickly pear, in places called Dripping Springs, Blanco, and Luckenbach, where white-tailed deer abound.

Think of all the cowboy movies and, if they weren't shot on the cheap in a back lot within fifty miles of downtown Los Angeles, they had to come way out here to the real thing, where those stories actually took place. Most of the time, the bad guys got their comeuppance.

The Austin Film Festival had already begun at The Driskill, a classic hotel which has been around in one form or another since

1886. It is a four-story affair with only sixty rooms, but is simply saturated with regional history, in the heart of the capital, in the heart of Texas. It was built by a Confederate colonel-turned-cattle-baron-turned-hotelier to be one of the finest in the state. Its exterior is dark red-brown brick with white limestone trimming every door, balcony, and arched window. Lighting in the evening gives the impression of the largest gingerbread house in the world.

It is the entry that draws you in, through a two-story columned portico, leading to high ceilings inside lined by more white columns, like soldiers in a row, carved leaves at the tops, gray stone bases, and polished mosaic inlaid marble floors. There are ornate coffered ceilings with dark stained, intricate wooden patterns, then recessed stained-glass ceilings and massive matching chandeliers providing light and color for so many occasions.

The expanse of this open area surprises new visitors, and the accoutrements scattered about, mounted on walls and in large display cases, burst with old Texas artifacts. There were horns from longhorn cattle, antique six-shooters, original paintings from the early days, and sculptures where Frederic Remington and so many artists chose cowboys as their favorite subject.

At The Driskill, you can stay in a slice of history. Living under its roof for even a few nights, whatever the event, adds to your sense of the Old West.

I pondered this last point, knowing what we planned in the next several days and that it would be part of The Driskill's newly made history. But no one at the festival would know anything about it—did not have a need to know—however momentous I hoped it would be.

You could almost hear the jangle of spurs on the heels of western boots, and then you realize you did, for here and there, real cowboys were encountered. This is where oil and cattle businessmen gather to plan the future. High-tech companies—Google, Qualcomm, Oracle, and others—had joined the party in Austin, using these historic rooms for history-making deals.

But starting today, The Driskill had a completely different clientele, as it had this same set of ten days, five years in a row.

Polly Platt, in an extraordinary way, had taken the bull by the horns and repurposed every suite and meeting room into a film festival venue par excellence.

By the thousands they came to meet and greet and place their screenplays down beside the others, and all would do their best to sell or buy these products by the hundreds.

The only problem—and it was a big one—was that while dozens of sessions had begun, with meetings going on, and presentations made, Ivan Kurylenko was nowhere to be found.

He had picked up his visa from the American consulate in Moscow, but then there was a problem with his airline ticket. They had given out all of the business-class seats. He could pay his own money to be raised to first class, but Russia's financial crisis precluded the withdrawal of funds. He could just drop down to economy class, the easiest solution, but he wanted to make sure we knew what was going on.

The only thing that really mattered was boarding the first plane out of Moscow, crossing the damned Atlantic Ocean, and getting the hell over to Austin!

I couldn't express it quite like that, but it was certainly how I felt.

The International Film panel discussion had been pushed back to the next to the last day of the festival, giving the greatest length of time for Ivan to arrive.

Of course, the inconvenience for the other panel members—insignificant compared with what Ivan was dealing with—brought out only a little of their prima-donna factor. Polly had far too many other issues to worry about them. They were getting their freebies, food, and lodging, so the heck with their temper tantrums. I didn't want to burden her with my part of this scenario—but I did need to stay in touch with her.

During the delay, waiting for Ivan, Polly and I went to see one of many movies previewed at the festival. She picked a promising one, *Pleasantville*, which would go on to win several awards.

There was something else that might seem inconsequential but was not. My undercover backstopping was harder to sell to normal Americans than it was to a Russian—much harder.

When the FBI sought solid undercover positions within established companies in order to meet our Cold War intelligence targets, the title on one's business card was crucial. We had to rely on the good graces of the company granting the cover slot for what that title would be. You didn't want to cause turmoil in the company with someone who was looking to raise himself to the position listed on your undercover business card. You must do whatever you can *not* to provoke an actual employee to do battle and start asking, "Who the hell is that guy, and where did he get the nerve jumping ahead of me in the food chain?"

Taking this lesson to heart, my cover as an independent movie financer was fine as a title in Los Angeles. Now, in Texas, it took on a dimension I had not foreseen. While I ended up smiling a lot, it did bring angst.

In Santa Monica, I said I had wealthy clients, oil and cattlemen in Texas, who wanted to get their feet wet in the movie business. But in Texas, some rather influential people at the festival asked the follow-up question: "Who are they?"

This was a moment to gulp hard and come up with the best answer I could.

The people who asked actually knew the oil and cattlemen. Some hoped to be exactly the person I pretended to be. Why had *I* been chosen for this cherry of a job and not them?

So, yes, it is always good to think through your cover, be able to think on your feet, and quickly rearrange your backstopping to fit the needs of the case. You don't want anyone to say something that might take down your operation. I didn't need a would-be oilman-agent saying too loudly, "Hey, this guy isn't what he says he is!"

You could not find a hole deep enough to crawl into if that happened, and Ivan could be standing right nearby.

And, by the way, all America assumes there are a plethora of multimillionaires in Texas. While they also exist in Minnesota, Maine, and Montana, those states simply don't exude the reputation of having so many people with so much disposable income that they would be expected to dabble in the movie business.

On the following day, all systems seemed to be "Go!" Ivan was expected to touch down at the Austin-Bergstrom International Airport. But when I called for the arrival time so I could pick him up, only a twenty-minute drive, I found his flight was cancelled.

He had been scheduled from JFK in New York to Houston, and then on to Austin.

They landed safely in Houston, but the skies broke open with thunder, lightning, and there was even a tornado watch. Everything was grounded with no timetable for flights out.

I am not a mystic. I don't believe in luck or buying lottery tickets, but I was thinking—things-gone-wrong had reached a new dimension of Murphy's Law—*a tornado, really?*

Because the festival had many more attendees than The Driskill could handle, the Omni Hotel, a block away, with its all-glass visage for fifteen floors, was enlisted as backup.

The delays, and obtaining authority from FBI Headquarters to get our ducks in a row, meant even I was not staying at The Driskill, and Ivan's reservation was also at the Omni.

I did have the forethought to make sure he was in a suite, thinking this was where an approach might be made and wanting the most comfortable setting possible.

What to do?

I could stay in my room and wait for a call. Remember, this was still the pre-cell-phone era in the US, and especially so in Russia. I could go about my business and hope for the best. At the least, I would have to leave my room for meals and to touch base with Polly and her assistant, Kelly, in case she needed something or had news for me.

Finally, I received a message through the front desk from Ivan. He was in Austin and had checked in at the Omni.

"But, how…?"

We agreed to meet downstairs in half an hour.

To give the Omni its due, it was quite impressive, based on the same pattern as the Loews in Santa Monica: a gigantic atrium, rooms entered by open corridors facing the great open space, and windows with panoramic views looking outward.

I had arranged for Ivan to have a suite that faced the Capitol building. He could even look to the foot of the Texas version of Capitol Hill and see the Governor's Mansion. He didn't know it, but courtesy of his invitee status at the Film Festival, along with other special festival guests, in a few days, he would gorge himself at that mansion on Texas-style ribs.

I met Ivan in the lobby after he had hurriedly showered and changed. He was neat and clean, well-dressed and dapper. You could see he had pride in himself, even if he did not exude it. As many good journalists, he was content to be in the background.

We sat for a meal which gave him time to catch his breath, jetlagged that he was, but excited and happy finally to be in Austin, having suffered his own odyssey along the way.

He didn't even want to discuss the mess that had taken place in Moscow but started his tale from landing in Houston with the storm brewing in the distance. Threatening clouds soon overtook the airport so no flights could take off, and inbound planes were turned away.

This was all new to Ivan, and his story was as much about the excitement as the danger.

I didn't know the weather patterns in Moscow but had never heard of tornados there. So, the weather in flyover country had, all of a sudden, become his favorite topic.

Still excited, he explained that on the New York-to-Houston leg, he was seated beside a man also bound for Austin, although not the film festival. The man's business meeting would not wait. He told Ivan he would rent a car and drive the two hundred miles, hoping to avoid the worst of the storm. He invited Ivan along.

I had not pictured Ivan as a storm-chaser, but with great enthusiasm, he described the potentially deadly weather. He was overcome with emotion and revisited the swirling black clouds in his mind. The farther west they drove, the calmer it became, until they arrived safely in Austin.

The tempest had put Ivan in the thick of things. It made me laugh inside. As a journalist, he was usually far on the outside of breaking stories. That might be why his accompaniment of Anahit in Armenia, and then all the way to Santa Monica, had had such a great effect on him. In some small way it put him *in the arena*, and not up in the stands, reporting. Now, to have been within a whisker of a Texas tornado—*wow!* That was something new for Ivan.

I told him how good it was that he had survived!

Now he was ready to get into things. He had hoped the panel discussion would be postponed and was relieved it was still on. I was glad for him to have his moment in the sun.

Sitting at a restaurant table in the vast Omni atrium, Ivan couldn't help himself. He kept looking all around—a kid in a candy store.

I told him I had first passed through Texas many years before, visiting a friend in Dallas. After a couple of hours walking downtown, I told my friend, "I have to buy a cowboy hat!"

My friend said, "Down here, we just call 'em a *hat!*"

Ivan chuckled, which let me know he was finally relaxing.

We went to The Driskill and checked him into the conference. He was given his Panel Member tag in a plastic case on a lanyard. He draped it around his neck with pride.

As we walked, every once in a while, he brought his hand up to the tag and pressed it to his chest. He seemed to be reassuring himself this was all real.

On another level, it meant that he had no inkling of what was coming: the real reason all of this had been so meticulously orchestrated.

It wasn't until the next morning that he could see Polly, but I had already advised her "the package has arrived." That was an example of our humorous use of "FBI talk," which she had come to enjoy. She was doing so much for us, I had to make sure it was also fun for her.

Feedback from her later indicated it had gone perfectly with Ivan. He would attend his choice of dozens of meetings, panel discussions, and breakout sessions over the next few days.

Although I would see him a few times, the goal was not to babysit him. We didn't want him to think he was being monitored. While we would share some highlights together, I think he enjoyed being on his own in this completely new setting.

I had briefed him on the appropriate clothing—none of which he could purchase in Moscow. Also, if he did buy any togs in Texas, it was unlikely he would wear them back home. Sequins, rawhide fringe, boots, and the like were all far too Western—not meaning *cowboy*, but the entire *western hemisphere*. Anything he bought in Austin would be mere mementos in Moscow.

While there were many similarities between the two film festivals, and some of the same people from the west coast had flown in for this one, there were Texans here who would never go to the one in Los Angeles. Ivan had to get accustomed to their accent, and them to his.

I told him a story of why it is sometimes difficult for non-native English speakers to understand the southern accent. A friend, raised in the streets of Jerusalem, who speaks several languages, told me of his first encounter with an American, and it was a Texan. He overheard the man order breakfast at a sidewalk café, asking for "a *bald* egg!"

Ivan's eyebrows shot up. I explained the pronunciation of "boiled" egg, in "Texan."

It was not until spending a couple more days here that he finally got the joke.

What I did not tell him was that this story had come from an old friend, Dimitry Droujinsky, one of the FBI's best agent-linguists, who had been the street urchin in Israel.

Something I would also have to be alert for was any indication that Ivan suspected he was under surveillance. Several SSG teams, which had come from Washington and Los Angeles, were following his every move as part of what they did for a living.

The logistics for all of these support personnel were not my concern but something Gene took care of. Truth be told, I cannot recall if he came to Austin, but I think not, because, up until the last minute, he was still working out the details of the female FBI agent.

That would have been plenty on anyone's plate, but both of us saw this operation as coming to a close fairly soon. We were giving our all to make it a good one.

And, don't forget, for all of those members of the surveillance teams, there were hotel rooms, vehicles, food, vouchers to fill out—and all of it still completely under the radar in the FBI's paperwork.

Whenever I saw Ivan, I could tell he was having a good time. Sure, he would punch out some articles from the conference, but now he was part of the story.

I dodged him most of the time because it could not look like I was following him. I also had minimal contact with the Gs to avoid compromising their efforts.

I wondered how they finessed the $900 entrance fee, and which ones purchased just day passes. Even Polly was not aware of the presence of all the surveillance.

There seemed to be enough young Gs to have their own breakout session, and I had to smile at that. They did a wonderful job, always with appropriate tradecraft.

Then the evening of the Governor's Barbecue was upon us. I really didn't care whether I went. That was my mission-oriented mentality. It boiled down to, "Would going contribute to our operation?"

I stopped Ivan in one of The Driskill's tall corridors to ask if he planned to attend.

He withdrew a crumpled brochure from his pocket to look for a check mark beside it.

Seeing none, I told him it was a good idea and I would go with him.

Of course, not all of the conference people were authorized to attend, but his status as a "dignitary" was his admission. I, too, had finessed an invitation, but that came with being pals with the founder of the film festival.

In a couple of hours, we met and walked the half a mile to the Governor's Mansion. It is everything Tara was in *Gone with the Wind*, but bigger and more so.

For a moment I thought it might even have been modeled after the mansion in the movie, but then I nearly kicked myself.

From the 1880s, this building preceded the era of *Gone with the Wind*—that is, the book *and* movie, and might even have been the model for Tara in the film. *Stupid, stupid!* So Ivan wasn't the only one who was not in his element.

The interior of the Governor's Mansion was like stepping back in time, with its hundred-plus-year-old furnishings, chandeliers, drapery, carpeting, ornate convex mirrors—everything perfectly placed, just so. In Ivan's view, it may as well have been the White House.

His wide-open eyes told me a lot, and he even compared it to the Hermitage in St. Petersburg, Russia, formerly the Winter Palace and the museums of the Tsars.

The boys from Texas would like to have heard that, but they would probably say, "Whatever they have in Russia, the one in Texas is bigger!"

Actually, the Hermitage is more on a scale of the many buildings of the Smithsonian Institution in Washington, but I am sure Ivan was talking about the exquisite presentation of the mansion.

In a special moment, I saw the governor across a large room, and Polly was with him. I took the opportunity to take hold of Ivan's elbow and guide him that way. He complied.

It was a surprise to Polly, but extraordinary woman that she was, she took it all in stride.

"Governor, I would like you to meet two friends of mine, my colleague, Wayne Johnson, and this is Ivan Kurylenko, who has come to our festival all the way from Russia to be part of our International Film panel. Gentlemen, this is Governor Bush." (That would be "George W.")

Easygoing handshakes came next. None of us knew we were standing with the next president of the United States.

When we finally got outside where smoke ascended from what looked like acres of cooking ribs, it was Ivan's olfactory sense that was intoxicated.

In minutes he was handed a plateful but seemed uncomfortable with how to proceed. He saw finely-dressed men and women grabbing the ribs and chewing the meat off the bones.

Ivan's face took on a when-in-Rome expression, and then—he went for it!

If only I had a photo of the barbecue sauce covering most of the bottom half of his face and his almost crazed look with how good it all tasted. He had sunk his teeth into the meat and was gnawing away at it, enjoying himself even more than *he* knew. And there was plenty more where that came from, more than the whole garden full of people could eat.

I casually walked over to Ivan and said, "Now, you understand Texas better."

His mouth was too full to speak, but his profuse nodding meant he got my point. It seemed they didn't do barbecues in Russia—at least, nothing quite like this one.

The next day would be one Ivan would never forget. I was glad for him and a bit fearful. It is okay to have an emotional involvement with the target of your undercover operation, as long as you keep your perspective.

The International Film Panel

The International Film panel, scheduled for the early afternoon, received so much attention that it was given the largest room. Hundreds packed the place, which no one had foreseen.

When Ivan was marched in with the other two panel members, he had a sharp intake of breath. This was the moment he had been waiting for, no matter how it turned out.

I thought Polly would run the panel, but another person was there who I didn't know. So I would be the only one in the room who knew what was really going on. That is, how all of this had been a massive setup for a single very special set of moments, planned to take place just a few hours away.

The moderator made his opening statements and explained how the panel would work. Each man would make an introductory statement, then they would take questions. Discussion would ensue naturally.

For Ivan's part, he pretty much recited his resume in his slight Russian accent. There was some evidence of nervousness, but it was how he started it off that surprised me.

He said he was honored to be invited to participate and was learning all sorts of new things in Texas. "For instance," he said, "I had lunch with a friend, and I told him I wanted to buy a cowboy hat."

"He said to me," Ivan using his newly minted Texas accent, "'Down here, we just call 'em a *hat!*'"

All the Texans laughed, and then so did the outsiders, mostly from California. Ivan was accepted, and it was a great way to begin the session. But I was thinking, if he tells them about the "bald egg," I'm suing for copyright infringement!

After his opening comments, Ivan said he wanted to make one more point. It was about his expertise on filmmaking in foreign countries. He heard about an English professor in America who was an expert on Australian literature. When asked what made him an "expert," the professor said, "The farther you are from the point of origin, the easier it is to be an expert!"

Again, there was laughter, but it was more than the humor in the joke. This was about as self-effacing as one could be. Everyone understood Ivan had flown fifteen hours to be here, and he would be fine. But my old Penn State professor, who coined that line, deserved a hat-tip.

After the others went into their credentials, the first question was addressed to Ivan. It was quite general, about how making films abroad was different than in America.

If I had pushed a button, I could not have started Ivan giving the answer he did. It was almost as though he had studied for hours, just to be able to respond to this question.

He began with, "For example," which I was sure was his *only* example. He mentioned Anahit Avakian and the film she was working on in Armenia. I was pretty certain 90 percent of the audience could not have found Armenia on a map, but the exotic nature of the place began to win them over. They were listening intently.

He told them that no matter where a movie is made, it is most important to have a good story, a strong plot. The backdrop for Anahit's film would be the genocide of a million and a half Armenians by the Turks in 1915. But while that was the setting, there must be a human-interest narrative to lay before it. In this film, he said, it was a love story, which would ring true in any culture. He went on to mention the dashing young Ottoman officer and the beautiful Armenian girl who fell in love with the Turk, but she was also out to save her family.

Ivan had the audience enthralled, and I don't think he knew just how much. He was, essentially, telling them that movies are the same the world over. But then he went on about the actors chosen to be in the film. Should they be "western," meaning from Europe, America, or even Australia, recognizable headliners on the marquee, or local actors?

He answered his own question discussing whether the movie would have "legs." If one wanted a worldwide audience, Anahit would need first-rate actors to reach beyond the Armenian audience. Sure, secondary actors could be from the country where the movie was made, but most small countries could not support an epic movie without a guarantee of greater distribution.

Then he spoke about the language of the film, which he said would have to be in English, with subtitles to accommodate any country where it would be distributed. Dubbing it was preferred and collaboration between foreign and American movie studios was essential because, "of course, America is the movie-making capital of the world."

He certainly knew how to work an audience: not just telling them the truth, but also what they wanted to hear.

I was more than impressed, I was dumbfounded. Many of these exact words I had said to Ivan on the very first day we met, and I had learned all of them from Polly Platt not long before. But the ones I had not told him, he and Anahit heard from Polly's lips during our long dinner at the Shutters on the Beach restaurant—which was half a year ago!

I would have sworn that, had he not been recording those conversations, he must have had something close to total recall, or maybe it was merely his journalist's knack. I was hoping his visual memory was that good, too.

Remembering so clearly when Polly had been instructing those two novices on what would make their movie work, I realized Ivan really did not know anything further about making movies than what he had learned in Los Angeles. But he didn't have to. He was a hit!

The other panel members chimed in with their bits and pieces, commenting on certain issues raised, and it went back and forth for a while.

Another question was asked about distribution of the foreign-made films.

The panel members looked among themselves, and Ivan took the lead. He spoke about how many screens a country had and the importance of knowing what the gross receipts would be from a certain number of showings. The movie's legs would enable other countries to be factored into the equation for its overall gross receipts.

Going back to Anahit's movie, he said the people in Turkey would not want to see their own brutal history revealed, but countries such as Israel would readily pay to watch what other murderous regimes had done, besides knowing their own brutal history with the Third Reich. Ivan added that this would be of interest to many western countries.

He made the point that the love story brings you in, but the backdrop is the history you learn as you go along, which brings it all together so your film can be "an international phenomenon."

Had Polly been there, I am sure she would have been nodding her head, knowing what was going on. But she would also have been pleased that her lessons had been learned.

All of this was very good for the film festival to which she had devoted so much time and effort. It was promoting screenwriters, who got a better picture of how their words could be transformed and shown in movie houses around the globe.

If Ivan could contribute to that, no matter how it happened, she would be happy. And it was something she could not have paid for. When she did hear about the results of the panel, I knew it was heartwarming for her—more positive karma.

When the session ended, running longer than anyone had thought, a line of people formed at the head table. Many had follow-up questions for Ivan, and some even wanted his autograph, although he had never produced a book that could be sold or signed. That was too bad, but I am sure it stirred his brain in directions he had never thought possible.

We stayed in The Driskill for another hour, walking the corridors. It gave Ivan time to calm down from a mental high he'd never had before.

We spoke randomly with well-wishers and peeked in on other sessions.

When I thought his buzz had receded, I told him we should have dinner in a while, maybe a drink first. However, I had been up late and needed to take a nap.

We agreed I would come to his room around 6:00 PM.

Mentally, I was now much more excited than Ivan, because I had heard from Red Pop that morning. The designated—and long-awaited—female FBI agent would be coming to my room later that afternoon. I had so much to tell her.

CHAPTER 24

REBECCA KING

My room in the Austin Omni had a door which, fortunately, was not visible from Ivan's on the other side of the cavernous atrium.

I put together papers I had prepared to give a proper briefing to my expected guest. I saw this as a kind of conclusion—at least for my part in the mission—and would do anything I could to improve her chance of success.

There was a knock on my door, knuckles hitting three times, pretty strong, too.

I opened it and took a moment for my first impression. It would be similar to Ivan's.

Not wanting to leave her standing there too long, I bid her to enter.

I wouldn't want women reading these words to think anything other than that I was totally immersed in this operation, body and soul. But now I had to assess the woman who had just entered my room and see if there was anything I needed to say or do about her appearance, demeanor—her personal presentation—for what lay ahead.

She walked past me and, in a few feet, spun around, extending her hand.

"Rebecca King," she said, and we shook.

It was a firm grasp, the one you would use when meeting an FBI Special Agent-in-Charge of a field office for the first time and you wanted so badly to get this job.

But she already had the job, and her firm grip was only part of it. More than that, it was her straight look at me, eyeball-to-eyeball, very direct contact, which was impressive.

This wasn't a beauty pageant or a talent show, and anything like tryouts were long over. This was the realest of real things one could ever do—meet face-to-face with a Russian target to end the KGB's compromise of US Intelligence.

Appearance-wise, assertive-wise, and overall-picture-wise, she was the perfect female agent—exactly what I had scripted for the part. I thought she was a magical fit.

It was not until much later that I learned of the almost unbelievable bureaucratic turmoil that had taken place in order for it to be so. And there was still no database from which to choose an undercover operative.

Rebecca had been on Mike Rochford's squad for two years. There was a very small cadre of female agents to choose from, and this was the one who *had* been chosen. Under such narrow parameters, who would have believed this would have worked? Oblivious to all of that, I was overjoyed with the woman who stood before me.

She was plenty tall enough, and with her black stiletto heels on pointed pumps, she would be taller than Ivan. She was slender and fit and could probably take most men in two-out-of-three falls—which would include Ivan.

He wouldn't have said that, but he might have thought it, too.

Her hair was blondish and pulled back to be businesslike and efficient, yet also sensuous. It was gathered in a black ribbon tied at the base of her neck so it flowed down just past her shoulders.

She wore a dark, straight skirt and a pale blouse that showed her form, yet she did not appear voluptuous.

I was certain she would take Ivan aback—and hoped she would have him eating out of her hand.

This was not a woman you could have told what to wear. You might have made a suggestion, and if she agreed, she would go along and dress that way.

Her countenance was not exactly harsh, but it didn't give much room to negotiate with her, either.

I took a seat in the hotel's easy chair and motioned to the one by the desk. She was already pulling it over to be directly in front of, and a little above me. She seemed to balance herself, sitting on the front edge.

She had a slim, black briefcase, with no room for more than a single folder. I knew it had a dozen photos of those who were potentially our unsub.

I picked up a sheath of papers with the notes I had prepared. Having briefed senior FBI management in the past, I often found they had not read the prerequisite information so my updates would make sense. I didn't know the level to which Agent King had done her homework in reading the many pages of my memos, so I began with what I thought was most important.

I started with Ivan's complete and utter involvement with strong women and quickly brought the timeline through to the Austin conference and what had happened there with Polly.

If Rebecca fully understood how Ivan would see her, in advance, it would better enable her to control the situation.

She sat patiently and listened.

Prior to her arrival, I had thought our conversation would take about half an hour.

I recalled wanting to brief SAs Suchan and Cardillo back in Los Angeles before they confronted Ivan, but neither had any interest in what I had to say.

Too bad, I had thought, but they had their cold-pitch mission, and nothing I said would have altered that. Now we knew there was nothing any of us could have done to enable them to succeed—starting with having the *wrong genitalia!*

To Special Agent King, I mentioned Ivan's encounter with Polly and Governor Bush at the massive Texas barbecue a couple of days before, then his great success earlier in the day at the panel discussion, noting he might still be on a psychological high.

I told her I planned to knock on his door around 6:00 PM for a drink and dinner, and it was now a few minutes before 5:30. She would have another twenty minutes with me.

But Rebecca stood up, abruptly. She said, "I've got it. That's all I need."

I was surprised and stood, too. I had prepared more for my briefing, things she could incorporate into her encounter with Ivan.

There was no smile or handshake, no indication of appreciation for any of this, the setup, the analysis, or that she was "glad to be the woman chosen for this role," and no, "Thanks for all you did." *Nada*!

She spun on her heels and was out the door.

Dismayed and in a huff, I plopped back down in the chair.

What the hell, I thought.

I sat for a few minutes, hoping she was sufficiently prepared for what she was about to do. I was going over what I had not covered, suggestions I wanted to make so she would be able to get into Ivan's mind.

But then it dawned on me. *Stupid, stupid, stupid!*

I laughed out loud, my maniacal laugh that sometimes makes others uncomfortable. It comes from deep within, a place of comprehension. I had realized something very special.

Sure, Rebecca could have sat with me for another fifteen minutes and listened to my spiel, but that was not why she had been chosen for this role. It was not the kind of person she was. She left so abruptly because she had everything she needed. She had drawn her own personal line, and it said, "That's enough!"

At first, I was disappointed, but then I had a realization. It was exactly this woman, and this personality, which the operation needed, and the hell with anything I might think about it.

I laughed one more time with my head back, and knew that whatever happened, it would be the very best outcome we could expect with Rebecca King now at the helm.

Rebecca and Ivan

Just after 5:30 PM, Ivan Kurylenko heard knocking on his door. It was a solid knuckle-rap, three times. Actually, it was too early to be me, and I wasn't particularly known for being punctual. He went to the door, straight away.

When he opened it, he stopped and stared.

This was a person he had never seen before—not in Russia, Washington, Los Angeles, or even earlier at the film festival. She was a completely new entity to him, and it took more than a moment for him to gather himself together.

If Ivan had been asked what kind of person—appearance and personality—he would want to come knocking on his door, uninvited, the answer would have been exactly what stood before him—Rebecca King.

She took advantage of his moment of hesitation.

"Ivan," she told him. "We have to talk."

She pushed the door open and walked deliberately right by him. Several feet into the spacious suite, she stopped and spun around, staring at Ivan. Her eyebrows went up in silence. He looked almost embarrassed.

He closed the door quickly and walked over to her.

He did not ask who she was, why she was invading his space, or what he could do for her. In fact, he said nothing at all. He could have been tongue-tied, but it was more than that.

She told him, "Have a seat!" and pointed at a nearby chair.

He did as instructed—*in his own hotel room*—and sat himself down.

Sadly, I was not a fly on the wall. But from everything I was later told, you could almost have written the script, at least the dominant-versus-submissive aspect of it.

She did not dance around and tell him she was glad to meet him, or happy he had come to the United States to attend the conference.

It was clear that she, and her people, had been monitoring everything going on.

If Ivan had concerns that Big Brother was watching his every move, this was the shocking proof that they were well-founded—*and here in America*.

She told him it was important to her that he had information she wanted to know.

That it was important went without saying, because *she* was there, wasn't she, in Austin, Texas? It's not a place where you just dropped in while passing through to somewhere else. You really have to want to be in Austin to be there.

In Ivan's eyes, the bureaucracy and logistics were secondary. What was primary was that this strong and assertive, doesn't-take-crap-from-anyone woman had entered his room and his life.

He was quite speechless.

Rebecca let her words simmer, probably having a better idea what thoughts were rolling around in Ivan's head than he did.

She said when he was assigned to Washington in the 1980s, an event occurred which he likely thought little about afterwards, but it was now very important.

She wanted him to think back and recall the face he had seen, for not more than a few moments, but one he would never forget, due to the most curious circumstances around it.

Ivan's attention was riveted on what she was saying. He was part of the picture she was painting, not on the outside looking in, but right there within the frame. He was an insider—important to *her*.

She described the specific building, the surroundings and the facts, as much as she knew of them, with sufficient detail so he could take his mind back to that rainy day in Washington.

It did not occur to Ivan to ask how she knew this information, but she did, and that was enough. She was not guessing about any of it. Most importantly, he was there when the man had come in, right off the street, and wanted to speak with someone in the KGB. "*Kah-gay-bay*," she said, and so had the visitor more than fifteen years ago.

She wanted Ivan to think back and put himself in that place—recall what the man looked like. Even if it took closing his eyes, he had to *be there* and *see it happening*.

When the two overt-prong FBI agents had approached Ivan back in Los Angeles, now several months ago, Ivan had not *heard* them. In fact, he had hardly even *seen* them. What was now taking place with Rebecca King was the opposite, so far beyond that scenario that it would take an expert psychologist to analyze it.

Ivan was seeing her and hearing her to a degree which would be difficult to describe, and he was listening to her, doing what she was asking—actually, telling—him to do.

He sat with his eyes closed, taking his brain back a decade and a half.

Agent King did not identify herself, her organization, or what her ultimate goal was—*to catch a spy!* That was not part of the conversation, if you could call it that.

She was dealing with only one piece of a much larger puzzle, but one that had to be placed into the framework before the rest of the mosaic could be completed. For Ivan, it was only about what this magnificent woman had instructed him to do.

None of this makes Ivan an aberration or so out of the norm from the rest of society. But these personality characteristics, his penchants and proclivities, pinged in just the right way, could produce the desired result. If you have the right key, you can open any lock. Rebecca King was the key to Ivan.

At one point, Ivan grabbed hold of himself. He had begun to grasp the consequence of what was happening, and his instinct for self-preservation took over.

He did not want to see the photos, but he didn't have the gumption to kick this woman out of his room, either. He wanted her to stay, but he also wanted her to go. He saw a long and sheeny feline before him, who could pounce at any moment.

Unlike Americans, people who have lived in a totalitarian state have ingrained feelings about their families, which they put before themselves regarding their own safety and security. This family factor had risen to the surface and was nudging aside the assertiveness of Agent King—but not completely.

Ivan was betwixt and between. He simply could not do what she was asking.

But would he in the future?

I would love to have seen a diagram of the synapses firing off in Ivan's mind and the fireworks display they would have given off, maybe looking like his cranium would explode.

He stood up, and so did Rebecca, maintaining her height advantage. He looked troubled, yet still subservient, but it was a push-comes-to-shove moment, and so much hung in the balance.

For Rebecca, it was gaining the final piece, the firing pistol going off to start the race for a whole new massive investigation that would come next.

For Ivan, it was potentially losing everything he had ever worked for and accomplished, especially the future of his family, which included a whole set of other strong women. Perhaps none was ever as assertive as the one before him, but it was a great deal to weigh on his conscience.

Finally, he cinched up his nerve. He told her he could not do this—at least, not now.

Fortunately, Rebecca had a fallback option—the potential for a future contact.

She did not know when or where, but she would be there whenever Ivan was ready to talk to her. She made sure he knew she was, personally, pushing for this meeting to take place, and sooner was better than later. It could be a very short meeting. His name would be kept out of it.

Of course, it would be impossible for Rebecca to guarantee that his identity would be protected once he provided the FBI agent with what she needed.

At a kind of impasse, there was little more to be done.

Hanging around and talking about the film festival was not an option.

Rebecca could not drop any of her established cover, make a change in her strong personal presentation, or say anything that might be a pullback from her dominant posture.

She took out her business card and extended it to Ivan. On the back, she had handwritten her home telephone number.

It was the first time Ivan had become aware of her name, but the organization was no surprise. Yet it didn't seem to faze him. This was the way to get back in touch with her, her *persona*, the one making the request of him, no matter the organization. It was Special Agent Rebecca King standing right in front of him, in the flesh. That controlled everything.

He had been having the conversation of a lifetime, and it enthralled him. It was this woman, her power-look, how she asserted herself, and even how she had treated him, if that could be an adequate description of her overbearing nature. Add to that the mysteriousness of it all. That was the ribbon wrapped around this encounter for Ivan.

The card would be going back to Moscow in Ivan's wallet. This was no longer the Cold War, but not enough had changed in Russia to easily distinguish it from the old days of the Soviet Union. The KGB was now the SVR, but was it really any different?

He held onto her card in a way that was not lost on Rebecca. She knew—we all would have—that he would be holding on to it tightly for many minutes after she left. In the days to come, looking at it, or just thinking about it, would bring a recollection of this most extraordinary encounter, that is, until he could meet with her again.

I never did show up at Ivan's room that evening, and he never asked me why. We never had that drink, either. I had no reason to believe he was suspicious of me because I was so involved in the film festival for Polly and was busy ostensibly seeing all of my Texas-based clients.

By the time he left the next morning, I had faded out of the picture.

CHAPTER 25

IT ALL COMES TOGETHER

My father was always supportive of his two sons growing up. He had been orphaned as a child, yet was self-educated and quite well-read. We were involved in the Boy Scouts, so he became a counselor for the Reading merit badge, potentially benefiting all of the scouts in Philadelphia.

Boys came to see him with the list of books they had read. In 1960, this often included Jules Verne's *Twenty Thousand Leagues Under the Sea*. The Disney movie had come out in 1954, so the question was, did they read the book, or just see the movie?

There is a scene where Captain Nemo, in his futuristic submarine, the *Nautilus*, traveled to a far South Pacific island, the result of a volcanic eruption. Through an underwater tunnel, he traveled deep inside where the caldera had collapsed to form a small sandy island.

An extraordinary individual, Captain Nemo found himself alone in that most remote place. Strolling along the beach, he came upon something very special. He bent to pick it up and examine its beauty. It was a seashell which twisted in the opposite direction of almost every other one—a left-handed seashell.

This special moment compared a unique Captain Nemo, so different from the rest of humanity, and the seashell, in its own way, equally unique.

My father asked the young scouts about this vignette and what Nemo had picked up on the beach. It was what separated the wheat from the chaff among them. The ones who didn't know the answer had seen the movie but hadn't read the book. They were sent home, only to return after reading *two more books*!

In every field there can be such a unique individual as Captain Nemo. While I have enjoyed considerable success with scores of investigations and have been described as a "maverick" and thinking "outside the box," it was not myself who I considered the unique special agent in the Graysuit counterintelligence operation. That would be Rebecca King.

I was doing my job as the set-up guy. But her role was to do the touch-and-pitch.

She had to leap that high hurdle at the very first meeting and was not even allowed the eight days I was originally given. She had to make an impression, have Ivan bow to her wishes, and do her bidding in a matter of minutes. Failing that, getting another bite at the Ivan-apple would be the next best thing, even if there was no meeting scheduled. But this did not diminish her performance.

The immediate result would be written up similarly to my case with the Romanian correspondent, who had gone home to Bucharest to ask his wife what he should have done when approached by the FBI. That one ended up working out well for US Intelligence. So, both the old Romanian case, and this approach, were described as "Not immediately successful."

While it seemed to be over, we were all hoping it would come back to life. With the unique Agent King, I was confident.

Rebecca and Ivan, Redux

Several days after Rebecca and Ivan parted company in the Omni Hotel in Austin, her home phone rang in Northern Virginia. She had given him that number for security reasons—so he wouldn't call the FBI field office. Also, he might have felt more comfortable calling her private residence. He had been invited into her personal space.

Her husband answered the phone, giving a ring of authenticity to the idea that this *was* her home. He called out to his wife to come.

Ivan's accent was unmistakable. He didn't have to identify himself, but he did. That was another indication of his lack of intelligence training.

Ivan told Rebecca, "I will look at your pictures."

He was in New York City and would meet her there. As nebulous as it sounds, they agreed to meet at Rockefeller Center the next day at 3:00 PM, "at the ice-skating rink."

Come hell or high water, Rebecca would be there, via train, plane, or automobile, whatever it took, to get to New York City and find her man. This is not something she could delay, and she made plans to get up there right away.

She advised her superiors of the contact and readied herself for the journey.

The next morning, she was on an early shuttle flight from the newly renamed Reagan National Airport to La Guardia and took a taxi to the meeting place.

Rebecca needed no further preparation, other than to put herself back in the mindset she'd had in Austin. With the analysis of how *un*-KGB-like Ivan was, there was little thought that this might be a setup against her.

Rebecca had a great deal of inner strength but didn't need to exude it all of the time. It was a natural thing for her on the job. Now, it would be especially designed to meet with Ivan.

During an interview, if you know your subject is about to lie, you watch him carefully to see what he does and how he prepares for it: the buildup, and then the slight deflation in tension in the immediate aftermath of the big moment. Some have smaller "big moments" than others, because they are practiced liars. I didn't think any of this applied to Ivan.

Likewise, if you know what to look for, you can also determine if a person is *not* lying. It comes in their certain motions, their physical reactions to things, especially if you have a baseline of past encounters to compare, and their overall calmness or anxiousness in the face of any given circumstance. Importantly, was this person different on a previous occasion from the one now under the microscope?

Rebecca had to consider all of this and whether Ivan would lie to her.

She would once again know that Ivan would be looking up to her, not because she was an FBI agent, but in the classic submissive mode of doing her bidding. While he had apparent anguish in Austin about looking at the photos, certainly with his family's future in mind, something must have enabled him to overcome that apprehension. Maybe he just figured a way around it in order to meet with this woman again.

Rebecca would have to get back into her dominant female "uniform," but not perfectly so. After all, they had met before, and first impressions, being what they are, almost anything she wore now, within reason, would not change the impression of her in Ivan's mind. Besides, it was fall weather and he might not even see what she was wearing beneath her overcoat.

Rockefeller Center is a complex of nineteen commercial buildings covering twenty-two acres in midtown Manhattan. Even when it is not the holiday season, the area around the ice-skating rink is more crowded than most places on earth. There are scores of skaters going around the oval, just as many waiting in line to enter, and ten times that number watching from all levels around the venue. Throngs of tourists, not moving in any particular direction, made it one of the worst places to try to find someone you were looking for.

Once at Rockefeller Center, Rebecca moved to the rink and took up a position where she had the clearest view of the greatest number of people. It is a knack good agents have: to be in just the right place when the action begins.

Then she saw Ivan.

He was across the rink from her, and they made eye contact. Apparently, he, too, was proficient at taking up a good vantage position, perhaps from years of reporting.

He signaled with his hand in the direction of 49th Street. He started walking and she did too, from the other side of the rink.

He hailed a cab and got in. He left the door open, and she followed him.

They pulled out into slow traffic, with no particular destination.

There were no hugs or high-profile greetings. That was not the basis of their relationship. This was a dimension beyond merely all-business.

She took out the thin folder with the photos of the Americans suspected of volunteering to spy for the KGB.

She opened it across Ivan's lap in the back seat. He began to examine them.

I had seen this maneuver many times in my career, through the lengthy process of debriefing defectors, to learn the story behind anyone they recognized. Each photo was an individual project. They were being counted on to examine all of them carefully.

Had they seen the face at the embassy, in an intelligence-school class, in college, or at a pub? In what regard did they remember him, superior or subordinate, friend or foe? Every face was given their utmost concentration until it was "I *don't* know him" or "I *know* him." If the latter, they would be debriefed in great detail. Then the session would move on to the next photo.

Ivan was going through that same process with the images before him. His level of concentration was as high as one could possibly imagine.

He started at the upper left, pausing at each one, slowly moving across the faces.

It was overcast, and the light could have been better, but it was sufficient to see.

Rebecca watched him going through them meticulously.

That is how I assessed he would take on this task: truly a detailed person in all of his articles and nearly every aspect of his life. That same penchant, it was hoped, would enable him to recall a once-seen face from fifteen years before.

It had been a rainy day. On that afternoon, he happened to be in the reception area in the residential duplex house in Northwest Washington, the smallest Soviet establishment office.

With no notice, a man had simply come through the doorway and asked to speak to someone in the KGB. He had a commanding voice and wouldn't take no for an answer.

How, Ivan would have thought, could he ever have forgotten that face?

Now in the backseat of the taxi, he was going over the photos in Agent King's folder. When he came to one of them, Ivan pondered it longer than the others. Then he went on to the next. It had not been for long, but it was the only one he treated differently from the rest.

When he had looked at all of them, he stopped.

Having said absolutely nothing about any of the photos, either way, Ivan pointed his finger at the one face where he had paused, then said, "I can tell you this is *not* the man!"

This was as shocking as it was surprising. It could only be interpreted as an incredibly cryptic Russian way of saying this *is* the man you are looking for. However, if Ivan were ever questioned, even polygraphed, by Russian Intelligence as to whether he had identified a Soviet agent to American Intelligence, he would unequivocally be able to report that he had absolutely *not* done so. With this wording, he might just be able to pass their polygraph.

The cab pulled over, and Rebecca got out. That was the last time they saw each other.

PART TWO

CHAPTER 26

AFTERMATH

Now I laugh when I hear someone say, "I don't want to be the one to point fingers, but…" because it has a completely different meaning for me.

Ivan was never paid any money. That wouldn't have occurred to him. But he was compelled to go to New York to respond to Agent King's overture. In fact, this favor—his *gift*—for a woman of such authority, for whom he had such admiration and held in high esteem, was probably at the top of the list of high points in his life, which was filled with so many strong women.

I never learned if this was an offshoot from other scheduled travel, or if he arranged the trip for a completely different reason. It did enable him to sneak away for a short time and spend those few minutes with Rebecca King.

Ivan had not been in the KGB and had no allegiance to a set of people he feared and loathed. He had no reason to report his contact in Austin to them, particularly when all he could possibly get from it was grief. And this was so long after the Berlin Wall came down, and his country had changed so much—even its name and the name of its intelligence service. Many in the KGB went on to other work, although always using the skill sets employed while Soviet Intelligence officers in the service of a totalitarian government.

My view is that Ivan was following the Japanese proverb, "The nail that sticks out gets hammered down." He wouldn't have wanted to draw attention to himself by discussing any of this with the new version of the KGB.

Would he have pointed at the wrong man? What would be the point? Ivan was so full of integrity within his own internal system, it would not have allowed him to do that.

He would have just said the man wasn't there, if he had not been. But to make up a story only to please this strong woman, even temporarily, would have been outside of the psychological makeup that was Ivan Kurylenko.

Similarly, he would not have lied to Anahit Avakian or Polly Platt. It wasn't within him.

There would be discussions in certain circles, among those with the clearances, as to whether this had been a setup by Russian Intelligence. But why go to all the trouble?

If they wanted to frame an innocent man as the possible mole, they didn't know whose photos might be there. Anyone who was *not* the unsub should have been able to prove it was not him. Like with police lineups, there might have been only one potentially guilty party. The rest were cops in plainclothes, so if the only pickable one was not picked, they could all go home.

There was just too much for the new KGB to have foreseen in order to set up a reverse scam against the FBI.

And would the KGB ever use a non-intelligence officer to try to dupe the FBI?

After hundreds of hours debriefing a record number of actual Cold War intelligence defectors, it was clear to me they had such a low opinion of non-intelligence officers, they would never let someone who did not wear the KGB class ring participate in one of their operations. And this goes back to the question of whether Ivan would have reported any of this to the KGB/SVR.

I thought it was less than unlikely. They had no strings on him, and no noose, either. Everything pointed to what he did as real, and that he had just been planning for his future self-defense if all hell broke loose.

A few days after the Rockefeller Center meeting, when things began to settle down, Gene McClelland called me. He said "our man" had come back, called, and met with the "lady from Texas." He had pointed out a photo in the back seat of a taxi in New York. Other details I would learn later.

With this information, I was overjoyed. I could see more of my family and even get going on some great healthcare-fraud cases which needed close monitoring. I had been reluctant to start them while Graysuit was in play—in play for me, anyway.

I had a feeling of self-satisfaction that would be difficult to match, but even then, no one else in the San Diego FBI could know anything about it. In the overall Graysuit case, the bad guy was yet to be caught.

It was a waiting game. But if the unsub had been identified, why didn't they arrest him?

Simple—evidence!

No United States attorney could make the case that this was the man who had caused such damage to the United States without a whole slew of evidence. There was only one tiny piece, thus far. The man who would never—*could* never—testify as to what he knew was now back in Russia. He was not what prosecutors would call a "reliable witness." Actually, he was, but not in terms of presenting information in court.

Now there was only one event which would enable all of this to come to the ultimate conclusion. The spy had to be *caught in the act.* In espionage cases, he had to be in the process of delivering classified documents to his Russian handlers.

How the hell do you make that happen?

The process is long and arduous, so it might not take only a few days or weeks, but possibly months—and maybe years.

Meanwhile, I was in San Diego living that dream—up to a point. I was waiting with bated breath every time I turned on the news, hoping to see an alert, or a newspaper headline: "Spy in the FBI!"

But there was nothing like that in the news—and yes, for *years.*

In the summer of 2000, I was on a temporary duty assignment in the Miami Division, still working healthcare-fraud cases. For the last three months of that year, I worked on the Columbia HCA taskforce in the Tampa Division. It was the first billion-dollar healthcare-fraud case. I had my share of that one, bringing $93 million back to the federal coffers. It was very fulfilling and put the icing on the cake of my FBI healthcare-fraud career.

Then I retired and was out, but there had still been no word about the Graysuit unsub.

I did enjoy, in semi-retirement, sitting at my desk, occasionally wearing a black T-shirt with a big red *V* on the chest, the Roman numeral five. It had been the official shirt of the fifth year of Polly Platt's Austin Film Festival in 1998. It was a memento: the only physical evidence I had of having been there.

Then, two and a half years after my last involvement in Graysuit, the news finally broke.

On February 18, 2001, President's Day, Robert Philip Hanssen was arrested in a park in the Northern Virginia suburbs of Washington, DC. He would be described by FBI Director Louis Freeh as having committed "the most traitorous actions imaginable."

Five months later, a plea agreement saved him from the death penalty. He would live out his life without the possibility of parole in the supermax prison in Florence, Colorado. For twenty-three hours of every day, he would be in solitary confinement. He would have no human contact, no touching skin-to-skin. He would be separated from humanity—guards and other prisoners—for the rest of his life.

I later learned Hanssen had believed, during his two decades of treachery, that were he ever caught, he would serve his time in a federal facility with white-collar crime offenders. It would seem like a minimum-security country club, but this was the opposite of what happened.

The day of his arrest had been a cause for celebration, the long-awaited result finally come to fruition—and for everyone in the FBI.

The pride I felt, personally, made me nearly burst at the seams.

But my part in all of this was still not something I would discuss with others. In fact, something I did not know then, and might not have thought was relevant, was that I had no clear evidence that the identification of Hanssen, as the long-sought unsub, was the result of what I had done. I certainly had no reason *not* to think I had been involved. No one could have doubted my efforts, all of which Gene McClelland had monitored and been part of back in Washington.

No matter that I had put in most of a year of my life planning and scheming, organizing and finessing this case, reaching into my undercover closet for a new identity, all the logistics and travels, the surveillance teams, everything, more extraordinary than any other time in my twenty-nine-year career. It was not until the movie *Breach* came out in 2007 that a realization hit me that this might actually not have come as a result of that supreme effort. It was a shocker!

Breach was the story of the hunt for a Russian spy in the FBI, with Chris Cooper playing the dastardly Hanssen, Ryan Phillippe as the clerk in Hanssen's outer office, Eric O'Neill, and Laura Linney playing his supervisor.

The movie began with the knowledge of *who* the unsub was. The entire plotline was the effort to catch him in the act of passing classified documents. What the movie did not sufficiently explain to me—and also to any other moviegoer who might have been concerned about it—was *how* Hanssen had been identified, so they knew he was the one to monitor.

At one point, the clerk told Linney that he didn't think Hanssen was a bad guy. He even went to Mass every morning!

She told him the FBI had paid a KGB officer $7 million for that information. Wow!

I knew that neither I, nor Agent King, paid Ivan anything, nor would he have wanted any compensation. More likely he would have preferred that we forgot we ever met him. Well, maybe for Rebecca King, because I think, to this day, he would still believe I was exactly who he always thought I was—a guy looking for a great movie for Texas millionaires to dabble in.

So this moment, while sitting in the theater watching *Breach*, besides loud *gongs* going off in my head, it brought me to question everything I had done and—*had it all worked?*

Four months after Hanssen was arrested, Polly Platt received a letter from the director of the FBI dated June 12, 2001. When agents receive communications in this format, it is referred to as a "Letter of Commendation." When a private citizen receives one, it is a "Letter of Appreciation."

> *Dear Ms. Platt,*
>
> *I share the appreciation of my associates in our Washington Field Office for the important role you played in a matter of national security, and I join them in thanking you for your valuable assistance. Through your initiative, positive results were derived, and you can certainly be proud knowing that your outstanding cooperation enabled us to achieve our mission. We are grateful for your support, and we offer you our sincere gratitude.*
> *Signed/Louis J. Freeh*

This was impressive, and I was so glad for Polly. She deserved more, but she was most pleased with this understated appreciation. She framed it and hung it on the wall in her peaceful home on the canal in Venice, California.

For me, I had felt this operation was the culmination of my undercover career. I had worn Hoover Blues for nearly three decades, with dozens of cases, each new one as interesting as the last, yet none could be discussed in public at the time. That was especially so with this one, now known simply as "the Hanssen case."

At the time, in 2001, no FBI agent had ever written a book about the work he had done in foreign counterintelligence while serving in the FBI, fiction or nonfiction. I don't think anyone ever submitted such a story to the FBI Prepublication Review Unit, and none had been approved.

But if you are reading this, things have definitely changed, and more of the great tales from within the FBI might yet see the light of day—and they deserve to be told.

Whatever happened to all of those memos I had written, printed out, and FedExed off to Gene McClelland? Did they sit in a pile over in the corner, or were they placed in something like the old FBI files, with beige cardboard covers, front and back, and two holes at the top for prongs to hold it all together? Were they ever scanned so they would finally make it into the FBI's FOIMS system, as all other case files, for the record?

It was three years after my part of the operation that Robert Hanssen was arrested, and so much had happened in the interim. Did anyone think to reach over to that pile of memos and say, "Hey, now that the bad guy has been caught, and no unsub is searching our computers to see if we are investigating him, we can scan them into the system." To the best of my knowledge, that never happened.

Making an appropriate Freedom of Information Act request for these documents was met with no results. That is, if there were such documents in the system, at the very least, the response should have been to bring them out into the open, and, if so determined, redact the heck out of them, then provide an almost entirely blacked-out set of pages to the requester—me!

Why would there be reluctance to reveal this story? Hanssen was long caught, long serving multiple life sentences in supermax, and there was nothing "SECRET" about the investigation anymore, or so one would assume, with at least a dozen books written about the Hanssen case and two movies made.

The fact is—and it is a sad one—it is likely that, today, there is absolutely nothing in the FBI's recordkeeping system that indicates this case—*my case*—ever happened. Some have suggested that everything I have written is "fiction," which, by the way, would have had clear sailing through the FBI's Prepublication Review Unit. But if you know me well enough, or know me at all from reading this book, you know I am extremely detail-oriented. I try to write so readers can *feel* they are right there, in the room with me, even looking over my shoulder, as the action takes place—about to fall into the Loews hotel pool, at the dinner table at Shutters on the Beach, or walking down the ornate hallways of The Driskill Hotel in Austin.

I would match my details with anyone else's denial that all of this ever occurred. I have said many times, "It is not the devil, but the truth, that is in the details."

I submitted my narrative nonfiction manuscript to the FBI Prepublication Review Unit in 2016. They are required to respond within thirty to forty-five days. However, it was a full three years later when it was sent back to me about 95 percent redacted with thick black markers having run through all of those lines. (The lawyer joke I told at the dinner with Polly, however, did make it through uncensored.)

Over months of back-and-forths, I traveled from Florida to the FBI in Washington for three personal visits to *discuss* my submission. I finally resubmitted it, in full, and it took another year and a half for its final approval—*a battle which took a total of seven years!*

That would seem to indicate they took the matter very seriously. They didn't want me to reveal FBI "sources and methods," and didn't want me to "give the KGB a manual on how the FBI catches spies." I would personally hope this book might be better seen as a recruitment tool to bring the best and brightest—agents and analysts—into the Bureau, rather than a book which tells the bad guys how we do what we do. As good friend Gene McClelland told the folks at Prepub, "This book isn't about how the FBI catches spies, it is about how *Wayne* catches spies." (I will be forever indebted to him for making that distinction.)

Another aspect worth noting is that, while it sometimes seems every other television show is about law enforcement, and every other one of those is about the FBI, it should come through quite clearly that the FBI you see presented in those programs is not the Bureau I worked in. They only come in close proximity to the actual reality on infrequent occasions.

One requirement from the FBI Prepublication Review Unit was for me to reach out to all of those named in the book and ask permission to use their true names. Certainly, this is not a legal requirement, but it was a strongly worded administrative request. I would have followed any proscriptions issued by Prepub in order to reach the finish line.

This new project took weeks and more investigation to reach some people who, in retirement, had moved off the grid. But find them I did. Even non-former-FBI personnel needed to give their okays, like cover-backstopping pal George Ramonas, who gladly gave his.

Through this process, something else was reemphasized to me. It was exactly how closely held the ultimate objective of this case had been.

When I was about to leave my house in San Diego for Santa Monica in 1998, anxious to begin my undercover role, I had been told by Gene McClelland to stop into the Los Angeles Field Office. There, I met Special Agent Philip Jing, who was on the foreign counterintelligence squad. He would be my contact in the office if I needed something.

Twenty-five years later, in 2023, I managed to locate him, now long retired. I told him who I was and that I had written a book, wanting permission to use his name. This was a poser for him because he did not remember me. He recalled Gene from Washington, who had been in the office a couple of times, and the two cold-pitch agents, Suchan and Cardillo, but my name and what I was doing there drew a complete blank.

With hindsight, I can understand this. For Phil, this case was about covering a Russian at the American Film Market and nothing more. He was not in the loop of the most extraordinary aspect of the case—to identify a spy in the FBI. Had he known that, he certainly would have remembered—and celebrated along with the rest of those who had been involved in this massive project when the announcement of Hanssen's arrest was finally made. But even on the day I spoke with him, a quarter of a century later, he was oblivious to the fact that he had actually been a part of it. This had been the most closely held secret, and even as an on-duty FBI agent, he simply did not need to know.

At the film festival, there were a couple of dozen Special Surveillance Group members constantly monitoring Ivan Kurylenko. But for them, even with the Berlin Wall down for nearly a decade, he was just another Russian to watch. None knew they were participating in the most sensitive case in the Bureau.

I have since been in contact with three of them: Hooker (John Powers), Crab (Keith Patrick), and Pepper (Sherry Green), who agreed to let me use their street handles in the book. But no one on the SSG in 1998 had any idea this case was more than a normal surveillance of a Russian. They never learned the ultimate reason why they were conducting these surveillances in Los Angeles, and then months later in Austin.

Sheila Horan, in 1998, was the senior female in the FBI, and the one Gene McClelland went to when he was administratively stifled about using a female agent to pitch Ivan. When I reached her in 2023, while she had been in the Graysuit loop, she said she could not recall giving Gene authority to use a female in our operation. To me, her back-and-forth with Gene had been so crucial that the operation would have died on the vine without her. But that day had apparently been just like any other for a top FBI official, filled with major decisions to make. No matter how crucial it had been, ours had apparently just been one of them, no longer recalled.

Last is the man on the night desk at the Department of State in 1998. This was another make-it-or-break-it aspect of the case. From my West Coast midnight, calling to his 3:00 AM in Washington, DC, I had finally reached the man who I hoped could make the decision I needed—authorizing Ivan to receive a visa to travel from Moscow to the Austin Film Festival.

After a great deal of investigation, I located David Pierce, who had been that decision-maker. Partway through our conversation in 1998, I hadn't been making much headway with him but kept at it. I was careful not to break cover and use the magical letters *FBI*.

Speaking with David in 2023, he pointed out that he had worked the State Department night shift during that time frame but did not remember my phone call. I told him that today's phone call was both to seek permission to use his name, and also, after long last, for him to become aware that he had been a key piece in a case that had the goal of preserving our national security. The International Film panel in the Austin Film Festival, and Ivan's attendance, had been a ruse in order to accomplish what was needed.

He made an interesting point, addressing the bureaucratic rules. Back then, he said, if I had told him I was in the FBI, he would have been prohibited from clicking a button on his computer screen to give the US consulate in Moscow authority to issue Ivan's visa. He said those three letters would have changed everything and required him to send the whole matter to Moscow, which would have been the ultimate arbiter over any inter-agency request. By the time they would have acted on it, Ivan would have missed his plane. Beyond that, we both knew the consulate had already made the decision to reject the visa request, which was why I made the call to State at midnight in the first place. The point is, if I had done anything besides exactly what I did, twenty-five years before, I would have been banging my head against the wall of the US government bureaucracy, and Ivan would never have left Moscow.

Just listening to David on the phone, even so many years later, gave me chills at exactly how close this case had been to coming to a screeching halt in the darkness of the night.

***

In debriefing Cold War defectors, almost all of the Romanians and many Russians, one point they all stuck to was that US Intelligence was penetrated by their own intelligence service. We didn't laugh it off—but didn't fully believe it, either.

When Romanian General Ion Mihai Pacepa, director of their Foreign Intelligence Service, defected in 1978, we asked about this. He said it was something they told their new officers during training to prevent them from being recruited by the US.

They would fear being found out by the ostensible Romanian penetration of US Intelligence. But it was not true.

Soviet defectors who said the same thing were taken more seriously, but further information—evidence—was needed to back up their assertions, which they did not have.

When I was given my assignment in the Bahia Hotel in San Diego by Mike Rochford, Dave Greb, and Gene McClelland to attend a film festival in Santa Monica, they told me we were penetrated at a senior level. They did not supply the details for why they believed it was so. However, we were losing our covert sources in the KGB at an alarming rate.

Much later, they said a KGB defector, who had made the familiar penetration-of-US-Intelligence assertion, also brought photocopies with him of internal FBI documents which had been provided to the KGB by their sensitive source. That is to say: *evidence*!

So, it was clear we had a mole—but how to ferret him out? This is what was such a long and arduous task, and with so very few investigating it inside the loop.

Who in the FBI or CIA had access to these documents when they passed across his desk, or someone else's nearby?

Efforts were made to track the administrative path of each document. A list of names was compiled of those who had access to all of them. This, as Rochford understated, "was not easy."

It initially included scores of names connected to any one document, further narrowed down to those with access to two or three of them.

Finally, they came up with a dozen senior US Intelligence officials believed to have had access to them all. The faces of those individuals comprised the photo array which was to be shown to any former Soviet Embassy assignee from the 1980s who might have seen their American spy. That would be in the embassy's security/counterintelligence section, or those involved in the tradecraft of dead-drops, but perhaps others too, like Ivan Kurylenko.

With this explanation, I no longer felt on the outside of the investigation and understood why all the ornate contrivances to identify him had been deemed worthy. I was no longer one of Alfred, Lord Tennyson's six hundred, blindly walking into battle—*Theirs not to reason why*.

It was a good feeling, but there had been, back then, still so much to do to recruit Ivan so, at long last, he could be shown the photos.

***

So, why write the book? It is part of the history of the FBI's counterintelligence effort during the Cold War. Should we not document as much of our history as we can? Importantly, very few knew this story as it was unfolding, and fewer still knew the outcome when it did take place. I actually felt bad for my Healthcare Fraud supervisor in San Diego in 1998, Eric Birnbaum, who had to be kept in the dark about all of the gyrations I was going through, not one bit of which had anything to do with catching a cheating lab or an outrageously overbilling doctor.

If not me, who else would write it all down?

In 1991, I met Cliff Stoll, an astrophysicist from the Lawrence Berkeley Lab. He was also the author of the bestselling *The Cuckoo's Egg*, about his 1986 odyssey of tracking down an East German hacker of American military base computers, working on behalf of the KGB.

He told me that if nighttime observers over the centuries had not written down that they had seen a certain bright light in the heavens every seventy-five years, today we would not know that, all along, it had been Halley's Comet. It wouldn't be as though the sightings had not been written down, he said, rather it would be as though they never happened at all.

After Cliff sat in on a presentation I gave at a counterintelligence school at the FBI Academy, well before the Graysuit case, he said these stories were too good, too important, not to write down. Analogizing, he said, if they were not, it wouldn't be as though they were just not written down. It would be as though they never happened at all.

At that point, I was two-thirds of the way through my career and it was not time to write such a book. Now, thirty years later, it *is*, for this recounting and more. So many cases are buried under the dust of long-closed FBI files, now at the National Archives and Records Administration, that truly deserve a place in our nation's history. And most of the agents who worked these cases—made them happen—have passed away. All of these stories are pieces of the larger puzzle—the FBI's role in winning the Cold War.

I am proud to have been part of it.

***

On June 5, 2023, in the federal supermax prison in Florence, Colorado, at 7:30 AM, Robert Hanssen was found on the floor of his cell in solitary confinement. When examined, he was found to be unresponsive and was declared deceased a short while later.

Ironically, if not poetically, he spent about the same amount of time in prison as the number of years he had worked as a turncoat FBI agent for the KGB.

CHAPTER 27

BRIAN KELLEY

Now would be a good time to address the question that should strongly be going through the mind of anyone who has read this far. It is actually more than one question.

The ultimate unknown subject in the massive, yet intricate, and often very confusing Graysuit investigation was Robert Hanssen. That is a given—now.

How that ultimate conclusion was reached has been written about in more than a dozen books, and at least a couple of movies. Those books and movies, and especially a 2013 C-SPAN presentation at the International Spy Museum in Washington, DC, with Mike Rochford, the agent who supervised the Graysuit case, do not clearly set out, in a definitive way, what really took place. It was years after my part in all of this, and even many years after I retired, before some of the details became public. Even now, much is still up in the air. Perhaps the worst part for me was the day Rochford told me, directly, "You know, we put out a lot of disinformation" about the Graysuit case.

What!

I could understand that the identity of the ultimate source, who provided the most sensitive information that led to Hanssen's arrest, would need to be protected. But his name, and other details about him, are already out there in the public domain. It would be understandable that creating a story to protect him might leave enormous holes, if there remained something that was still sensitive. But it is all now so far in the past—plus Hanssen is dead—that there hardly seems to be a reason to keep any of it secret. All of that could be another book but, for now, let's stick to my part of the case, with Ivan and Polly and Rebecca.

When Ivan and Rebecca met at Rockefeller Center and entered a taxi, Ivan reviewed the array of photos of the possible unsubs, then clearly pointed out one of them. That was all I was told, because, of course, the man was yet to be investigated, and in an all-encompassing way, the depth of which had never been done before in the FBI. Or so I thought.

I was not in that loop, and when I retired, I was told nothing further, like the name of the individual Ivan did point out. I had known that, prior to the taxi-ride event, and over many months, some of the photos had been pulled, for various reasons, while others replaced them in the photo display. This did contribute to confusion about the exact set of photos that were shown to Ivan. For all of the years since then, I assumed it had been Hanssen's face. But I never *knew*.

So, what really happened after the back-seat-of-the-taxi identification?

A number of months before the endgame of my part in the Los Angeles–Austin–New York scenario, a senior CIA officer had come under more than suspicion—Brian Kelley. Again, in several other books, and the C-SPAN two-hour presentation by Mike Rochford, further details can be learned about him. But relevant here is that, for whatever reason, Mike Rochford zeroed in on Kelley as the unsub, hellbent to a degree that is difficult to comprehend. I am sure he had good reasons to believe this, but something was amiss in the syllogism that led him to that conclusion—because it was an invalid one.

Unlike the close-to-the-chest investigation that took place later with Hanssen, once Kelley was "identified," there seemed to have been a lot of out-in-the-open with the suspicions about him. In fact, he was so strongly considered to be the spy for the Soviets in US Intelligence that all efforts, logistics, and funds were put in high gear to prove it.

With hindsight, this seemed more like an agenda-driven conclusion—the focus on Kelley which steered away investigating anyone *but* Kelley.

He was interviewed, which, it seemed, turned into harassment, and he was moved to a diminished position at Langley, to no avail. His family members were even interviewed and threatened with conspiracy charges if they did not divulge the depth of Kelley's ostensible double life of working for both US and Soviet intelligence. It was truly harrowing—unforgivable, really.

Then came the taxi-cab identification of the unsub from a dozen photos. The belief by Rochford, and necessarily followed by the entire Graysuit squad, was that it was a certainty that Ivan would point out Kelley's face. When the information came back to Graysuit HQ that Ivan's finger did not point at Kelley, it was like the proverbial pin piercing the large balloon that was the Graysuit investigation. To say that Rochford was disappointed would be an understatement.

I was later advised that the Ivan-identification was, essentially, cast aside because it did not match what had been considered *gospel* for so many months.

I want to point out one piece of "evidence" against Kelley to demonstrate the flawed nature of what, in part, supported investigating him.

A search of Kelley's house in Great Falls, VA, located a map in his sock drawer. Someone decided it was a map used for dead-drop activity—that is, non-personal communication with the Russians. This was in the same general vicinity where there had been other Soviet dead drops, and for decades. But it was right near where Kelley lived.

Confronted with this, Kelley said it was a map he used as part of his daily exercise routine, the routes he jogged on trails through the woods. That would have sounded reasonable, unless you had already decided Kelley was the bad guy.

A significant problem with this analysis is what Soviet (KGB and GRU) maps actually looked like. They are very specific, and we had many in our FBI files, obtained from our double agents during the Cold War. Comparing some of the real maps to the one found in Kelley's sock drawer, one should have realized it was not made by the hand of a Soviet intelligence officer. And, if this appeared to be a map Kelley had drawn to provide to the KGB as the location for a future dead-drop site, that was not the way those maps worked. There, essentially, had to be an "*X* marks the spot" notation, for where US secrets would be disguised and put into a drop site, but it didn't have that. It simply didn't match the Russian pattern. Besides, in our experience, it was the Russians who created the maps, secreting them in a dead drop, with the plan for the next non-personal contact, and not the American spy as the cartographer. Also, would Kelley really have left his next planned Soviet Intelligence communication in his sock drawer?

I would like to have been the agent to interview Kelley, as I had debriefed about two dozen Soviet Bloc intelligence defectors, eliciting information on their intelligence activities. It seems that nothing Kelley did would have matched the lessons learned from all of those debriefings about drop-site exchanges with American secrets going to the Russians.

What was probably the most egregious aspect of the misidentification of Brian Kelley was when the Graysuit squad learned the true identity of the target of their investigation, Robert Hanssen. It would take many months, and a very complicated scenario, to set a trap to catch him in the act of passing classified documents. Over all of those months, there could be no indication that Kelley was not still the primary suspect. They could not let Hanssen believe there was any indication that the investigation was closer to identifying him. This enabled Hanssen to have sort of a comfort zone while they continued to hound Kelley and his family members. The ruse may have been justified, but the toll it took on all of the Kelleys was absolutely horrible.

Balancing the security of the operation and its single-directedness, at the time, was seen to far outweigh the suffering of the Kelleys. Even a hint that another person was suspected, or that Brian was no longer under investigation, could have resulted in Hanssen going dark in his relationship with the Russians. Then he might never have been caught. It was a brutal decision, any way you looked at it. In the end, there would be apologies to Brian Kelley and his family, not for the early error of believing he was the Russian spy, but for the delay in informing them that, for months, they had known he was innocent. Sadly, operationally, it could not be helped. The security of the investigation was paramount.

[Recall that one of the early suspicious incidents about Hanssen was only later reported by his brother-in-law, an FBI agent in

Chicago. He had found a roll of $100 bills in Hanssen's sock drawer, for which he had no good explanation as to where the money had come from. Now *that* would have been a lead worth covering, in comparison with Kelley's jogging map. But the roll of big bills, as a lead, fell by the wayside.]

So, if Ivan did not point out Hanssen, who *did* he point out?

That is a question to which I could never get a straight answer. Was that man ever investigated?

My thoughts on Ivan's integrity is that it was highly unlikely he would have lied to Rebecca, or done anything to deceive her. If he wasn't familiar with any of the faces in the photo array, he would have just said that. It could make one incensed that there was never any follow-up with this lead, but that seems to be the case. Instead, Rochford, admittedly, had doubled down on Kelley.

For me, that was the worst of the worst for the lack of a clear-thinking investigation. Rochford had his man, or at least he thought he did. So, the weeks and months of my efforts—the travel, contacts made, and dollars spent—seemed simply to have been snuffed out, like a candle in the wind.

I can now understand why no one gave me further feedback: because there wasn't any. But it didn't make me feel any better, with no answer, as opposed to an explanation that the identification was a washout. And still, we don't—*I don't*—know, for certain, that it was....

What I believe now is that Ivan did not point at a photo of Robert Hanssen, but that could not be clarified, either way. Who he did point out was lost in the paperwork, with no indication there was any follow-up.

Talk about egregious!

CHAPTER 28

WHATEVER HAPPENED TO REBECCA KING?

I had been with Rebecca King for a total of fifteen minutes. Yet everything I had done for the previous nine months, whether or not I knew it at the time, was paving the way for her to meet Ivan.

After our part of the larger Graysuit operation and Robert Hanssen's arrest some three years later, I wondered what had happened to Rebecca. Had she received *her* letter of commendation?

When an agent performs especially well, in addition to a letter from the director, they may receive an incentive award. That is with really big cases. The dollar amount, the actual figure on the check in the envelope, is never commensurate with the work done or the outcome. It is a small token of appreciation from Uncle Sam, as determined by FBI administrators.

If you received an incentive award for as much as $250, it was a big deal. You were expected to take your squad out and buy a round, or pay for lunch, maybe bring pizza into the office, nothing less than a bag of bagels the next morning. (Of course, make sure none of them have poppy seeds, or someone may flunk a random drug test. That is how the bagel guy knows you are an FBI agent!)

Such squad camaraderie tended to knock the stuffing out of most monetary prizes, but it was more the point of *receiving* the award, and not the financial remuneration.

I thought Rebecca should have received one—a big one—for a job extremely well done.

I later learned she did not—not even close.

Her Bureau career was fresh and new when the Graysuit case came along. She had only been assigned to Mike Rochford's squad for a couple of years. As Gene McClelland later said about her being selected as the contact point with Ivan: "She was the right height, shape, demeanor, and was perfect for the job." Her degree had been in psychology, her true calling.

Sometime well after the incident with Ivan in the taxi, she was offered a lucrative position by a businessman. He needed someone to travel with him for psychological assessments when meeting clients. He would use her keen observations to make business decisions valued in the hundreds of thousands of dollars at each turn. He would truly rely on her judgment. It sounded challenging.

To me, it seemed like she would be his muse.

The available spots at the FBI Academy in the Behavioral Sciences Unit were quite coveted and few and far between. To Rebecca, the outside-the-Bureau offer appeared to be the best use of her skills and inclinations.

But there is an old unwritten rule: Once you are in the FBI—*don't leave!*

It is not because it is difficult to find a better or more fulfilling job, but if you leave the FBI, *you will not get back in.* When the door closes, it hits your butt and slams you all the way across the street.

Studies show the job of FBI agent has one of the highest retention ratings. A very high percentage of those who come on board stay until retirement. The position is not seen as a stepping-stone to some other job or something to look good on a resume. Once you are in, for almost all of us, you have reached your goal. Then you go about doing your life's work and love it every day.

When you get up each morning, you don't feel like you are going to work; rather, you are doing what you do—catching bad guys. Most agents are happy to carry the little gold badge and credentials with the big blue letters. They wouldn't consider doing anything else.

FBI manuals have forms and instructions for all sorts of things, right down to how many pencils agents may keep in their desk drawers. But there are no forms or instructions about how to resign, because resignations so seldom occur.

In 1971, my training class started with thirty-one men, typical at the time. We were from all around the country and had different backgrounds, but no women, Blacks, Asians, or Hispanics. That is just the way it was. There were Black, Asian, and Hispanic agents in the Bureau, just few of them, and there was certainly no quota per class.

Truth be told, most young Black men who had gone through law school were much more easily enticed into accepting positions at major law firms than to take a relatively low-paying job in the federal government. It was actually hard for our recruiters to find qualified young Black men willing to work for the Bureau, although the numbers would begin to build up over the next few years. The same could be said of other minorities and women.

A few months after the death of Director Hoover in May of 1972, women made it into the first co-ed training classes. They came in two at a time, and then more, which was a very good thing. Each one surely felt she was under a microscope, but a barrier had been rightly broken. Also, the later change in the height requirement, from 5′8″ to none at all, greatly increased the number of female applicants.

My New Agents Class (NAC-4), in 1971, was one of the last to graduate before there even *was* an FBI Academy at Quantico, Virginia, which was under construction.

One of my classmates was from Harrisburg, PA, not far up the road from Washington, DC. He had been a high-school principal with strong ties to his community.

About the fourth week of class, he told our counselor, Edgar Best, he needed time off to visit his family. He was homesick. The previous evening, he had been on the phone with his wife and they talked about it. His little boy got on the line and said, "Daddy, I really miss you. Can you come home?"

It just about tore his heart out. He told Best he would be gone for only a few days.

Best told him it was a bad idea because he had to stay and attend classes.

That afternoon he left. He didn't know it, but his budding career in the FBI was over.

The door back into the FBI was not just locked, it was sealed over so it no longer existed.

Our class graduated thirty new agents.

As for Rebecca, she left the Bureau for another job, which worked well for a few months. Then her employer had a change of heart, or perhaps a change in his finances, and he let her go. It was a crushing blow. She had to pick herself up and start again.

She spoke with her former Bureau colleagues about getting back in.

With all she had done for the Graysuit case—and, at the time, I thought she had been the crucial lynchpin to identify the ultimate perpetrator—it seemed to be an easy decision. Her colleagues and supervisors were glad to go to bat for her and make the proper overtures. Even if she had not been the lynchpin for identifying the ultimate Graysuit unsub, her part had been played with such aplomb and distinction, no matter the outcome. Surely, with her knowledge, experience, and her track record, she should have been greeted with open arms.

The administrators who had been in a vertical line over her asserted that they wanted her back. She had been, and would continue to be, a great asset to the FBI.

However, it is a different section of the Bureau that decides who gets to come back in. The managers there didn't see any of these reasons as valid. Those were the views of *operational* people. The decision-makers were *administrative*, and they had their sheet of requirements to block-check.

Rebecca was finally told she could come back and be a special agent once more. All she would have to do was go through the FBI Academy—again.

Well, that was patently ridiculous. No one who had ever gone through that process before would want to do it twice. There were not merely the months of studying at Quantico, which would be completely redundant, but the grueling aspect of the physical requirements—getting back into tip-top shape—which would lie ahead.

For example, there was the Yellow Brick Road, where mostly hidden rocks and tree roots on paths through the woods had been painted yellow, so they could be seen more easily, and you ran around them to avoid spraining an ankle. There were rope-climbs, obstacle courses, distance runs, and other physical requirements. It may not have been the Parris Island Marine Corp boot camp, but it was challenging.

Rebecca had already performed well enough to become a street agent, but the bureaucratic rules would not bend, even for a recycled applicant with her demonstrated capabilities.

To me, this sounded more like college fraternity hazing, some level of punishment for leaving in the first place, but the gatekeepers were adamant.

There were also financial issues regarding her severance and future annuity, but that could be resolved. It was the idea of being a *retread* at Quantico that stopped her, and maybe it even pissed her off at the entire Bureau.

The administrators got the result they wanted. Once again, the door back in was sealed.

When I started to write this book in 2010, I had not remembered Rebecca's name from a dozen years before, and I had almost never heard it, even back then. The many things going on at the Austin Film Festival were almost a blur. The short time with Rebecca had been more about the mission than getting to know her. I had never seen her before, and never saw her again.

Yes, she had read all of my stuff about the case, but I knew nothing about her, other than she was the *chosen one* who had what was needed for the picture-perfect woman to meet Ivan.

It took months of contacting people within the FBI to try to learn her name, and no one I talked to had known her. Of course, no one knew what she had done in the Graysuit case because the behind-the-scenes activities of that unique case were still completely hidden.

I even went to the convention of the Society of Former Special Agents in the FBI in San Diego in September 2012, hoping she might be there. At that time, I was unaware of the difficult time surrounding her departure and non-return to the FBI. She would never have come to such a gathering, but I didn't know that.

I spoke with many of my old friends, especially former female agents, and told them Rebecca's part in the Graysuit case. None had ever heard it. None had been aware of the woman who had conducted herself so brilliantly. Each former female agent said they would like to have met and worked with her.

But Rebecca had worked where none of them could have known her, not in the normal office space of WFO, but behind double-ciphered, locked doors. She would never have commiserated with other female agents, no lunches or coffees; such was the nature of Graysuit.

Rebecca King had been a ghost agent.

My goal was to find out what had happened after she met Ivan in the hotel in Austin. I had only gotten a blurb of feedback, and that was off the record.

Ivan, "pointed at a photo," was all I was initially told.

It was as though she, and the rest of the case, had fallen off the edge of the world.

When Hanssen was arrested three years after those events in Austin, I'd had every reason to believe it was a direct result of what we had done. The not-knowing made me feel like a front-line worker on a long production line in a factory, who had no idea what the final product looked like.

I wanted to get all of my facts straight, and this was frustrating.

Finally, I went back to Gene McClelland and he clarified Rebecca's name. (I am using an alias for her). He told me of her departure story. That was the first I'd heard it, and it was truly crushing to me. He had no idea where she was currently located.

Through modern databases, I finally found her.

I called her and identified myself, saying I had met her at a hotel in Austin in 1998 and wanted to talk to her about what happened after we parted company.

On the other end of the line, she froze.

Then she said she couldn't talk about it.

I was willing to fly from where I lived in Miami to speak with her, even for only a few minutes, but I didn't get that far.

She said, "You will have to talk to Mike Rochford."

She would not speak on the phone again to arrange a meeting, and she would not meet with me if I came to see her. She wanted nothing to do with any of this.

She had been a great resource and a tremendous agent. All of her talent, in my humble opinion, had been truly wasted, cast aside by the FBI.

The more I thought about it, the sadder I became about how Rebecca King had been lost to the Bureau. It was as though someone had taken a unique and beautiful left-handed seashell and dashed it to pieces.

ADDENDUM

I have almost no regrets about anything I have done in my life. That is how I fall asleep the moment my head hits the pillow each night.

Further, I have no regrets about anything I did in the FBI, operationally or administratively. I know—*bo-o-o-ring!*—but that is how you stay for a full career, even receive the eighteen-carat gold charm for your twenty-fifth anniversary, later fitted into a gold ring crafted by a friendly Vietnamese goldsmith. It is, at least, *something* to show for your efforts.

There are, however, some things I do regret, sadly, because I could not control them. That translates into a high level of frustration.

In the early 1980s, a man with US Intelligence clearances walked into a building in Washington, DC, which housed an official office of the Soviet Union. He asked to speak with someone from the KGB but was told there was no such person.

The visitor said he knew there was and told the receptionist to go find one.

A few minutes later, a KGB officer appeared at the reception area. The visitor went to a back office with the KGB man and was never seen again.

If this story is unequivocal, and there was such a man and such a visit, and if it was *not* Robert Hanssen, *who was it?*

Over time, Hanssen's stories of what he did became clearer, but with his defective personality, telling the truth, plain and simple, was almost impossible—for decades.

He had lied to so many, and every day of his adult life, that trying to get back on track and tell it all straight was just not something he could do. Honest-to-goodness truth-telling was no longer part of his repertoire.

The same mentality which inspired him to commit treason for the Soviets—our main enemy—against his own freedom-loving people might have led to the ultimate end: the downfall of the nation that gave him the freedom…*to become a spy*!

But then he wouldn't have been either free *or* a spy any longer. Ironic!

With this kind of logic, unperceived but meandering through Hanssen's cranial cavity, as well as his—and I keep using this word—*defective* personality traits, there is nothing to say that anything he ever told the debriefing agents was completely true or accurate. Of course, much of it was, but there was no certain line which, when he would cross it, would cause blips in his brain waves. He would say anything that would soothe his ego.

Hanssen always thought he could trick anyone, including those at FBI Headquarters, right down the hallway from his office. He looked down on everyone, had respect for no one, and was mired in a high opinion of himself—which he could not overtly share with others. His attitude presented as self-righteous and bullying, not the personality of someone who debriefs well. Even in solitary confinement, his psyche still saw himself as "the smartest person in the room."

The FBI thinks it knows when Hanssen first volunteered himself to the KGB. As to his *motive* for his actions, his treachery—an issue that must be resolved with every defector we interview—it is not clear how many degrees in psychiatry or psychology one would need in order to decipher what was really going on in Hanssen's mind. There were so many rationalizations, compartmentalizations, and egocentric justifications for what he did that there can be no reliable sense made of any of it, although highly qualified professionals have tried.

For the man who walked out of the rain, and into that Soviet office, if not Robert Hanssen, what Bureau or Agency did he work for then, and where is he now?

EPILOGUE

I know, I know, the book is complete and the story is over—maybe....

The title of this book, when first submitted to the FBI Prepublication Review Unit, was *The Last Spy*. With further research, there were so many books with something so close to this title that it would have become mired in a sea of *The Last* this and that, even *The Last Spy* this and that. It finally became *The Traitor Among Us*, which did not portray the important aspect of *catching* the individual, so it became *Catching the Traitor Among Us*. But even that wasn't my story, which was to *identify* the spy—*finding* him—to me, the most difficult part.

Here is the important question: Was Robert Hanssen actually the last spy, meaning in the FBI, or in the US Intelligence Community, from the Cold War era? After all, he was arrested in 2001, twelve years after the fall of the Berlin Wall, so maybe he was. If you think that—if you even contemplate it—you would be sorely mistaken. The simple reason is because there are always spies, and on both sides, who could be almost anywhere. Even with the utmost vigilance, that is simply a fact of life—the second-oldest profession, and all that.

Below is a vignette which is stuck in my craw—maybe yours, too, after you read it.

David Major was a brilliant and innovative FBI special agent, and later, a supervisor in counterintelligence. With many successes, he was transferred to Washington Field, the nerve-center of foreign counterintelligence in the FBI. He came up with an ingenious idea, which was assigned the codename "Spiderweb."

Dave conducted an analysis of dozens of known dead-drop sites around the Washington area, which the Russians had used with our double-agents over many years. He realized there were only so many options for the kind of location they would use. One fall season in the mid-1980s, we had reason to believe, on a particular weekend, there would be dead-drop activity on the outskirts of the suburbs of the nation's capital. The many agents working the case humorously referred to those suburban-to-rural areas as "Spider-country."

While our double agents had participated in this non-personal communication with their handlers, there were very likely others who we did not know about. This included Johnny Walker, infamously spying for Soviet Intelligence, with several family members, arrested in 1985. We wanted to zero in on certain locations and hoped to get lucky. One was near the Potomac River in Northern Virginia. A number of agents were assigned to patrol the area, including me.

The timeframe was typical of evening dead-drop activity, 10:00 PM to 1:00 AM. It would involve both a Soviet Embassy intelligence officer and an American furnishing secrets.

They often used what we called a "GRU rock," (the GRU was Soviet military intelligence), which was specially fabricated for dead-drop activities. When a Soviet handler would leave one, it would have money and directions inside for the next drop for the American who was spying for the Russians. When an American used one, it was filled with our secrets.

On a designated evening, the American turncoat drives to a specific spot where he can pull off the road at a bend, but cannot be seen from either direction, and exits his car. Fifteen feet into the woods is a flat stump, behind which he places his homemade hollow rock filled with US secrets in a plastic bag. Then he returns to his car and drives a large figure-eight pattern on the backroads, until he spots what he needs to see.

Along his route, somewhere, is a particular sign. It could be for a Railroad Crossing, a Narrow Bridge, or maybe even a Stop sign: something permanent that will not be moved.

The American gets out and leaves a mark on it, perhaps a three-inch strip of duct tape to signal to the Soviet, who is also driving in a circulating pattern, that the drop has been filled, or cleared/emptied, whichever the case may be.

Then both the American traitor and the Russian leave the area, secrets exchanged, and they were never within several miles of each other.

Johnny Walker's contacts were so prolific that he did a double drop. That was two in the same evening, both leaving a package in the woods with American secrets, and picking one up which a Russian had left, containing cash and instructions for the next contact.

Preparations for these operations are meticulous. The maps have to be hand-drawn with the nearby converging streets and a close-up map of the specific drop location.

You cannot purchase such maps. Someone must, physically, drive there in the daytime to scope out these areas so the specifics will be accurate. In my experience, every passing of money and instructions for an American had a map, hand-drawn by his Russian handlers, for the next scheduled dead-drop activity.

These covert activities would continue, uninterrupted, without the need for personal contact, which would be dangerous for the American. He could have been recruited through blackmail, or maybe he volunteered himself due to critical financial needs, or simple greed. Some might have become philosophical traitors to our land of freedom and didn't want any money—which would have been rare—but they would still use the dead-drop system.

The drop is filled—the drop is cleared. It should be simple enough.

When both parties have done what they came to do, they depart the area, with absolutely no indication they were ever there—neat and tidy.

On this evening there were a dozen agents flooding the locale in Northern Virginia with streets named Utterback Store Road and Seneca Knoll Drive. Some were parked and watching chokepoints. Others, including me, were assigned to cruise the backroads.

If a Soviet Embassy vehicle with a diplomatic license plate was seen in the area, where he would have absolutely no reason to be for his normal duties—but would, if he were involved in espionage tradecraft—we were to write down the license plates of every vehicle we saw, thereafter.

One of us would radio in about the Soviet tag, on a designated channel, to all the other surveillance cars. It would be like firing a starting pistol for everyone to begin writing down all the license plates of vehicles in the target area.

When the plates were later run through the records at the Department of Motor Vehicles, those owners who didn't live in that immediate vicinity became suspects.

If the vehicle's owner was in the military, or from another state, it could cause the initiation of a *preliminary inquiry*, and a case would be opened to find out why the driver was out there that night.

But it was all predicated on first seeing a Soviet license plate.

There was no certainty that a non-personal communication operation would take place that evening. Occasionally, when one party showed up, the other might not. Even spies have emergencies or good reasons to miss a meet.

That is why there is always a backup date for each meeting in two weeks or a month. Espionage can be a long, slow process, but that ensures a certain amount of security.

It would be very bad if a Russian were driving a non-diplomatic vehicle, or even tried to rent one. There would be repercussions in both capitals, so for these clandestine operations, an "official" car was always used.

The evening wore on, and it looked like there would be a no-show for the Soviets. It was approaching 1:00 AM. Another evening well spent by a dozen FBI agents on what had been a good lead which didn't pan out. Maybe next time.

Just before our activity was to conclude, I drove back down Springvale Road, where it crosses Beach Mill Road, near the restaurant L'Auberge Chez Francois. About another mile past there, I saw a late-model sedan pulled off to the side of the road. No other vehicles were nearby. The driver held a flashlight and was looking at a map. He looked to be early-thirtyish, with a haircut the military calls "high and tight." I thought this was a strange place to pull over. Maybe he was lost, or his car broke down. Was he looking for the home of a friend? Or something more sinister?

In intelligence terms, this was an anomaly and matched what I was looking for. I would rather have seen an accompanying Soviet license plate, too, to make it a perfect match.

I had traveled many miles of figure eights and knew the area really well.

I pulled off the road to park right behind the man and walked to his window. He rolled it down. I asked if he was having car trouble "out here in the middle of nowhere."

No, he said he was fine, just looking to meet someone and was lost. A map was open on his lap.

I was able to see what he was referring to, but it was not a commercial book map, with a spiral binding, popular at the time, or a large accordion road map. Rather, it was exactly the kind of map the Soviets give to their spies for the next meeting.

The roads on the piece of paper were hand-drawn, with the bends clearly marked, as well as certain buildings and large trees drawn in. On the passenger seat beside him were other papers, a larger map, also homemade, and even some photos of...I could not tell what.

I had seen hand-drawn maps in preparation for this case from some of our FBI files, and what this man had matched those exactly. Of course, it could have been made by a friend who lived out there somewhere, and he truly might have been lost, but the degree of *coincidence* was overwhelming. Even the driver's most OCD (obsessive-compulsive disorder) friend would not have drawn the many details that were in the map on this man's lap.

My spy-bell was ringing loudly in my ears because this guy had a genuine spy map, and I didn't care if there had been no Soviet vehicle observed. His military appearance, to boot, told me this one should be investigated. This would have been an almost impossible situation to duplicate—so don't waste it!

I didn't want to raise his suspicions. I told him I hoped he found his way, wished him good luck, and bid him goodnight.

I wrote down his license plate and thought it was very important. At this point, I knew there hadn't been a Russian in the area, but he didn't. My thought was he had been driving around looking for a mark on a sign which would never appear, and now he was rechecking his Russian-made maps. What a curious situation—humorous, actually.

On Monday morning, all the agents were to provide license plates to the agent in charge of the case if there had been a Soviet tag seen, but there had not. So, there was nothing for anyone to turn in—except me.

I went to the case agent and told him what had happened, what I had seen, and gave him the piece of paper with the Virginia license plate written on it.

He took it but made the point I knew he would. With no Soviet in the area, there was no use running license plates.

But, I explained, there could have been a broken meeting, where the Russian couldn't make it, or some other glitch. What I did know was the guy in this car had a map drawn by a Soviet intelligence officer, with all the same markings and details they use.

Who knew? The guy could have been from the Pentagon!

The agent replied that the weekend work had been a washout. With no Soviet, there would be no further investigation.

I don't know why I could not get through his thick skull that sometimes following the given parameters—*the rules*—is not always the best way to do things. Even if my lead seemed to be outside of his particular bureaucratic box, that shouldn't matter. Not to follow up with this one was unimaginable to me.

Finally, he said he would, so I left it at that—his case, his prerogative. I had plenty of other leads to cover on my own cases.

A few weeks later I saw the case agent and asked about the tag from out near the Chez Francois restaurant.

He told me he had done nothing with it.

As it turned out, I no longer had my paperwork with the license plate on it either.

Bureaucratically, what he had done may have been fine, but operationally, it was the worst of the worst.

There was an American out there spying for the Russians who had slipped through our fingers. I had obtained his license plate, but now it was lost forever.

While I think of this book as being about the effort to identify "the last spy" of the Cold War, I have to ask myself, "Who was that guy by the side of the road?"

If he was in the military and thirtyish, maybe he could have gone from a captain, then, to a general now, possibly with a couple of stars on his shoulder boards. And it would all be possible because an appropriate investigation was not conducted when the sighting took place.

This case is *stuck in my craw* and will always be my *intelligence* regret.

AFTERWORD

This is a memoir. I have only written about what I did, and what I know. For aspects outside of my personal knowledge, I have given the proper attributions so all get credit where it is due.

Many will review and reanalyze the overall Graysuit investigation for decades to come. It has been my intention to add my piece to the much larger puzzle so more of the story is in the public domain.

Some names have been changed, and permissions were received from all of the others to use theirs.

It would have been nice to have my plotline end up with me as the hero of the story. But that would be fiction, not reality, and not how life often turns out.

We cannot foresee where a case will go when we are only partway through it. And if the cards dealt to an investigator do not contain the facts that will bring the ultimate, long-sought conclusion, then so be it. We can only cover the leads that are there, then walk up the stream, splashing around, turning over every rock to find another lead worth covering.

My part *might have been* what brought the overall Graysuit case to a positive conclusion, but it seems it just wasn't in my cards. And there was no rock to be found through splashing around which could have made it so. It was still such a very good feeling to have ferreted out what was there to be found in the fact pattern I did have. No matter what, you still have to cover all of the leads, create some if none seem apparent, and do everything you can to resolve all of the issues to bring about the very best conclusion possible. Gene McClelland and I succeeded with everything we had been asked to do—a near-impossible task from the start—and brought our part of the investigation to a fitting conclusion.

A picture was pointed out in the back seat of a New York taxicab.

It was a happy day!

I hope you enjoyed reading about it.

It was exciting to have lived through this case, and just as exciting to write about it.

ACKNOWLEDGMENTS

As this is my first book published, there are many to acknowledge, boiled down to: What got me here!

My parents, Florence and John Barnes, taught me to live the straight-and-narrow, which clearly helped pave the path to an appointment as a Special Agent in the FBI. My father's philosophy in raising his two sons was, "Do as I say, *and* as I do." Not much room for missteps there.

Sampson Freedman was my 7th grade homeroom teacher at Leeds Junior High in Mt. Airy in Philadelphia. When a short, platinum-haired me, arrived in his class, I was timid and shy. He took me on as a project to get rid of that, and he succeeded. A decade later, a student shot and killed him. In my despondency on the subway on the way back from his funeral to my dorm at Villanova University, I penned a letter to the editor of the Phila. Inquirer. They published it as the lead letter among many for my old teacher. It was my first piece ever published—so even in death, Mr. Freedman helped set the path for my writing life.

Irene Jameson was the faculty advisor at Germantown High for the Student Government when I was elected President. She taught me how to speak and be comfortable in front of an auditorium full of hundreds of students. This has come in very handy for over fifty years and scores of presentations.

Marilyn Froelich was my creative writing instructor at Penn State's Ogontz/Abington Campus. She was the first to take me seriously, and was midwife as my writing skills emerged.

Associate Professor Jim Lord, opened the vibrant world of art for me in his Penn State Art History class, an area I would revel in for decades. It led directly to my post-FBI career in art theft recovery of impressionist paintings. Follow-up articles about paintings and sculpture would be published, a precursor for many who submit manuscripts.

In my early days in the FBI in Washington in the 1970s, Dan Kiernan, a senior agent and master interviewer on our Foreign Counterintelligence squad, taught me everything he knew about interviewing. That knowledge is still serving me well, and I have passed it on to many.

Those named in this book, George Ramonas, Polly Platt, and Gene McClelland, aka, "Red Pop," were crucial for this case coming to a conclusion. Jim Stassinos, my Washington supervisor, years before, always gave me a very long leash to cover leads to the fullest. He first applied the description of "Splashing upstream" to my dogmatic persistence in investigations. Jon Siverling, my partner in the San Diego FBI, was a stalwart in the field and an excellent observer of the human condition.

Harry Gossett, longtime friend and criminal supervisor in Washington Field, came up with a title for the multi-topic, difficult-to-describe Chapter 22: Cascading over Sharp Rocks in the Stream.

Thomas V. Cash, a former senior ATF official, started me off in my post-FBI career of worldwide investigations.

Jack Dobbyn was my Villanova Law professor in 1970. We reacquainted 45-years later when he finally retired. As for "life after…" he has now written eight legal detective novels, my model on a pedestal for my writing efforts.

The ladies of The Epoch Times, Channaly Phillip and Sharon Kilarski, published fifteen of my essays on art and feel-good pieces, laying open my style of writing where the public could see it.

If you take a writing-to-get-published course, and it finally works, then you thank Kathy Ver Eecke—Queen of the Query letter—and her Pitched-2-Published, GetaBookDeal101 staff. A follow-up with Diane O'Connell, readied me for the finish line with her course, Sharpening Your Manuscript.

Cynthia Chambers, former department director in Broward County, and longtime girlfriend, would stand back far enough from my manuscript to give me a broader perspective on my stories—and kept me grounded.

Daughter Natalia was in a talent show when she was only nine, in the Skyline Elementary School in Solana Beach. Her performance simply demanded to become an essay. *Natalia's Dance* is my most published piece, and I thank her, again, for enabling her success to become the essay that helped launch my writing career.

Daughter Ariel set up my www.WayneBarnesWriting.com webpage so those who wanted to could take a look at my craft of writing, posting dozens of my essays—and with editing skills, as well.

Ron Chesin had been a classmate at Leeds Junior High and Germantown High, in Philly. We reacquainted 55-years after graduation. He has become my close confidant and the Jiminy Cricket voice over my shoulder, always with thoughts of *the next step, and the one after that.*

There are those most recently responsible for this story seeing the light of day: Barbara Ledeen, Virginia Hurt, publisher Alfred Regnery, his staff at Republic, Katherine Ruddy and Caitlin Burdette, and then rounding out the effort, my literary agent, Alexander C. Hoyt.

Rebecca King did not want her true name mentioned in this book, but she still needs to be given credit as my hero in the story.

Then there is Ivan Fyodorovich Kurylenko, the man of the hour, who, to this day, probably still thinks I am working to finance independent films for Texas millionaires....

ABOUT THE AUTHOR

Wayne Barnes was a counterintelligence special agent in the FBI for twenty-nine years. He worked KGB espionage, ran double agents, recruited hostile intelligence officers, and found his niche debriefing Cold War defectors. He is now a licensed private investigator, a signature expert, and he also recovers stolen impressionist paintings—the "Dirty Harry" for billionaires. He is a graduate of Penn State and Villanova Law.